STEPPING
STONES
SUCCESS

EXPERTS SHARE STRATEGIES
FOR MASTERING BUSINESS,
LIFE, & RELATIONSHIPS

Stepping Stones to Success
Copyright © 2010

Published in the United States by
INSIGHT PUBLISHING
Sevierville, Tennessee • www.insightpublishing.com
ISBN 978-1-60013-546-0

Cover Design: Emmy Shubert
Interior Format & Design: Chris Ott

Disclaimer: This book is a compilation of ideas from
numerous experts who have each contributed a chapter.
As such, the views expressed in each chapter are of
those who were interviewed and not necessarily of the
interviewer, Insight Publishing or the other
contributing authors.

A Message from the Publisher

There are many things I've come to understand throughout the many years I have been in this business. I've learned that it's never too late to grow and learn, to change course, to expand perspectives, and to admit I don't know everything.

Because I know it's important to learn from the experience of others, I reached out to many experts when putting this book project together and I gained some valuable information from them. The people I talked with have presented some insights that will expand your horizons and make you realize that you can be the key to your own success.

This book, *Stepping Stones to Success,* is your golden opportunity to profit from the knowledge of others. It will give you the facts you need to make important decisions about your future.

Interviewing these fascinating people was a unique learning experience for me. And I assure you that reading this book will be an exceptional learning experience for you.

—David Wright

The interviews presented in
Stepping Stones to Success
are conducted by David Wright,
President and Founder of
ISN Works and Insight Publishing.

TABLE OF CONTENTS

CHAPTER ONE

F.L.I.P. the Switch

An Interview with . . . **Patrick E. Alcorn**

DAVID WRIGHT (WRIGHT)

Today we're talking with Patrick E. Alcorn. He is "America's eXtreme Motivator" and founder of TTG Transformations, LLC. He is a successful entrepreneur who builds courage, faith, and hope through interactive and entertaining presentations. From inner city youths to corporate peak performers, Patrick knows how to get you from where you are to where you want to be. He is a member of the elite group of motivators who enable the world to live more amply with greater vision and with a finer spirit of hope and achievement. Patrick works *with* you in a way that works *for* you to provide individual and organizational improvement. He is available as a keynote speaker for conventions, corporate training, and youth enrichment.

Patrick, welcome to *Stepping Stones to Success*.

PATRICK ALCORN (ALCORN)

I am so happy to be here; I can hardly wait to get started.

WRIGHT

I've heard of extreme sports and extreme makeovers. How do you define "extreme motivation"?

ALCORN

I've been asked that question many times. Extreme motivation is extreme consistency in your thoughts and behaviors as it relates to achieving worthwhile, predetermined personal goals. Paul J. Meyer once said that success doesn't come from doing anything extraordinary—success comes from just doing the ordinary, consistently well. I believe that you have to be extreme about being consistent. You have to take consistency to a whole new level. You have to do a radical, mental, quantum leap in your thinking and your behaviors if you want to be successful.

The strategies that I share are simple, yet they enable you to maintain extreme consistency. For me, this is the definition of *extreme motivation:*

WRIGHT

I noticed that you sometimes use acronyms when you share empowering information. How does the acronym FLIIP relate to the steppingstones for success?

ALCORN

Acronyms are an effective tool for remembering key concepts. My audiences more easily remember the concepts because I use the acronyms. David, if you look at it closely, FLIIP is an extension of the word *flip* that Webster's dictionary defines as, "to change from one position to another and especially turn over."

The same way that you turn on a light in a dark room by flipping a switch and the room instantly turns from darkness to light is the same affect that the message FLIIP can have on the life of someone who applies four very simple principles. Thus, the acronym FLIIP is central to a strategy that I share with

2

anyone who needs to make a radical change or break out of the pack. In other words, the people I share this concept with are people who really want to break the cycle of failure.

Principle Number 1 is Focus. Focus on the reason that you have to make the change. Remember, you most often get what you focus on. Focus on success not failure. Focus on where you're going, not where you are. Focus on who you are becoming, not who you've been. Focus on what you want, not what you lack. If you want to flip the switch and turn things around in your life, you must begin with the right focus. You gain that focus by visualizing in your mind's eye, by drawing a picture, by taking a picture with your camera, or by cutting the picture out of a magazine. You gain focus using any method whereby you can see your future. The bottom line is that for your vision to be in full Technicolor, your focus must be clear and unclouded.

Principle Number 2 is Leverage. Webster also defines *flip* as, "to move with a small quick motion." Bring together and leverage all of your resources for the most dramatic effect. Don't go at it alone. Leverage your experiences and past successes as well as the knowledge, skills, and relationships necessary to produce your desired outcome. Leverage can shorten the learning curve—the production process. Leverage multiplies your actions and speeds the process along by creating an exponential component. Accessing the knowledge and skills of others using LinkedIn, Facebook, MySpace, Twitter, and other social networks expands your library of resources beyond the traditional four walls and book shelves. Leverage is the L in FLIIP.

Principle Number 3 is to Immediately Implement. Procrastination kills dreams. The I in FLIIP combines a sense of urgency with the importance of productivity. The double I highlights the need to *immediately implement* your plan of action. Yet most people are waiting until their situation changes. They're waiting until their kids graduate from college; they're waiting for their stimulus check; they're waiting for that special day. In essence, they're waiting for the proverbial ship to come in.

The reality is that we are the captain and the crew of the ship. Thus, the ship is not coming in—the ship is already sailing in the direction in which we are steering it. Every action—or inaction—moves the rudder of the ship, ever so slightly. But that small movement of the rudder has a huge affect on the direction the ship sails. The key is to *immediately implement* those actions and behaviors required to break away from the past and to launch into the future.

You never do anything, or have anything, unless you do it now. The only way that you can get from where you are to where you want to be is to take consistent daily action. Don't just plan to do it. Actually do it, and do it now. Flip the switch. The only way that you will ever break out of the past—break the cycle of failure in your life—is to do it now. Make the call. Deliver the goods. Accept the offer. Join the club. Read it. Write it. Say it. Give it. Do it. Do it now! The third principle is to flip the switch and *immediately implement* your plan of action.

And finally, Principle 4 is Persistence. Once you start, don't quit. It does not matter what others think you can or cannot do, don't quit. It does not matter how futile things appear. Don't quit. Be consistent. Persist and do not quit. Water your tree. Adjust your rudder. Jettison some fuel if you must. But whatever you do, don't quit. Persistently pursue your destiny. Og Mandino wrote,

I was not delivered unto this world in defeat, nor does failure course in my veins. I am not a sheep waiting to be prodded by my shepherd. I am a lion and I refuse to talk, to walk, to sleep with the sheep. I will hear not those who weep and complain, for their disease is contagious. Let them join the sheep. The slaughterhouse of failure is not my destiny.

Webster's dictionary also says to *flip* is to "lose one's mind or composure . . . to become very enthusiastic." Grammy Award winning rapper Eminem versed it this way in his song "Lose Yourself:"

Look, if you had one shot, or one opportunity
to seize everything you ever wanted—one moment
would you capture it or just let it slip?

To persist is to lose your mind and refuse to let it slip away.

FLIIP: *Focus, Leverage, Immediately Implement* your plan of action, and *Persist.* It's a simple acronym that I use to help my audience remember a simple strategy— a powerful strategy for anyone who desires to flip the switch and go from where they are to where they want to be.

WRIGHT

What do you remember most about your West Point experience, and how has that memory served as a steppingstone for your success?

ALCORN

David, first of all, most people understand that West Point is a difficult institution to get into. When I think about West Point—although I was not at West Point when the speech was delivered—my most significant memory of West Point is in reliving the moment that General Douglas MacArthur gave his final address to the Corps of Cadets, May 12, 1962. In his address he said,

Duty, honor, country: Those three hallowed words reverently dictate what you ought to be, what you can be, what you will be. They are your rallying point to build courage when courage seems to fail, to regain faith when there seems to be little cause for faith, to create hope when hope becomes forlorn.

David, those words resonate with me. They keep me incessantly focused on the three things that build my courage, that enable me to regain faith, and that create hope within me. That's what I remember most about my experience at West Point. It's the relationship and the connection I have with the words from the speech delivered by General Douglas MacArthur long before I graced the halls of the Academy. It goes beyond the military training. It surpasses the leadership development. It exceeds the intellectual foundation that any institution could provide. The memory is not physical or mental or spiritual. The memory is a combination of all of the above.

WRIGHT

So what three things have been your foundational steppingstones for success?

ALCORN

Faith, Fellowship, Freedom: They are my rallying points. They are what keep me in the fight. They keep me moving forward and readjusting my strategy and my plan of action.

Faith—Faith that what I desire to achieve is possible, not because it has been done before, but because I was able to vividly imagine doing it.

Fellowship—Fellowship reminds me that I am never alone. I have the fellowship of family, of friends, and of colleagues who lift me up, encourage me, and share my vision. I'm surrounded by people who are positive and effective. I have a supernatural spirit within me that is greater than anything in this world.

Freedom—I have freedom. I live in a time and a place where I have freedom of choice. I have the choice to rise or fall, the choice to win or lose, the choice to step up or step back on the road to success.

Thus, for me, the foundational steppingstones are faith, fellowship, and freedom.

WRIGHT

You talk a lot about choices. What is your philosophy regarding choices and the influence of one's choices on success?

ALCORN

I believe, incessantly, that wherever we are in life (or for that matter wherever we end up in life) at some point in our past we made a choice to be there. Either we chose to do it or we chose to not do it. Either we chose to accept things as they were or we chose to make a change. Either way, the choice is always ours—and so are the consequences. Life revolves around choices.

Success is simple. Every plan for success works for those who work the plan. Not everyone chooses to work the plan. Success begins with making good and effective choices.

WRIGHT

So what would you say is your number one key to success?

ALCORN

David, people have asked me that over and over again. I have always, without fail, responded that the most important thing one can do to achieve greater success is to work on oneself.

When I was expelled from high school in the ninth grade, I began to ponder my future. I realized that the only way my life would change was if I changed. I understood that my life would not get better until I got better. And, I was responsible for unleashing the winner within me.

For me, that meant learning more about myself, learning what I was good at, and what I enjoyed doing most. It meant discovering my uniqueness and the value I could bring to the world around me. It meant recognizing the effect I could have on the lives of others.

You see, David, to fulfill my purpose it is critical for me to study my craft, to research my audience, to understand their needs, and to prepare for the privilege to deliver the message. Many a good man has failed because he's had his wishbone where he should have had his backbone. I had to stop wishing and start working.

Johnny Wimbrey, who wrote *From the Hood to Doing Good*, says that your want has to become your must—not just a want, but a must. When you must have it, when you must do it, when you must become it, when you must get it or give it, you remove the likelihood that you'll ever give up. When it must be achieved, it becomes an inextricable part of who you are. In essence, it becomes impossible for you to separate yourself from getting it done.

My success began with just wanting it—truly wanting it. Les Brown, my personal mentor says, "You have to want a thing bad enough to go out and fight for it, to work day and night for it, to lose all your sleep for it . . ." He emphasizes the importance of desire. He says, "You gotta be hungry!" Whether you're hungry for the thing itself or you're hungry for the person you become in the process, you have to be hungry.

David, you must be hungry enough to consistently work on yourself to make yourself more valuable to the world around you.

WRIGHT

So, how do you maintain balance in your life? How do you work on yourself and stay organized and focused?

ALCORN

It's tough. Staying balanced and figuring out how to maintain my personal life and my business life, doing all the things that I truly enjoy doing, and interacting with all of the people I enjoy interacting with is tough. With the support of a coach, I compartmentalize my life into six main areas:

1. My spiritual growth, which I focus on daily
2. My family heritage and the type of legacy I come from and the type of legacy I want to leave
3. My physical well being. David, if I'm not physically healthy—if I'm not physically strong and if I don't have endurance and strength—I can't do what it is that I was created to do.
4. My professional development. And for me, that means gaining more knowledge and gaining more experience in the area that I want to have an influence.
5. My community involvement. Being able to give back and find those organizations that I can be a part of and those individuals whose lives I can influence. That's my passion.
6. My financial goals. Accumulating financial resources that allow me to be more, to do more, and to give more is important.

I'm supported by a mentor in each area of my life—someone I want to emulate in each specific area. My mentors help build my faith. They provide the fellowship I need, and they remind me of the freedom I have to choose my future. My mentors are my mastermind group. They help me maintain my balance and stay organized and focused.

WRIGHT

So why did you become a motivational speaker?

ALCORN

Someone once said a job is what you do to earn a living—it's how you pay the bills. A career is what you build to create a life. And, a vocation is what you were created to do to bring value to the world around you. Your vocation is hidden in your unique skills and gifts; it's revealed in your passions. The key to success is to align your job with your career and your vocation. Becoming a motivational speaker and sharing empowering information to help others grow, improve, and prosper has been my passion since I gave my first speech.

I was nine years old. I remember it as though it were yesterday. I stood in front of a small congregation, in a small church, in a small town in Monrovia, California. My knees were shaking. My palms were sweating. My stomach was churning as though I were lactose intolerant and I had just consumed a gallon of ice cream. My eyes rolled back and forth until I began to speak. Amazingly, when I spoke, it was as though a higher power was speaking through me. I became a vessel, and words flowed without thought or worry. When I finished my presentation, I realized that I had momentarily entered another zone. The world around me had momentarily disappeared and I was providing what it needed to reappear with more life, energy, and purpose.

I didn't become a motivational speaker. I was always a motivational speaker. I needed to learn how to position myself in front of the appropriate audience and deliver the message that had been given to me by the spirit within me.

WRIGHT

So what has hindered you the most in your pursuit of happiness and success, and how have you been able to persist through the hindrances?

ALCORN

That question brings to mind a comment that Tony Robbins once made. Tony Robbins said that "bad things are always around us, but, so are the good things." That's the same response I have with respect to your question about hindrances. Hindrances are always there, but so are the avenues and the opportunities to get around them.

My own self-perception has always been the biggest hindrance to my success. As a result, I have had many jobs. I have done many things. I have worked in many different areas. And although each role helped to develop me into who I am and what I'm good at, each role has delayed the passionate pursuit of my calling.

Once I recognized and accepted my calling, it became easier to resist lucrative job offers. I learned to work for "Me Incorporated" full-time while working a full-time job. Today, I am able to pursue my passion, and I am able to immediately recognize any hindrances. I now know when the thing in front of me is blocking me from doing what it is that I was created to do. In essence, I have flipped the switch on my own self-perception.

WRIGHT

If you had your life to live all over again, what would you do differently?

ALCORN

People are always asking questions like, "If you could start your life all over again, what would you do? If this situation were different, what would you do? If you won the lottery, what would you do?" I never think about "if I could've, would've, or should've." I prefer to focus on the things that I can change.

Every day I'm blessed—you're blessed, we are all blessed—with a new beginning. Each day comes with the opportunity to think, act, and be different than we were the day before. I begin each day by giving thanks for not only who I was, not only who I am, but also who I am becoming. Then I put my feet in motion, doing what I've been blessed to do—speaking for a living and empowering others with information to help them go from where they are to where they want to be.

WRIGHT

So what advice can you share with our readers—those seeking greater success in their lives?

ALCORN

Well, there are three things, quite frankly, that I'd like to share.

Before you place a stone under your feet as a steppingstone—while it's in your hand—remember that stones can either polish you or pulverize you, depending upon how you position them. Avoid positioning yourself for poverty through slackness and procrastination. Get to work and immediately start on your dream.

Work harder on yourself than you do on your job so that you can bring more value to your job and the world around you. You should spend full-time working on yourself. Recognize that you must *be* before you can *do* or *have*. So study yourself and work to enhance your own strengths while finding ways to minimize your weaknesses. Maintain a healthy spirit, a healthy mind, and a healthy body. Pray. Read. Exercise.

To have more, you have to give more. The more often you release what you *do* have, the more room you make for what you *can* have. Give love and you will be loved. Listen and you will be heard. Sow a seed and you will reap a harvest. I encourage you to give and it will be given back to you. That's my advice.

WRIGHT

Well, Patrick, now I know why you're "America's eXtreme Motivator." I really appreciate all this time you've taken with me today to answer these questions. I have taken notes here:

Focus, leverage, immediately implement, and persist. What an empowering presentation that must be. And working on one's self—my life will not get better, until I get better—really insightful.

I really do appreciate your sharing this with us today. I have learned a lot, and I know our readers will be empowered as well.

ALCORN

Well, David, thank you so much for this opportunity. I really appreciate it, and I hope our readers recognize that our goal is for them to *do* more, *be* more, and *have* more in their lives. Our ultimate desire is to help everyone to achieve the ultimate success they were created to achieve.

It's been a wonderful time visiting with you. I appreciate you and everything you are doing to help provide the steppingstones to those individuals who are trying to go from where they are to where they want to be.

WRIGHT

Today we've been talking with Patrick E. Alcorn. He is "America's eXtreme Motivator and founder of TTG Transformations, LLC. He is a successful entrepreneur who builds courage, faith, and hope through interactive and entertaining presentations.

Patrick, thank you so much for being with us today on *Stepping Stones to Success*.

ABOUT THE AUTHOR

PATRICK E. ALCORN is "America's eXtreme Motivator" and founder of TTG Transformations, LLC. He is a successful entrepreneur who builds courage, faith, and hope through interactive and entertaining presentations. From inner city youths to corporate peak performers, Patrick knows how to get you from where you are to where you want to be. He is a member of the elite group of motivators who enable the world to live more amply with greater vision and with a finer spirit of hope and achievement. Patrick works *with* you in a way that works *for* you to provide individual and organizational improvement. He is available as a keynote speaker for conventions, corporate training, and youth enrichment.

PATRICK E. ALCORN

America's eXtreme Motivator

PO Box 1074
Rowlett, Texas
877-297-8273
patrick@patrickalcorn.com
www.paidonpurpose.com

CHAPTER TWO

There are No Limits . . .
An Interview with... **Scott Schmaren**

DAVID WRIGHT (WRIGHT)

Today we're talking with Scott Schmaren. Scott is the owner and creator of Mind Performance Training™. He has used the techniques he has developed, Mind Performance Training to transform himself, losing one hundred and eighty pounds and taking control of his life. He brings that passion of transformation to his work. He has studied many different "mind technologies" for almost twenty years. His techniques are being used for weight management, overcoming fears and obstacles, achieving goals, managing stress, and many other things. Athletes and sales professionals are using his BAGUBA™ system to achieve peak performance, consistently. Scott is a husband, father to three incredible sons, motivational speaker, author, and a personal coach.

Scott, welcome to *Stepping Stones to Success*.

SCOTT SCHMAREN (SCHMAREN)

Thank you. I am happy and grateful to be here with you.

WRIGHT

Scott, the obvious question is: how did you go from three hundred and fifty pounds to one hundred and seventy pounds?

SCHMAREN

Most of my life I had been morbidly obese. Just as so many other people like myself, I had been looking for a solution with different diets, medications, and crazy off-the-wall programs. None of them worked for me, which we know is also true for many people. I had lost and regained hundreds and hundreds of pounds repeatedly, since I was thirteen years old. I had lost more than fifty pounds, I don't know how many times, and I can think of at least three times in my life that I had lost over a hundred pounds, always regaining the weight I had lost and putting on a few extra pounds just to make up for losing the weight to begin with, punishing myself.

I was feeling depressed, angry, and disgusted with myself for not being able to lose weight and keep it off. I was feeling lost and desperate—the emotional agony of feeling like an outcast, a freak, a monster (five feet, seven inches, and three hundred and fifty pounds). I hated myself and what I looked and felt like. The pain—physically, mentally, and spiritually—was destroying me as a person. It was all too much for me. The suffering I was enduring was completely and totally unbearable. My life at that time had no purpose I could see, I wanted to die. This is how I felt, inside myself, my prison, my torture chamber, yet I was very careful to hide my anguish and despair, letting the world only see me as a happy jovial "fat man." I was always hiding. The only person I was fooling was me. I wanted desperately to feel good about myself and make the pain and suffering go away.

Physically I was being tortured—I was a prisoner in a body that could not do much of anything. When walking up a flight of stairs, I was not able to breathe and I sweated profusely. My heart would beat a hundred miles an hour just walking to my car. The worst thing was not being able to experience physical activity with my three sons and be an active part of their lives. I could not do anything except watch them. The excuses I had included: I am too tired, my back is hurting, my knees are bad, etc. The excuses really only served one purpose, justifying in my mind my inability to participate physically in my sons' active lives. Just having to sit on the sidelines and watch as other fathers had a chance to do what I could not do—interact with my boys physically.

At five feet and seven inches and three hundred and fifty pounds I was big—*very* big. People noticed me because of my size and stature. There was nothing worse than having an uninhibited four-year-old yell out in public, "Look at the fat man!" I know how the Elephant Man felt—I was an enormous freak of nature.

I tried everything from crazy diets, different medications, whatever it was, to try and get rid of the weight and trying to relieve my emotional pain, always searching for the happiness I could not find. I was always looking outside myself to find happiness and to solve my problems. My thinking back then needed me to attach myself to something (a diet, medication, acceptance or love from other people) in order for me to achieve happiness. I was looking for and I thought I needed that "Magic Pill" that would transform me into a person who was happy and feeling good. It just never seemed to work.

I can remember specifically once in 1988, I lost one hundred and sixty pounds; I was on a quest to run the Chicago Marathon. I thought that losing the weight again would make me happy (what was I thinking!).

A local newspaper did a story on my losing weight and my quest to run the Chicago Marathon. Then a news station saw the article in the newspaper and they did a story on me. They were in the same building in Chicago where Oprah Winfrey was doing her show, and one of her producers saw my story. I was asked to appear on her November 15, 1988, "Weight Loss Show." It was the show where she had gone on a liquid fast system and had lost a lot of weight.

I was in the best physical condition of my life, yet I was miserable and unhappy. My first son was born almost exactly a year after that show aired and within eighteen to twenty-four months of being on that program, I had gained all the weight back that I had lost—again. I weighed three hundred and fifty pounds. The definition of insanity is doing the same thing over and over and expecting something different to happen. That was my life in the past—lose weight, gain weight, over and over.

I was so angry and disgusted with myself, and it has taken me many years to "wake up" and to become "aware" of who I really was, what I thought, why I was torturing myself, and what I needed to do to be happy and solve my weight issue.

I began studying about the conscious mind and the subconscious mind, how they worked and why some people could change and overcome life's challenges and why most people couldn't. I studied and learned different techniques, skills, and disciplines, including: hypnosis and Neuro-Linguistic Programming, creative visualization, different forms of meditation, and many other "mind technologies" (that's what I call them). I experimented on myself and my children. I developed some of my own systems and techniques and titled my program Mind Performance Training. I started to look within myself to explore, looking for answers. I sought to change my values and beliefs such as, why did I believe that I had to be obese all the time, when I didn't want to be, at least consciously.

As I began to explore my mind and my thoughts, I realized that happiness did not come from a "Magic Pill" or any other external source. The "Magic Pill" was really within me—it is within all of us. My thought process had always been in the past that once I lost the weight I would be happy and my problems would be gone. Boy, was I wrong. It is exactly the opposite. Once you become "Awake" and you become "Aware" of who you are, your thoughts, values and beliefs (many values and beliefs we have are self-limiting and destructive), you can begin to control them and change them. You first have to accept yourself for who you are at that moment in time and learn to like yourself.

My weight was a manifestation of my unhappiness. Once I became aware of that, I could begin to work on it and change myself. The feelings that were deep inside of me were not hidden anymore. I was aware of what was going on inside my head.

I began to work on changing my values and beliefs, using some of the techniques that I learned and some of the ones I developed. I focused on changing my values and my beliefs at a deep level of my subconscious mind. I began to allow myself to enjoy my life, my children, my wife, and all the things I really wanted to do in my life. I realized how wonderful my life was (it still is) and I was thankful for everything that I had in my life. For the first time in my life I allowed myself to experience true happiness—the happiness that had been inside of me my entire life.

At some point in this process, I no longer had a need to hold on to the excess weight, for insulation, protection, or anything else that I thought I needed to protect myself from the world. I started to lose the weight. I felt better. I lost more weight. And, I can say literally and figuratively, the heaviness of my past was lifted from my shoulders. It was time for me to start living my life and to start sharing what I learned with other people—something that I am passionate about.

Most overweight people know logically at a conscious level what they need to do to lose weight. In fact, most of them probably know more than many nutritionists and exercise physiologists because they've been through it and they've done it all. At a conscious level they really want to lose weight, but almost all of them have gained the weight they have lost back. People who have lost a tremendous amount of weight in their life, who feel good physically and have been exercising regularly, *do not* want to consciously go back to where they were. It's not a fun process, yet they always seem to do it.

More than 50 percent of the people in this country are overweight. I heard on the radio just last week that 70 percent of all men in the United States are overweight. That's a huge number and obviously it's not getting better. So all the programs and diets are not working. It seems that more health clubs are being opened and people are trying to get you to the gym, but yet we seem to be getting heavier, and heavier, and fatter and fatter. Being overweight obviously has to be a manifestation of something else. That's what I want to address in what I'm doing and I want to share it with everybody who wants to change and to be happy.

WRIGHT

What was the defining moment in your life that caused you to change your life and lose the weight?

SCHMAREN

For many years, I continued to study (I still do) how the mind works, how it makes changes, and how it sometimes prevents us from making the changes we need to make in our lives. I became focused on using what I learned to help my children, my friends, and everyone I knew who needed help and wanted to make positive changes to their lives.

All my energy was focused on everybody—except me. I was blind and I didn't want to know what I really needed to do to change my life permanently. I was hiding from the truth. I felt safe, insulated in my heavy body, protected from the world. I had my weight as a built-in excuse for failing and not accomplishing my life's goals. After all, in my mind, I was morbidly obese; it was my crutch, my handicap, and my justification for not participating 100 percent in my own life. The changes I desperately needed to make, I was avoiding, not at a conscious level, but at a subconscious level. I was so frustrated and angry with myself. The changes I wanted to make in my life were coming into conflict with my old values and beliefs that not only did not serve me, but were killing me. My values and beliefs were leading me slowly down the path of self-induced suicide. What is sad about that is I was holding on to all of this garbage in my mind and I would not let it go. My values and beliefs got in the way of my being happy, losing weight, and living the life I had envisioned for myself.

The cycle of losing weight and gaining weight continued, as did all the pain, frustration, depression, and finally the disappointment and hopelessness I felt. Like a mindless robot, my subconscious mind had me carrying out its orders and I remained morbidly obese, unable to participate in life physically, mentally, and spiritually. I was angry at the world for my predicament and I blamed everyone else except myself for what I had become. I was just going through the motions of my life, asleep and unaware, not knowing what I was doing to myself.

The defining moment for me came when my oldest son, Josh, came to me one day and said, "Dad, what are you doing to yourself? How can you expect to help other people when you aren't helping yourself? Dad, you need to take care of you, first. The work you are doing is so important to you and to the other people you are helping. You have to take care of yourself first. I need you to be here for me."

I will never forget that moment in my life, it changed everything for me. It felt like I had been struck by a lightning bolt (I had been). There is a saying that "when the student is ready, the teacher shall appear." I was at the right place at the right time. I was in the right emotional state, and it was as if a bullet had just pierced through all the layers of my mind, penetrating all the layers of garbage, clutter, and self-limiting beliefs that had accumulated throughout the years that kept getting in the way of my becoming happy and then losing the weight. At the deepest levels of my subconscious mind I was affected, I had awakened. It was like a slap in the face.

Politely, I thanked my son and agreed with him very nonchalantly; and then I had to go off to be by myself. When I was alone I was overcome with emotions that had been building up inside of me for many years. These were feelings I had not felt in a very long time and included responsibility for my actions and shame for blaming others for my troubles all these years. I spent a long time crying, releasing and washing away so much of the pain and unnecessary suffering from my past that I had put myself through. It was just a huge emotional release, a powerful cleansing of my mind and my soul.

It was just what I needed—I needed that moment with my son. For the first time in my life I was really, "Awake," "Aware" and "Alive." (You will hear me say that a lot: Awake and Aware). I became aware of what I was thinking, of what I was feeling, and what I was experiencing physically, mentally, emotionally, and spiritually. At that moment I realized that I was the source of all the pain and anguish in my life. It was my fault, no one else's and if I caused it, I could change it and get rid of it.

A huge burden had been lifted from my shoulders and my life. The heavy "rocks" of guilt, disappointment, jealousy, fear, anger, and so many other awful things I had been carrying around on my back that had been "weighing" me down had been lifted from my shoulders. The pain and sadness I had carried around for years, like a black cloud—a feeling of heaviness—was all gone. I was "Awake," and I felt good, free to change the course and direction of my life. I could accomplish all my goals, dreams, and visions. I knew what I needed to do. I was no longer in life's "coma," using avoidance, excuses, and denial to justify the reasons for my unhappiness and my heaviness physically and emotionally. I had

21

a new sense of clarity and vision that I never had before. It was as though all the pieces had suddenly come together just from a simple question from my son. I will forever be thankful to him for asking that question.

The process of change began. I changed all aspects of my life. The cleansing, healing, and forgiving of myself began and I allowed myself to let go of the limiting values and beliefs I had that were really hurting me, that got in the way, and weighed me down (literally and figuratively), preventing me from living an incredible life.

The process continues today. It will go on for the rest of my life. Change is an evolutionary process that does not end. You have to decide if you are going to control and direct change or you will let whatever happens happen, like a ship without a rudder, drifting aimlessly.

What is interesting is that, as I began to change and heal, becoming stronger, my ability to help other people got better, more powerful and highly effective. I was practicing what I was preaching; I became more congruent with what I was thinking and doing. What I was teaching and helping other people do to make powerful changes in their life, I was doing for myself. The experiences they were having, I was having too. My ability to relate and communicate with other people helped me to help them better and to help myself, too. I wasn't just "talking the talk," I was "walking the walk." That made a huge difference in my life and in the lives of the people I was helping.

It's funny, I've been doing work with my boys for many years and I am still helping them with their performance in school, their athletics, and now more than in the past, how they feel about themselves, getting rid of the self-limiting beliefs and the "stuff" that accumulates in their heads. It's funny how they're always the ones who seem to be teaching me something new about life every day, instead of the other way around. I always seem to get exactly what I need from them to help move me forward in different areas of my life. They give me great ideas and insights to overcome a challenge or to improve myself. I have a wonderful connection with my boys and I am so grateful to have it. It is an amazing gift. By the way, their mother is pretty good herself. She gets a lot of the credit (honestly, most of the credit) for the way my sons have become fine young men and for putting up with me all these years.

WRIGHT

So many people set goals for themselves such as losing weight, achieving financial success, achieving peak athletic or sales performance, and many other worthwhile goals. Often they seem to get stuck, put obstacles in their own way, self-sabotage their successes, or they simply give up. Why do you think that happens?

SCHMAREN

Well, I think there are two things that keep most people from achieving their goals, dreams, and visions to achieve happiness in their lives. These two things are their values and beliefs. Values and beliefs drive you to take action or not to take action, for better or for worse. Your subconscious mind moves you down a path of your life toward your goals, dreams, and visions that you have deeply implanted in your subconscious mind. Your mind is a goal-achieving machine and is very good at accomplishing whatever you truly believe at a very deep level in your mind. Whether they are good or bad goals, your mind doesn't really care; it will achieve greatness and happiness for you or misery and pain.

Most people aren't even aware of their goals (good or bad) or they think they don't have any goals. Guess what? You do—it's how your mind functions. As I stated earlier, the greatest single thing you can do to effect change in your life is to become "Awake" and "Aware" of what and how you think. Ignorance is your greatest enemy.

So, you have values and beliefs in your mind that shape and form who you are, what you think, your judgments, and how you experience the world. How did you get them? You are the sum of all the experiences you have had since the day you were born. Your subconscious mind has recorded every single experience— good, bad, real, and made up—it is all there. Based on those experiences, your view of the world and how you will or won't react to it is shaped and formed. All these experiences have been imprinted at a very deep level on your mind defining who you are. What is interesting is that many of your values and beliefs (especially the self-limiting and the negative ones) do not come from you. They came from your families, friends, teachers, and sometimes traumatic events or extremely emotional situations you have experienced. The people who love you the most—your family members and friends—did not do this on purpose to hurt you. Sometimes you misunderstand things that were said to you and sometimes they do not realize that what they are constantly saying to you has an effect on what you believe about yourself and who you are.

You need to work on focusing on the positive goals, dreams, and visions you have that make you a happy and complete person. Most people don't really know why they react the way they do to the situations they encounter in their lives. They really aren't aware of why they stumble and fall, self-sabotage, or simply just lose interest in their goals and give up.

Your values and beliefs in your subconscious mind move you toward the path that you take throughout your life. It can be an incredible journey, it can be a horrible nightmare, but most people are not even aware of it. How did all these people have so much influence on what you value and believe? From the day you were born into this world, your subconscious mind is recording every single experience you have. It will continue until the day you die. It does not distinguish between reality and fantasy, good or bad. Whatever you continually tell your subconscious mind with conviction or in a highly charged emotional state, it will accept as the truth.

The subconscious mind then begins to shape and mold these views and experiences as you begin to make judgments about yourself. You use those as filters to judge the world around you and how you experience it. You see patterns of behaviors—good and bad—run generation to generation in families repeatedly.

For example, look at professional athletes. Eli and Payton Manning are two brothers. Both are top professional football quarterbacks. Their father, Archie Manning, was an NFL quarterback. Is this because the family has genetically predisposed to be good at what it takes to be successful playing football? I do not think so. What has made them successful is the environment Payton and Eli grew up in and the value and belief systems they were exposed to continuously every day that shaped and formed the expectations, the goals, dreams, and visions they had for themselves. They had no limiting beliefs to stop them; they believed they could be the best. They only saw possibilities.

24

It is the same with families that have been on welfare from generation to generation, never improving their self-worth. They only see the darkness and hopelessness of their lives as a value structure. They are using the same process as the Manning family, just the opposite end of the spectrum. Your mind will pursue and achieve good or bad goals, dreams, and visions relentlessly, every day.

Make a conscious decision to make a change in your life. Set a goal, whether it's to lose weight or some other positive change. Losing weight is always the easiest because you can see the results—positive and negative—easily. Begin to make conscious decisions to change.

For example, you start eating a little bit better and you lose some weight. You start to exercise a little bit and you begin to lose more weight. You will begin to consciously feel a little bit better and you will use your sheer will, determination, and discipline to force these changes to happen. You will begin to change physically.

Eventually, your subconscious mind begins to wake up. Sometimes it doesn't happen until you lose all the weight and you're thin and you feel really good and you're probably in the best physical shape you've ever been in your life. Your subconscious wakes up and you think, "Hey wait a minute, what are you doing? This is not who you are. You're the fat guy, you're the heavy guy. Being heavy protects you from all the pain in the world. You need this weight to be safe." There is a tremendous conflict between the conscious mind, which is trying to change by losing weight and being healthy, and the subconscious mind that thinks change is bad and that your weight is helping and protecting you by keeping you heavy. These are your values and beliefs. War rages between change and the status quo in your mind. Guess who almost always wins? It's going to be the subconscious mind. The subconscious mind almost always wins and the process of sabotage, subtle excuses, and obstacles are suddenly in your way. Your subconscious mind wants everything to go back to the way it was so that everything is congruent with your values and beliefs and, in this case, you gain weight. Many times you end up gaining more weight than when you started. The subconscious mind "takes no prisoners" and you need to be intensely focused on your values and beliefs and becoming "Awake" and "Aware" of your thoughts and your actions.

25

Most of us aren't even aware of the process and the cycle constantly repeats. We become depressed, angry, frustrated, and we don't know why we can't change. If making changes happens in your life as in this example of losing weight, then I think you would agree that no one who has lost a good amount of weight and become physically fit would ever go back to being obese, right? Wrong! Very few people ever maintain good physical fitness after having been overweight. It is not a conscious process. Your values and beliefs decide for you. You become what you think about and experience all the time.

It's important for us to become "Aware" of what we think. People need to become "Aware" of what they think and of who they really are. The moment you can achieve self-awareness in your life and you become truly "Awake," something new and wonderful enters your life. You are given a gift, the greatest gift you could ever want—the gift of choice. For many people, it's the first time in their life that they become "Awake" and "Aware." They become free to use their choice to decide what goals, dreams, and visions they want for their lives. A huge burden has been lifted from their shoulders and they begin the process. They start changing their lives and they experience happiness.

WRIGHT

How do people change and reshape their values and beliefs to get what they really want out of their lives?

SCHMAREN

Changing your values and beliefs happens at a very deep level of your subconscious mind. It's a process that is never-ending and it is an evolutionary process.

I am aware of that process today and I work on it every day. It may sound like a daunting task, but it really isn't. In fact, it is exciting and fun. When you "Awaken" yourself and become "Aware" of all the aspects of your life and realize that you are in control now, you wake up every day with the passion and excitement that life is going to bring you something spectacular today that will affect your life in a positive way!

26

The biggest, most important step you can take to make permanent changes in your life is to become "Awake" and "Aware" (there, I said again) of all the aspects of your life—your thoughts, beliefs, values, and what you say to yourself. You become "Awake" to the fact that your values and beliefs got you where you are today and you take responsibility for it. You become "Aware" that the thoughts you have in your mind may not be serving you and, more than likely, are hurting you. You become self-aware of your thoughts, your actions, what you say to yourself all day long, and how you react to the situations life presents to you. They are all critical to making permanent changes in your life. You cannot change what you are not aware of. Becoming "Awake" and "Aware" and really being honest with yourself can be painful at first. Having to accept yourself for who and what you are, owning your past, and letting it go is painful, for a short time. The process is freeing and it removes the burdens, the heaviness, and the excuses of your past. You will be free to be who you really are and be proud of yourself.

All the negative values and beliefs you have accumulated over the many years of our life since the day you were born come from constant repetition. All the negative input accumulates in your mind, primarily at the subconscious level, like clutter, baggage, and garbage, blocking up your mind and preventing you from making changes and taking control of your life every time you try. Things like guilt, obligations, fear, anger, jealously, self-limiting beliefs, and so on (I am sure you could make a list a mile long).

You need to reverse this process, of accumulating negative input and replace it with good, positive input. You will use the same process that you used to clutter your mind with junk. This time you are "Awake" and "Aware" and you can control what you put into your mind to reshape your values and your beliefs. It's the same process you have used in the past that you were not even aware of—repetition. Repetition can have a profound effect on the subconscious mind in a positive way and it is simple and powerful. There are several things you can do. I'll give these to you in simple steps that will allow you to use positive repetition every day to help you effect positive change in your life.

Step one: Take some time out of your day, every day, and write one page of positive affirmations. You will be affirming the behaviors you want to have and affirming the goals, dreams, and visions you want to achieve. They must be handwritten, not typed on your computer, and you must state them in the present tense or, if you write a goal, you must have a definite date for achieving it. State the date in the affirmation. Affirmations are more effective if you write them out in your own handwriting and you reread them back to yourself. Your mind, for some reason, accepts what you write, in your own handwriting as the truth.

The reason you state what you want to achieve in the present tense is because your subconscious mind does not distinguish between what is real and what is not. If you tell your subconscious mind something over and over again, it will begin to move down that path to achieving what you say. How many times have you heard that something was "a self fulfilling prophecy"? If you doubt what I am saying about your subconscious mind accepting a fantasy as a fact, think about this: How many times have you awakened in the middle of the night from a nightmare? You are in a cold sweat, your heart is racing—you are terrified. These physiological reactions happen because you are reacting to a life or death situation (in your mind). After a few seconds you realize it wasn't real, thankfully. That dream was a fantasy, your subconscious mind thought it was real and induced the "fight or flight" response in you that happens in a life or death situation.

Step two: You need to become aware of what you say to yourself. What you are saying to yourself all day long is very important. Whether you know it or not, you are talking to yourself all day long and much of it is not positive. You need to become aware of your negative self-talk and catch yourself when you are saying something negative to yourself, about yourself, or about other people. When you catch yourself saying something negative, immediately stop the thought. Tell yourself, "This is not who I am. This is not what I believe." Then reframe it and say it to yourself as a positive statement in your mind—a positive affirmation.

For example: "I will never be thin." Stop saying that immediately and reframe it. Restate it as a positive affirmation. Say, "Every day I am getting closer to maintaining my weight of—" Once you are "Aware" of what you are saying to yourself, you will catch yourself all day long doing it. When you do this for a while, it becomes a game and the chatter in your mind will change. This simple

28

exercise has a powerful affect on your subconscious mind. The key here is to be diligent and always be aware of what you are thinking. Like an armed guard, protect the most priceless treasure in the world—your mind.

Step three: Create a clear, sharp picture of the vision you have of what you want your life to be, whether it's a goal you're trying to set, something you're trying to accomplish financially, a habit that's not serving you or an obstacle in your life. You need to create a clear, sharp vision of what you really want. You need to make that vision the most exciting movie you have ever seen in your life. After all, it is a movie of your life accomplishing your goals, dreams, and visions; what could be more exciting? You need to make that vision real. You can see it, feel it, hear it, and experience it in every way. Then every night as you're lying in bed, with the television off, visualize that image. Make it real; make it bright, clear, loud, vibrant, and rich in experiences and emotion, just as though you're watching the best movie you've ever watched in your life. As you are about to fall asleep, tell yourself, "This is who I am. This is what I want and I will accept nothing less than this!" then allow yourself to fall asleep.

When you are in that process of falling asleep at night, your mind begins to slow down as you begin to enter your creative state of mind. It is a direct access to the subconscious mind and the state of your mind where you dream. (You are also in this state of mind in the morning, just as you are waking up. You should repeat the process in the morning). Do this every night right as you go to bed. Focus on what you want. It will have an effect on your values and beliefs. Again, repetition is the key.

If you doubt the power of this exercise, read a book about any great businessperson, world or religious leader, or great athlete. You will find that great people all had a clear vision of what they wanted to accomplish and they focused on it all the time.

Repeat your affirmations out loud to yourself every single day and they can change your life.

As you begin to reshape and reform your values and your beliefs, there are things you can do to affect the subconscious in an instant. You can enter a very deep level of your mind and penetrate all the layers of "stuff" to effect change. It happens all the time. We see change happen to people in a highly charged emotional or sometimes a traumatic situation. A permanent and lasting imprint is made and their path is forever altered.

The techniques I developed for my Mind Performance Training allows you to make quick and permanent changes to your values and beliefs. The techniques allow you to open up that doorway in your mind so you can access your subconscious mind directly.

Our lives are always changing and evolving and the process of change for all of us continues throughout our entire lives, whether we're aware of it or not. Be "Awake" and "Aware" and you decide what you want in your life. Take control and begin to reshape your values and beliefs so you can live the life you want to have and have always wanted. You deserve it; we all deserve to live a life full of happiness, achieving all of our goals, dreams, and visions.

WRIGHT

Scott, why now, at this point in your life, did you decide to pursue this quest—to help people make incredible and positive changes to their lives?

SCHMAREN

As far back as I can remember, I've always been driven and I've always wanted to help other people. I cannot even begin to describe to you the incredible, blissful, loving feelings that helping people gives me. It is better than any drug one could ever take and it is highly addictive. When you help people and you see them actually make positive changes to their life and they feel good about themselves, it is awesome! I've always been a person who wants to give of myself.

Like many people, throughout the years I became caught up in my own issues and I allowed them to get in the way of my helping others and fulfilling my life's purpose. I used excuses such as life, my family, work, and my weight for not doing what I was truly driven to do. Unfortunately, I stopped listening to that little voice in my mind, my gut feeling, and my intuition. After I stopped listening to that voice, it slowly began to fade away until I could not hear it anymore. It was buried beneath all the excuses and self-limiting beliefs I had. That voice was trying to tell me to help other people any way I could, that it was my true purpose in life, and it was the key for me to live a happy life. Not knowing it at that time, that passion to help other people was my salvation and a direct path for me to living a happy and fulfilled life. It was, and is, where my heart and soul are and have always been; this was and still is me.

All that baggage I had allowed to get in the way for so long prevented me from experiencing happiness.

As I stated earlier, I reached "rock bottom," knowing that if I did not change, my obesity would end my life at an early age and destroy my family. My family is so important to me that when I was at my wits end, my family became more important than my self-destructive behavior. A wonderful thing started to happen and I began to change. I became "Awake" and "Aware." I really began to work on myself, finding out who I am, what I feel, and what I wanted out of my life.

When that happened, my focus changed and my subconscious mind began to direct and guide me down a new path in my life. Those gut feelings and my intuition came back to me. The desire I had that had always been important to me—helping other people—came back to me.

The "Little voice" in my head returned to me, this time it was screaming and yelling, so I could not ignore it. I knew that I had to pursue the path that I was passionate about—making a difference in other people's lives. I wasn't exactly sure what it was going to look like and how I was going to do it, but I just started to go down that path, focused on the image I had planted deeply and constantly in my mind. As my awareness of what was important to me increased, the pieces of the puzzle began to fall into place. The process for me was nothing less than transforming and amazing. I started to develop my Mind Performance Training program and pursue the path I'm on now.

I can think of nothing else I'd rather be doing right now; it has truly electrified and enriched my life. I am happy and so grateful that I have been given this clarity, focus, and the driving passion every day to go out and help other people. It is a gift that I am grateful for.

WRIGHT

What is Mind Performance Training (MPT) and what makes it different?

31

SCHMAREN

Mind Performance Training (MPT) grew out of my frustration of my past—the misery I had caused myself in my life. As I became more "Awake" and "Aware" in my life and how I experienced it, I became increasingly fascinated about how the human mind works and in some cases, how it works against us. I learned how and why the things people constantly try to accomplish didn't always work out. People often get into a cycle of making a diligent effort to change just to revert back to their old behaviors.

I began to read a lot of books (I still do) on the human mind and how it works. I also studied of what I call "mind technologies" such as Neuro-Linguistic Programming, hypnosis, creative visualization, different meditative disciplines, and many other powerful techniques that help people make changes to their lives.

I went to school and became a certified clinical hypnotherapist and, as my knowledge grew, I realized, based on my own experiences, successes, and setbacks that everything I learned was great but it did not have the affect for me that I needed to change the direction of my life. I started adding new ideas to the equation to make the affect and results more powerful and more productive so that change for the average person can happen quickly and permanently. I wanted the average person to be able to use the techniques. Once they learned them on their own, as a new set of skills and habits, they could accomplish all their goals, dreams, and visions for the rest of their life and would be able to overcome whatever challenges they might face in their lifetime. MPT was born.

Mind Performance Training today is a powerful and productive tool for anybody who wants to make dramatic change to their lives and who wants to accomplish all their goals, dreams, and visions. Mind Performance Training, as effective as it is, is still evolving and changing, adapting and improving. I'm always looking to improve its effectiveness.

MPT is designed to work with people to help them make effective change at the deepest levels of their subconscious mind where their values and their beliefs are shaped and where they can be reshaped and changed. What makes MPT so different and powerful is that it allows people to see, feel, hear, and experience the information they need to experience to effect change in their life in the exact way they need to experience it. We all experience the world differently. That is why when we watch a movie, read book, or even witness an accident, each of us takes away from it something different and has a different opinion of what they experienced. MPT lets people experience the techniques and exercises in the way they need to, to effect change in their life. Two people using MPT will each experience what they need to make change happen and they'll experience it in their own unique way. Experiencing a message that is geared specifically for you is much more effective. The results you get and the changes you will make will be permanent.

WRIGHT

Who can benefit from MPT?

SCHMAREN

I'm going to make a very broad statement—I believe that anyone who wants to make changes to his or her life can use this program and to make those changes. This program can help people become "Awake" and "Aware" so they can take control of all aspects of their life. That may sound simplistic and it is. So many people want to change—whether it's weight management, to accomplish a goal, perform at peak performance level, consistently manage stress, overcome fears, or whatever worthwhile endeavor it is—and they just do not know how. We are taught to read, do math, and dissect a sentence. We are taught history, geography, how to drive a car, and just about everything except how to make changes to our lives and to accomplish our goals, dreams, and visions so that we can be happy.

Mind Performance Training is simple. I find that the simpler something is, the more effective it is. People can learn how to make permanent changes to their values and beliefs, and once they become "Awake" and "Aware" of their thoughts at all levels of their mind, they can begin the process of "change." I've said that often in this interview, and I really believe that it's so true.

Many people become "Awake" and "Aware" for the first time in their lives and it is a very freeing, emotional experience. They know what is going on in their head and that allows them to take control. Once they have awakened, they cannot go back to being in that "coma" again. They cannot go back to the way they were—not knowing who they are, what they think, what they believe, and what they want. The feeling is amazing and indescribable.

It's sad that most people go through life almost like zombies. They're born asleep, they grow up asleep, they work asleep, they get married asleep, and they live their lives asleep, not knowing what they truly want. Some of the things they are doing are very destructive to themselves. They just accept it as their burden in life to carry; sometimes they aren't even aware of it. They just accept whatever life gives them. They don't know why they have the values and the beliefs they have. They might not want them and those values and beliefs might not even be actually theirs—they may have assimilated them throughout the years from their family, friends, teachers, and so on. Most of the time, the damage is unintentional or was misunderstood.

Mind Performance Training is a system that allows almost anyone to make permanent and dramatic changes to their lives. It allows them to "wake up" and become free to live the amazing life they want and deserve to have. So when I say that MPT is for almost anybody, and everybody, I truly believe that with all my heart and all my soul.

WRIGHT

You use the words "Awake" and "Aware" you also talk about making "Permanent Changes." How does Mind Performance Training help with all of those things?

SCHMAREN

That's a great question, David. Our minds consist of our conscious and our unconscious (subconscious) mind. Our conscious mind records what we hear, see, taste, and smell when are awake. It helps us make decisions. It guards us and allows us to react and make conscious decisions in our everyday life. You want to believe that when you are conscious—awake—that you are controlling your life. In fact, it's your subconscious mind that controls everything.

Your subconscious mind controls every single function of your mind and your body, from your values and your beliefs to your heart rate. It uses hormones and chemicals that it tells the other organs to produce and release to keep you alive. The subconscious mind is the "general" giving the orders to the conscious mind and all the organs of the body, every second of every day. It tells you how to experience the conscious world as a whole. Your subconscious mind has recorded every single experience you have ever had since the day you were born—good, bad, real, or imagined. Those experiences are all stored in the subconscious mind and they have shaped your values and beliefs. They determine how you react to the world and how you feel about yourself, for better or for worse.

You are reacting using your values and beliefs at a conscious level, how you judge things, whether you like things or dislike things. When you see something and you instantly get a feeling that you don't like something or something else is great, those feelings and opinions are based on your values and your beliefs, for better or for worse. Your conscious mind is only the foot soldier, taking its orders from the "general"—your subconscious mind.

Using Mind Performance Training helps you make changes at a very deep level of your subconscious mind, at the level where your values and beliefs are shaped and formed. Those values and beliefs can be reshaped and reformed. Using MPT, you can remold your values and beliefs and get rid of the ones that are hurting you, as you become aware of them.

When you make those changes, and you do them at a very deep level of the subconscious mind, they become permanent and your subconscious mind begins to go down a different path. You develop a clear vision of what you want and where you are going, and that old road you were on changes. The changes might be subtle at first, as your subconscious mind now begins to chart a new course to a new destination. Your life begins to flow and day by day, step by step. It is like taking a trip on boat down a river to a new life, your life becomes congruent and everything is in line. What your conscious actions are and what your subconscious values and beliefs are match and there is no more conflict. You will begin to see the changes in your actions, in how you think, and how you react to situations. You have given your subconscious mind a new set of values, beliefs, and new orders of how you want your life to be.

Once your subconscious mind has those new values and beliefs, it will work 24 hours a day, 365 days a year for the rest of your life to create what you want

35

in your life and make it happen. It is your decision. MPT is an incredible tool to help people do just that. It has been a wonderful experience for me and is the process I still continue to work on today for myself and the people I work with. Your experience in life can be wonderful or a nightmare—you decide.

WRIGHT

How does Scott Schmaren define success?

SCHMAREN

To me, success is only one thing and that is a state of mind. Many people, including myself, have associated success with "things" such as money, cars, clothes, houses, and all the wonderful things they want. Most of the world currently associates and measures success with possessions. Don't get me wrong—it is great to have money, cars, and houses—they are all wonderful things to have. Abundance is a wonderful tool in your life. It's great to have nice things and to have financial abundance in your life, but they are not success; they are only the symbols of success. Possessions are there for us to enjoy and they enhance our lives.

Unfortunately, most people in the world want things in order to feel or experience happiness. It's almost like taking drugs to fill the emptiness in their life. That emptiness will never be satisfied by things.

If you doubt what I am saying, think about this and I am sure you will agree: We are now living in a world where people have more and more things. Our standard of living is higher than it's ever been in the history of the world and yet we seem to have more suicide, depression, drug and alcohol abuse, and addictions of all kinds (food is one). There are also more heart attacks, strokes, diseases like cancer, family problems such as divorce, people have problems with relationships. There is more crime such as murder, rape, and so many other physical, mental, and spiritual difficulties. So on one hand we have all these things and we are abundant in many ways, but we are lacking in many other ways. Something is wrong.

There are many people today who have abundance, but when you ask them if they're successful or if they are happy, they say no or they don't know or they just give a laundry list of things they own. They're never completely satisfied with what they have because they always want something new or different. They're trying to keep up with everybody else and they are trying to fill a need to be happy that they cannot fill.

I look at total success, in all the areas of life, like a very well built house. The foundation of your house is success as a state of mind. It's creating a mindset wherein you are happy and you love your life in your mind, body, and spirit. You must allow yourself to be happy, healthy, blissful, and appreciative for everything you have in your life. *You* create the image of what you want your life to look like.

Creating success in your mind is the foundation for having friends, family, love, abundance, and all the things that go with it. You must appreciate yourself and what you have. When you have created a vision of your happiness and success in your mind, you have the strong foundation of success. That foundation will support a magnificent home. It will support the abundance and all the things you want to accumulate. On a strong foundation you can build anything you want, confident that it is built on solid ground, strong and ready to withstand anything that may come your way in life. You will be able to weather any storm that life throws at you. On a strong foundation, you can build the most incredible home of your dreams and have all the wonderful and beautiful things life has to offer you. You can feel secure knowing that your home—your success—is strong and solid, and is built on an indestructible foundation of happiness and success in the most important place, your mind. Happiness and success are strong feelings and emotions that come from only one place—inside of you.

Most people are not building a strong foundation of success. Most people are doing the exact opposite; they're busy trying to make it in this world. They are trying to accumulate things that they think they need to be happy. They are building their house. Many times it is a magnificent house with one major flaw—no foundation or, at best, a very weak foundation instead of a strong foundation built on happiness and love and joy. So what happens during this process year after year?

They say things to themselves like, "One day I'll begin to love myself. I'll like myself. I'll have more time to spend with my children and my spouse, spending time together and growing as a family, and to enjoy life and to exercise and to eat right. I can do all those things later—after I have everything I want and need to make me happy." The problem is, that day probably never comes. They never take the time to appreciate all the wonderful things they have. They never take time to cherish them, to really enjoy them, and use them to build a strong foundation of success. Eventually, one day that house they built without a strong foundation of success crumbles and falls. Maybe it happens financially; maybe it happens emotionally. Then it falls apart. They have destroyed relationships with their spouse and their children. Perhaps they have a heart attack, a stroke, cancer, diabetes, or some other disease. Perhaps they develop an addiction. They end up with what they were avoiding most—sadness, an empty feeling of nothingness and worthlessness. They acquire all the things in life they didn't want to have. Sometimes that house they built is still standing and it's just an empty shell—there is nothing in it except just a bunch of things. There's no love and no happiness. Having abundance in your life and all the things that go with it are wonderful. But true success is a state of mind. When you can reach that state of happiness and bliss in your mind and you have a strong foundation of success, then you can manifest all the wonderful things in life, make them a reality, and truly enjoy them. You can share them for the rest of your life!

WRIGHT

Scott, you're currently working on a project that is very important to you—helping people who have lost their jobs and their careers. Please tell us about it.

SCHMAREN

The program I have developed is called "Programming Your Mind for Success" and I am donating my time to do this program at job fairs. I don't charge a fee for this program; all I need is a meeting room to do it in. The seminar is designed to help people create a more positive attitude and gain the skills they need to build a daily routine that will help keep that positive attitude and have positive expectations for their life. They will be taught a skill set that will allow them to expect great things to happen for them. It will allow them to put forth a positive energy and to attract great opportunities to themselves. When these opportunities come to them, they will be in a positive frame of mind—the right frame of mind—to go after them and to make a great impression with the people they interview with.

There is a reason this country was born and there is a reason that this country is the greatest country in this world. It's important that we help each other. Whoever wants a program like this for a job fair is welcome to contact me. I feel very strongly about improving the energy and optimism in this country.

There are many Americans right now who have lost their jobs. Some have lost more than their jobs, they have lost their careers. I want to help them to recapture their confidence, their positive attitude, and to regain the expectation of success in their mind. When they have a positive attitude and expect success, they can go out into the world knowing that the positive energy they are generating is attracting great opportunities to them.

If you doubt that, let me ask you this: If you were an employer who would you rather hire—a person who has a positive attitude and is excited about the job he or she is interviewing for or someone with a negative, defeated attitude?

It is obvious which one you would want to work for your company, isn't it? A positive expectation of success and happiness attracts opportunities and attracts great things in life. A negative, pessimistic attitude attracts a cloud that hangs over you, affecting your life negatively. That is a basic principle of our universe—you attract what you give out to the world.

We're living in a time in the United States of America where many people have lost their jobs or their lifelong careers. The prevailing energy and atmosphere in our country, in the newspapers, radio, Internet, and on television is extremely negative and dismal. What all that negativity does is create a very bad self-fulfilling prophecy of hopelessness and despair. The more we read the newspaper, watch television, and search the Web, the more we start believing all the negative ideas, forecasts, and predictions we hear and read about.

As I've been saying, if you are not "Awake" and "Aware," you will accept what's given to you in the world as the truth. Repetition, good or bad, creates your outcome. You have to decide if the negativity out there becomes your self-fulfilling prophesy or you can decide to create your own success.

When people lose their careers they lose their self worth, they lose their confidence, and sometimes they even lose their purpose in life. They don't feel good about themselves. They become very negative in their thoughts and the energy they put out to the world. The negative energy they are putting out attracts negative outcomes and they do not attract opportunities. They stop going after them and sometimes, when they have a chance at an opportunity, a job offer, or a career, they're in such a negative state of mind that the impression they make on their potential employer is not a good one.

I want to change that. I want people to have the expectation of success in their work and their career. Their negative energy needs to change to positive energy so they can attract great opportunities and have the expectation of success in their mind, in their body, and their spirit.

WRIGHT

Scott, if you were allowed to share only one message with the world, what would it be?

SCHMAREN

The one message I would share with the world is this: each of us, no matter who we are, where we live, or where we come from, has the absolute universal right to live a happy and abundant life. All of us deserve that. Happiness is what our minds are seeking out in life. Your life does not have to be the sum of all your past negative experiences. "Change" is your best friend, embrace it and, like a best friend, it will challenge you. Sometimes it will hurt your feelings or will frustrate you, but it will support you emotionally, physically, and spiritually. It will support you and push you through challenges, and will allow you to experience happiness and bliss in your life. Do not fear change. It is what you need; we all need it.

You need to take the first step and to invite your best friend, "Change," into your life by becoming "Awake" and "Aware." Wake up from the coma you currently exist in and change. Become aware of your thoughts—both positive and negative—and your actions so you can use your best friend, "Change," to help you. You will then be able to accomplish all of your goals, dreams, and visions in life.

Accept nothing less from yourself than what you really want; you truly deserve it. Never allow yourself to give up, surrender, or quit. And never let anybody, no matter what he or she says or who that person is, say that you're not good enough or that you can't do it. You *can* do it!

Listen to yourself. You can live a life of no limits. You need to believe in yourself. You need to believe in your ability to change, and to become exactly what you want. It is your choice. You have the power to either live your life in pain, misery, suffering, and physical and mental anguish or you can choose by using your best friend, "Change" today, right now, at this very moment in time, to create the incredible life you want and you deserve. Choose what you really want and I encourage you to invite "Change" into your life. If you do not change the direction of your life then you will get what you have always had.

What do you really want from your life? Now go get it!

WRIGHT

Well, what a great conversation. I really appreciate all the time you've spent with me, Scott. These are important topics that we've discussed, especially your Mind Performance Training program since it has worked for you. The things you have done in your own life are great accomplishments. I can just imagine how you can help others.

SCHMAREN

Thank you.

WRIGHT

Today we've been talking with Scott Schmaren. Scott is the owner and creator of Mind Performance Training. Scott has actually used the techniques that he's developed to transform himself by losing one hundred and eighty pounds and taking control of his life.

Scott, thank you so much for being with us today on *Stepping Stones to Success.*

ABOUT THE AUTHOR

SCOTT SCHMAREN is the owner and creator of Mind Performance Training™. He has used the techniques he has developed to transform himself from a lifetime of obesity to losing over one hundred seventy pounds and taking control of his life. He brings that passion of transformation to his work. Scott has helped many people manage their weight, control their anxiety, fear, and stress, and live productive lives by discovering their internal happiness. Sales professionals and athletes are using his BAGUBA™ system to achieve consistent, peak athletic and sales performance. Scott has helped people learn the skills necessary to accomplish all their goals and live the life they have always wanted.

Scott brings almost twenty years of knowledge, learning, and skills to his clients and audiences. Scott is a Certified Hypnotherapist and a Neuro-Linguistics Practitioner. He has spent thousands of hours studying different forms and disciplines in creative visualization, meditation, and guided imagery. He has also developed his own technique, Mind Performance Training™ (MPT) that allows people to make permanent and rapid changes to their lives, allowing them to accomplish all their goals, dreams, and visions.

When Scott Schmaren speaks, he delivers a powerful, positive, and passionate message to his audience, leaving them with the insight and the skills necessary to effect positive changes in their lives. Scott has designed programs for individuals, groups, and corporations using his knowledge, skill, and experience to adapt to his clients' needs.

His keynote speech, "Programming Your Mind for Success," teaches audiences how to unleash the power of their subconscious mind to accomplish all their goals, dreams, and visions so they can live the incredible life they want.

SCOTT SCHMAREN

Mind Performance Training™
2761 Acacia Terrace
Buffalo Grove, IL 60089
847-331-5848
Scott@MindPerformanceTraining.com
www.MindPerformanceTraining.com

CHAPTER THREE

To Change Your Life, Change Your Patterns

An Interview with . . . **Tumi Frazier**

DAVID WRIGHT (WRIGHT)

Today we're talking with Tumi Frazier. Tumi is the author of *Your Moment*. She is an international keynote speaker and coach. Tumi is also a change and diversity management specialist and takes time each month for keynotes, workshops, and seminar presentations. She develops and conducts leadership and coaching programs in organizations to improve accountability and commitment to cultivate high performance culture. She facilitates programs for women in business and leadership. Tumi is a co-founder and director of two other businesses: a business process re-engineering firm and a fashion house in South Africa.

Tumi Frazier, welcome to *Stepping Stones to Success*.

TUMI FRAZIER (FRAZIER)

Thank you, David. I'm very pleased and honored to contribute to this book.

WRIGHT

So why is it that two people with similar backgrounds and circumstances can have two entirely different outlooks on life—one becomes successful and yet one doesn't?

FRAZIER

Well, David, that's simply because success has nothing to do with background or circumstances. We all have one thing in common and that is the potential for greatness, no matter what our circumstances may be. It doesn't matter what advantages or disadvantages you were born with and it is not the conditions of your life that will determine your destiny. What will determine your destiny are the decisions that you make about how your life is going to be.

Those who succeed in life are not necessarily the most intelligent, or educated. Neither are they necessarily from well off and supportive families. In some cases, many of those from whom success is expected, fail, and conversely, many who seem doomed to failure succeed.

For instance, many would have thought that Helen Keller, who was left blind and deaf by an illness before the age of two, didn't seem to stand a chance of achieving success in life, but she did.

WRIGHT

So if we all have this great potential, then why do so many people never achieve great things?

FRAZIER

That's because many people allow self-limiting patterns control their lives. If we look at people who are successful and truly fulfilled in their lives, we will see that they have discovered the key to attracting the unlimited and immeasurable abundance that is available to all of us. These are the people who are prepared to pay the price in order to develop qualities and disciplines that average people lack. They refuse to accept the self-limiting patterns that most people exhibit. Success doesn't just happen—it comes as a result of doing certain things in a certain way repeatedly, identifying the many ways in which you limit yourself, and replacing these patterns with new ones.

WRIGHT

What are these self-limiting patterns?

FRAZIER

I will discuss them in a moment, but just to make things clear, success is built on a solid foundation of positive thoughts, beliefs, attitudes, behaviors, perspectives, and actions that are clearly observable. To achieve your goals you have to be willing to change old self-limiting patterns.

Now here are some examples of the patterns I'm referring to:

- *Thought patterns:* Thoughts can have a profound influence on our lives—both positive and negative. You are literally what you think. The thoughts you think about repeatedly eventually influence and shape you into the person you become. Think about someone who is successful in all areas of his or her life. What do you believe that person thinks about all day? Chances are, successful people are focused on their goals, how to improve what they do, love, joy, and so on.

  What about the thoughts of people who have achieved nothing in life? Would their mind be dominated by thoughts of success or ambition? I don't think so.

  Becoming aware of our thoughts is the first step in taking control of our destiny. Consciously changing repetitive negative thought patterns into positive affirmations can literally change our lives.

- *Belief patterns:* By constantly dwelling on the right positive thoughts you eventually convince your subconscious that these thoughts are true. These then become deep-rooted beliefs. Beliefs hold incredible power in our lives, and if you believe you cannot succeed because there are no opportunities for success, there will be no opportunities; if you believe you are a failure, you are a failure, if you believe you will succeed, you will. People have been known to achieve the impossible

47

when told they didn't stand a chance and when the odds of success were minimal simply because they believed in their own abilities.

- *Attitude patterns:* An attitude is the way you approach life and this colors the way you react to people and circumstances on a daily basis; it actually reveals your beliefs. For example, if you wake up tired and grumpy one morning, your attitude for that day may be quite different from how you would normally behave, and others can pick up on it instantly. Body language, tone of voice, and your entire demeanor reveals your attitude. It is important to also remember that your attitude can attract or repel others because we attract that which we are. So despite whatever is going on in your life or your emotional situation, even if you're faced with a setback, you can still have an attitude of gratitude.

- *Behavioral patterns:* It's easy to become stuck in the same old ways of doing things. Routines can serve us and give discipline and structure to our lives, but they can also stifle our creativity. Knowing that you can change patterns can liberate you from habits and behaviors that no longer serve you. You are probably familiar with the popular definition of insanity by Albert Einstein: "doing same thing over and over again and expecting different results."

- *Perception patterns:* This refers to how you view yourself and the world around you. We view our world through the prism of our experiences, feelings, and attitude. To understand why people behave a certain way, you have to understand the perception that drives others' behavior. Sometimes two people could be looking at the same situation but have different perceptions of it.

  Let's consider a salesman sent to sell shoes in the most primitive part of the world where no one wears shoes. He can either see this as an opportunity for shoes—an untapped market—or see no opportunity at all since no one knows what shoes are in this place.

- *Action patterns:* Keeping positive thoughts, beliefs, and attitudes constitutes an element of the mindset required to be successful. These will keep you in the game but will not necessarily move you forward. To be successful, you need to be action-oriented. Always remember that "The great aim of education is not knowledge but action"—Herbert Spencer.

The good news is that we can change old patterns if we choose to.

WRIGHT

So how does one change these patterns?

FRAZIER

One does this through a transition process. Transition enables us to make fundamental changes to how we see the world and respond to our new reality— good or bad. Now, transition offers crucial opportunities for personal and career development. Achieving closure on what you have been doing is critical during this period because you cannot move ahead with a constructive transition until you have finished with what was in your past. When you move into something new, you face a period of uncertainty and loss because you have to give up something. This response is normal because it reflects transitional stages that one goes through in life.

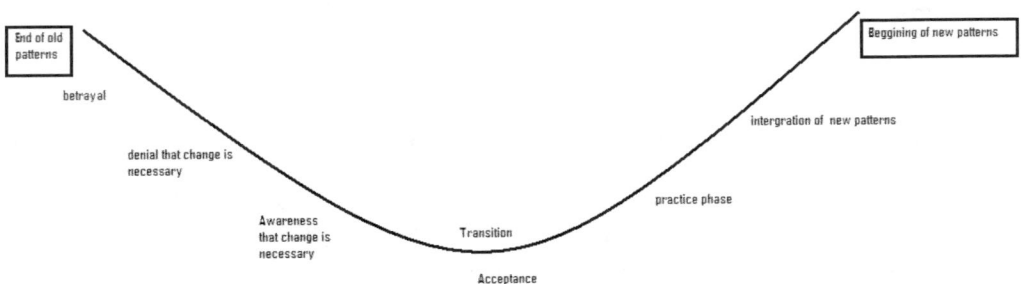

The first stage is marked by a sense of betrayal, followed by denial and anger, then awareness that change is necessary, acceptance, and finally, practicing doing things differently and integrating the new behavior into your routine, which eventually becomes a new habit.

The sooner you choose to get over the first two stages—betrayal and denial—the sooner you can experience the new beginning and seize the opportunities presented by the change itself.

During transition, it is easy to revert to old patterns because they keep you in a comfort zone. Sometimes you may be paralyzed by fear. It is important to remember that you always have a choice; even deciding not to choose is making a choice. You can continue to choose not to challenge your old patterns or you can courageously create new ones.

Every aspect of our life deserves to be constantly improved. This is what the Japanese refer to as Kaizen. If you want to change your life, you will have to change your patterns. Change is inevitable.

Similarly, businesses, governments, educational institutions, and other organizations have to alter how they operate. This is true now more than ever before. All organizations have been challenged by the current global economic recession and will continue to be challenged by new competition, new technology, new regulations, and socio-cultural shifts. Those who don't change will not survive.

WRIGHT

Is transition always an easy or smooth process?

FRAZIER

Not necessarily. Transition is not always easy or smooth because it always involves resistance and emotions. When you are in transition you may be caught up in anger, grief and pain. How you view your experience during the transition stages makes all the difference in the world. You may not have control about how things are changing in your life or in your organization, but you have total control of your attitude.

Now, let me give you a picture of my country, South Africa during the fifteen years of its freedom. This is a country that some people in 1990 thought would ignite in civil war, but instead, through the leadership of its remarkable former president, Nelson Mandela, South Africa has shown the world an example of peaceful and non-violent transition. However, the transition itself was not easy or smooth at all—we are still dealing with the effects of apartheid that still linger.

It is also important for us to remember that we are in a global cultural transition, now more than ever before. This is a transition to unite people all over the world and change old patterns that have been negatively affecting all of us socially, economically, politically, and historically. These will only intensify if not challenged. This is a new era that requires application of different patterns.

WRIGHT

Will you share with our readers the effects of apartheid on people in South Africa?

FRAZIER

Absolutely. Although the country has made a remarkable transition from apartheid to democracy, the challenge that remains is for some of our people to have a total paradigm shift—to emancipate themselves from self-imposed mental chains. Somehow some of us have allowed ourselves to become victims of the very same stereotypes and prejudices that we fought against by allowing ourselves to be labeled the same way as before the transition.

If you recall our history, the 1976 uprising marked a key moment in South Africa's struggle for liberation from apartheid. Taking up arms had become the only way to bring about the transition. The unfortunate part, though, is that people still resort to violence and destructive methods as a means of communicating their concerns or dissatisfaction.

For example, when communities are dissatisfied with the government's lack of service delivery they resort to destroying government property, including vandalizing other business property. When the train runs late, it is set on fire. These are the patterns that prevail, but the time has come for people—especially the young African people—to realize that the era of taking up arms is over. The battle is of a different kind now—the battle is against mental bondage. We will never be totally free as a nation unless we achieve mental freedom—freedom from ignorance, hunger, fear, mediocrity, and a sense of entitlement.

All over the world, self-imposed mental bondage is what prevents people from achieving success. Unless you have mental freedom, you will not be able to capitalize on any advantages, resources, or opportunities that come your way. The major responsibility for leaders in Africa and the rest of the world is to empower people to be accountable for their lives and to be self-sufficient.

WRIGHT

Speaking of leadership, what is it in your perspective?

FRAZIER

What comes to mind, David, is the definition that Dr. Miles Monroe has on leadership. It resonates deeply with me. He says, "Leadership is the capacity to influence others through inspiration, motivated by passion, generated by vision, produced by a conviction, and ignited by a purpose."

I believe leadership is the ability to take people where they wouldn't go by themselves. It is about motivating and influencing people toward positive attitudes, beliefs, and activities to reach specific objectives inspired by vision, bearing in mind that leadership doesn't only take place in boardrooms or presidential offices but it also takes place in villages and local communities. A leader is not only honored by the position he or she is elected to; but rather, enhances the dignity and the stature of the very position in such a way that the office complements the personal attributes of those who occupy it.

Let me tell you a bit about King Moshoeshoe, a beacon of African leadership. What distinguishes him from others, like Shaka Zulu and Dingaan, is that he wasn't a great conqueror—he didn't become famous because he was a warrior. He was a nation-builder, a supreme diplomat, a strategist, and a humanist.

There is a remarkable story that I will share with the readers about how Moshoeshoe dealt with his aggressor, Mzilikazi, who attacked him in his mountain stronghold. When Mzilikazi retreated after failing to take over the mountain, Moshoeshoe, in an unexpected turn of events, sent his enemy a herd of cattle and food. The kindness was too much for the enemy—they never attacked him again. However, some of Moshoeshoe's followers criticized his "unusual behavior" because they believed a defeated enemy should be completely destroyed, not fed.

The unusual way that Moshoeshoe dealt with his enemies suggests that the application of old rules to new situations will almost always compound the problem. The leadership challenge is in the ability to recognize that there is a new situation at hand and that it requires the application of a different or unexpected solution. The wisdom of Moshoeshoe's methods produced one of the defining moments in South Africa's historic transition to democracy.

Part of Mandela's legacy is counter-intuitive leadership—his ability to take practical steps, dictated by the conditions and circumstances he encounters. This is evident in the manner in which he and others took part in the struggle against apartheid. He had a way of disarming his enemies by offering them friendship as an alternative to enmity while maintaining his principles. One of Mandela's greatest virtues is his ability to truly listen and enable others to listen to and talk with each other.

WRIGHT

What is "Ubuntu leadership"?

FRAZIER

Although Ubuntu philosophy originates from Africa as a practical worldview that determines how people treat and interact with each other, the basic values of Ubuntu are so universal that various individuals throughout history have applied some aspects of the concept. As a matter of fact, the whole world could apply them to all aspects of life and leadership.

Ubuntu leadership style embraces the capacity to express compassion, dignity, humanity, and mutuality in the interest of building and maintaining communities of justice and mutual caring.

It is an innovative value-based leadership approach. One of my really good friends, Dr. Dumisani Magadlela, an executive coach and leadership development facilitator maintains that Ubuntu leadership includes flexibility and maturity that allows a leader to change his or her views when there is enough evidence to make the shift or when the shift in a leader's view is in the service of the collective good.

People and improving human relationships are central to this philosophy. It means people come first before products and profits. This doesn't necessarily

53

mean ignoring production and profits; but rather, concern for the rational measures of performance and the recognition of the importance of treating people right.

Raymond Ackerman of Pick 'n Pay, the leading chain store in South Africa, is known for the point of view that employees come first. In the years of apartheid, when housing for black people was limited, he arranged accommodation for his employees. This resulted in extremely committed staff, which in turn had a positive influence on productivity.

Ubuntu leadership is the critical ingredient behind successful human endeavors at all levels in organizations, as it motivates and energizes people who then willingly commit themselves to higher quality of work, which leads to productivity and profits. When people are entrusted with responsibility and are encouraged to use own initiative, they tend to adopt a responsible and accountable attitude.

The Shepherd style of leadership is a practical example of leadership in Ubuntu tradition. It was introduced by former South African State President Nelson Mandela. This style suggests that a leader stays behind the flock, letting the most agile go on ahead, at which point others follow, not realizing that all along they are being directed from behind.

Archbishop Desmond Tutu is a typical embodiment of the humanness of Ubuntu; he lives and leads with passion for collective human values.

Characteristics of Ubuntu:

- Integrity
- Accountability
- Respect
- Generosity
- Transparency
- Good faith
- Ethics
- Impartiality
- Transformation
- Participative
- Execution

Ubuntu philosophy enhances team spirit; the leader is central to and part of the team. Everyone is regarded as part of the organization's extended family in an atmosphere of solidarity. All team members are regarded as equal; people merely have different roles and responsibilities. Cooperation replaces individual competition and the dignity of all is respected, regardless of political, religious, and other convictions.

As the saying goes "umuntu ngu muntu nga bantu," which means, "I am because you are, and I became because you became and we are human beings through the eyes of other human beings, my dignity is your dignity"—Raiz Boneza.

It is imperative for leaders to encourage critical thinking and create an inclusive environment where teams can give feedback without leaders experiencing it as a threat to their security.

The bureaucratic and control techniques of previous generations are increasingly becoming ineffective. Today's leaders must be forward thinking, possess moral courage, and be skilled in diplomacy.

The changing structure of organizations, the growth of alliances between organizations, and the changing nature of work itself calls for new approaches to leadership.

WRIGHT

Is humility a sign of weakness in leadership?

FRAZIER

Absolutely not. Humility is an internal quality of a leader who considers the human being as the core, despite his or her position, and therefore worthy of honor, while realistically appraising his or her own worth. It is not putting oneself down, as some people may think. In fact, humility is central to the Ubuntu concept. It is about giving others respect because they are human beings. It is about serving and giving, rather than receiving.

We live in a world of self–absorption. Ego in leadership often leads to pursuit of self-gain at the expense of others. True leadership has no room for arrogance and self-promotion. Let's consider people like Mahatma Gandhi, Albert Einstein, Mother Teresa, Nelson Mandela, and Franklin D. Roosevelt; each one of them had a positive influence on the history of this world; they are the embodiment of humility.

WRIGHT

When faced with setbacks in life, what is your reaction?

FRAZIER

You know, David, I believe that setback, pain, and adversity are part of life, and life is about triumphing over adversity. So, when faced with setbacks, I consider them to be temporary detours on my journey. I therefore, do not complain or feel sorry for myself because I would be allowing myself to be a victim of circumstances. Instead, I focus on the ultimate goal. Can you imagine life without challenges? It would be a very boring existence. How then can we acquire coping techniques or competencies if we are not put through the test? We can't have victory without battles. "A captain earns his reputation during the storm"—Epicurus.

Most successful people will tell you that they've had their own share of setbacks or adversity, and what sets them apart is that they accept setbacks as natural phenomena. They have the ability to stay focused on their long-term goals.

"When you get in a tight place and everything goes against you, till it seems as though you could not hold on a minute longer, never give up then, for that is just the time and place the tide will turn"—Harriet Beecher Stowe.

Sometimes you are going to have to persevere—to have total commitment and determination to follow through with your vision—even in the face of insurmountable obstacles.

"Most people give up when they are about to achieve success. They quit on the one-yard line. They give up at the last minute of the game, one foot from a winning touchdown"—H. Ross Perot.

The truth is that we all face adversity in many forms, but even under the worst circumstances, we can still choose to focus on the positive rather than dwell on the negative aspect of our situation. We can find lessons and opportunities in that situation, no matter how hard it may be. Sometimes a problem may point out an adjustment you need to make to improve different areas of your life. I know of people who have lost their jobs, who have lost their homes, and even relationships, but who have risen above their circumstances to become successful businesspeople or own better homes than they had before. Many even find much more fulfilling and healthier relationships.

"When one door of happiness closes, another opens, but often we look so long at the closed door that we do not see the one that has been open for us"—Helen Keller.

How you deal with the circumstances of your life reveals many things about your character; adversity also reveals it. As Martin Luther King Jr., stated, "The ultimate measure of a man is not where he stands in times of comfort and convenience, but where he stands in times of challenge and controversy."

The two women whose stories really inspire me are Helen Keller and Wilma Rudolph. Helen Keller, an icon of perseverance, overcame seemingly insurmountable obstacle of deafness and blindness to become an influential lecturer and social activist. Wilma Rudolph is an example of struggle, overcoming setbacks, renewed hope, and ultimate triumph. Born prematurely to a poor family, she was struck by one illness after another—measles, mumps, chicken pox, and double pneumonia. She was eventually told she had polio and would never walk again. Despite all these setbacks, she became a remarkable athlete—the first American woman to win three gold medals in the Olympics.

No matter how trying the circumstances or how discouraging the odds, commit yourself to finishing the race and doing your best.

WRIGHT

We're proud of Wilma Rudolph in the United States. In fact, she was born in Clarksville, Tennessee.

What an interesting subject and I have really been enlightened here with our conversation. I'm sure that our readers will be also. I just appreciate so much the time you've taken with me today to answer these questions.

FRAZIER

Thank you so much, David, for giving me the opportunity to contribute and share part of my history and perspective with our readers. It has really been an honor; thank you very much.

WRIGHT

Today we've been talking with Tumi Frazier. Tumi is an author, international keynote speaker, and coach. She is a change and diversity management specialist who develops and conducts leadership and coaching programs in organizations to improve accountability and commitment. She facilitates programs for youth and women in business and leadership as well.

Ms. Frazier, thank you so much for being with us today on *Stepping Stones to Success*.

FRAZIER

It is my pleasure, thank you, David.

ABOUT THE AUTHOR

TUMI FRAZIER is the author of *Your Moment*. She is an international keynote speaker and coach. Tumi is also a change and diversity management specialist and takes time each month for keynotes, workshops, and seminar presentations. She develops and conducts leadership and coaching programs in organizations to improve accountability and commitment to cultivate high performance culture. She facilitates programs for youth and women in business and leadership. Tumi is a co-founder and director of two other businesses: a business process re-engineering firm and a fashion house in South Africa.

TUMI FRAZIER

5 Ealington, Sunninghill
Johannesburg, South Africa
Phone: +27 11 807 3669 / +27 (84) 206 7762
frazier@telkomsa.net
www.tumifrazier.com

CHAPTER FOUR

Find a Mentor and Believe in Your Dreams
An Interview with . . . **Jack Canfield**

DAVID WRIGHT (WRIGHT)

Today we are talking with Jack Canfield. You probably know him as the founder and co-creator of the *New York Times* number one bestselling *Chicken Soup for the Soul* book series. As of 2006 there are sixty-five titles and eighty million copies in print in over thirty-seven languages.

Jack's background includes a BA from Harvard, a master's from the University of Massachusetts, and an Honorary Doctorate from the University of Santa Monica. He has been a high school and university teacher, a workshop facilitator, a psychotherapist, and a leading authority in the area of self-esteem and personal development.

Jack Canfield, welcome to *Stepping Stones to Success.*

JACK CANFIELD (CANFIELD)

Thank you, David. It's great to be with you.

WRIGHT

When I talked with Mark Victor Hansen, he gave you full credit for coming up with the idea of the *Chicken Soup* series. Obviously it's made you an internationally known personality. Other than recognition, has the series changed you personally and if so, how?

CANFIELD

I would say that it has and I think in a couple of ways. Number one, I read stories all day long of people who've overcome what would feel like insurmountable obstacles. For example, we just did a book *Chicken Soup for the Unsinkable Soul*. There's a story in there about a single mother with three daughters. She contracted a disease and she had to have both of her hands and both of her feet amputated. She got prosthetic devices and was able to learn how to use them. She could cook, drive the car, brush her daughters' hair, get a job, etc. I read that and I thought, "God, what would I ever have to complain and whine and moan about?"

At one level it's just given me a great sense of gratitude and appreciation for everything I have and it has made me less irritable about the little things.

I think the other thing that's happened for me personally is my sphere of influence has changed. By that I mean I was asked, for example, some years ago to be the keynote speaker to the Women's Congressional Caucus. The Caucus is a group that includes all women in America who are members of Congress and who are state senators, governors, and lieutenant governors. I asked what they wanted me to talk about—what topic.

"Whatever you think we need to know to be better legislators," was the reply.

I thought, "Wow, they want me to tell them about what laws they should be making and what would make a better culture." Well, that wouldn't have happened if our books hadn't come out and I hadn't become famous. I think I get to play with people at a higher level and have more influence in the world. That's important to me because my life purpose is inspiring and empowering people to live their highest vision so the world works for everybody. I get to do that on a much bigger level than when I was just a high school teacher back in Chicago.

WRIGHT

I think one of the powerful components of that book series is that you can read a positive story in just a few minutes and come back and revisit it. I know my daughter has three of the books and she just reads them interchangeably. Sometimes I go in her bedroom and she'll be crying and reading one of them. Other times she'll be laughing, so they really are "chicken soup for the soul," aren't they?

CANFIELD

They really are. In fact we have four books in the *Teenage Soul* series now and a new one coming out at the end of this year. I have a son who's eleven and he has a twelve-year-old friend who's a girl. We have a new book called *Chicken Soup for the Teenage Soul and the Tough Stuff*. It's all about dealing with parents' divorces, teachers who don't understand you, boyfriends who drink and drive, and other issues pertinent to that age group.

I asked my son's friend, "Why do you like this book?" (It's our most popular book among teens right now.) She said, "You know, whenever I'm feeling down I read it and it makes me cry and I feel better. Some of the stories make me laugh and some of the stories make me feel more responsible for my life. But basically I just feel like I'm not alone."

One of the people I work with recently said that the books are like a support group between the covers of a book—you can read about other peoples' experiences and realize you're not the only one going through something.

WRIGHT

Jack, we're trying to encourage people in our audience to be better, to live better, and be more fulfilled by reading about the experiences of our writers. Is there anyone or anything in your life that has made a difference for you and helped you to become a better person?

CANFIELD

Yes, and we could do ten books just on that. I'm influenced by people all the time. If I were to go way back I'd have to say one of the key influences in my life was Jesse Jackson when he was still a minister in Chicago. I was teaching in an all black high school there and I went to Jesse Jackson's church with a friend one time. What happened for me was that I saw somebody with a vision. (This was before Martin Luther King was killed and Jesse was of the lieutenants in his organization.) I just saw people trying to make the world work better for a certain segment of the population. I was inspired by that kind of visionary belief that it's possible to make change.

Later on, John F. Kennedy was a hero of mine. I was very much inspired by him.

Another is a therapist by the name of Robert Resnick. He was my therapist for two years. He taught me a little formula: $E + R = O$. It stands for Events + Response = Outcome. He said, "If you don't like your outcomes quit blaming the events and start changing your responses." One of his favorite phrases was, "If the grass on the other side of the fence looks greener, start watering your own lawn more."

I think he helped me get off any kind of self-pity I might have had because I had parents who were alcoholics. It would have been very easy to blame them for problems I might have had. They weren't very successful or rich; I was surrounded by people who were and I felt like, "God, what if I'd had parents like they had? I could have been a lot better." He just got me off that whole notion and made me realize that the hand you were dealt is the hand you've got to play. Take responsibility for who you are and quit complaining and blaming others and get on with your life. That was a turning point for me.

I'd say the last person who really affected me big-time was a guy named W. Clement Stone who was a self-made multi-millionaire in Chicago. He taught me that success is not a four-letter word—it's nothing to be ashamed of—and you ought to go for it. He said, "The best thing you can do for the poor is not be one of them." Be a model for what it is to live a successful life. So I learned from him the principles of success and that's what I've been teaching now for more than thirty years.

WRIGHT

He was an entrepreneur in the insurance industry, wasn't he?

CANFIELD

He was. He had combined insurance. When I worked for him he was worth 600 million dollars and that was before the dot.com millionaires came along in Silicon Valley. He just knew more about success. He was a good friend of Napoleon Hill (author of *Think and Grow Rich)* and he was a fabulous mentor. I really learned a lot from him.

WRIGHT

I miss some of the men I listened to when I was a young salesman coming up and he was one of them. Napoleon Hill was another one as was Dr. Peale. All of their writings made me who I am today. I'm glad I had that opportunity.

CANFIELD

One speaker whose name you probably will remember, Charlie "Tremendous" Jones, says, "Who we are is a result of the books we read and the people we hang out with." I think that's so true and that's why I tell people, "If you want to have high self-esteem, hang out with people who have high self-esteem. If you want to be more spiritual, hang out with spiritual people." We're always telling our children, "Don't hang out with those kids." The reason we don't want them to is because we know how influential people are with each other. I think we need to give ourselves the same advice. Who are we hanging out with? We can hang out with them in books, cassette tapes, CDs, radio shows, and in person.

WRIGHT

One of my favorites was a fellow named Bill Gove from Florida. I talked with him about three or four years ago. He's retired now. His mind is still as quick as it ever was. I thought he was one of the greatest speakers I had ever heard.

What do you think makes up a great mentor? In other words, are there characteristics that mentors seem to have in common?

CANFIELD

I think there are two obvious ones. I think mentors have to have the time to do it and the willingness to do it. I also think they need to be people who are doing something you want to do. W. Clement Stone used to tell me, "If you want to be rich, hang out with rich people. Watch what they do, eat what they eat, dress the way they dress—try it on." He wasn't suggesting that you give up your authentic self, but he was pointing out that rich people probably have habits that you don't have and you should study them.

I always ask salespeople in an organization, "Who are the top two or three in your organization?" I tell them to start taking them out to lunch and dinner and for a drink and finding out what they do. Ask them, "What's your secret?" Nine times out of ten they'll be willing to tell you.

This goes back to what we said earlier about asking. I'll go into corporations and I'll say, "Who are the top ten people?" They'll all tell me and I'll say, "Did you ever ask them what they do different than you?"

"No," they'll reply.

"Why not?"

"Well, they might not want to tell me."

"How do you know? Did you ever ask them? All they can do is say no. You'll be no worse off than you are now."

So I think with mentors you just look at people who seem to be living the life you want to live and achieving the results you want to achieve.

What we say in our book is when that you approach a mentor they're probably busy and successful and so they haven't got a lot of time. Just ask, "Can I talk to you for ten minutes every month?" If I know it's only going to be ten minutes I'll probably say yes. The neat thing is if I like you I'll always give you more than ten minutes, but that ten minutes gets you in the door.

WRIGHT

In the future are there any more Jack Canfield books authored singularly?

CANFIELD

One of my books includes the formula I mentioned earlier: E + R = O. I just felt I wanted to get that out there because every time I give a speech and I talk about that the whole room gets so quiet you could hear a pin drop—I can tell people are really getting value.

Then I'm going to do a series of books on the principles of success. I've got about 150 of them that I've identified over the years. I have a book down the road I want to do that's called *No More Put-Downs*, which is a book probably aimed mostly at parents, teachers, and managers. There's a culture we have now of put-down humor. Whether it's *Married . . . with Children* or *All in the Family*, there's that characteristic of macho put-down humor. There's research now showing how bad it is for kids' self-esteem when the coaches do it, so I want to get that message out there as well.

WRIGHT

It's really not that funny, is it?

CANFIELD

No, we'll laugh it off because we don't want to look like we're a wimp but underneath we're hurt. The research now shows that you're better off breaking a child's bones than you are breaking his or her spirit. A bone will heal much more quickly than their emotional spirit will.

WRIGHT

I remember recently reading a survey where people listed the top five people who had influenced them. I've tried it on a couple of groups at church and in other places. In my case, and in the survey, approximately three out of the top five are always teachers. I wonder if that's going to be the same in the next decade.

CANFIELD

I think that's probably because as children we're at our most formative years. We actually spend more time with our teachers than we do with our parents. Research shows that the average parent only interacts verbally with each of their children only about eight and a half minutes a day. Yet at school they're interacting with their teachers for anywhere from six to eight hours depending on how long the school day is, including coaches, chorus directors, etc.

I think that in almost everybody's life there's been that one teacher who loved him or her as a human being—an individual—not just one of the many students the teacher was supposed to fill full of History and English. That teacher believed in you and inspired you.

Les Brown is one of the great motivational speakers in the world. If it hadn't been for one teacher who said, "I think you can do more than be in a special education class. I think you're the one," he'd probably still be cutting grass in the median strip of the highways in Florida instead of being a $35,000-a-talk speaker.

WRIGHT

I had a conversation one time with Les. He told me about this wonderful teacher who discovered Les was dyslexic. Everybody else called him dumb and this one lady just took him under her wing and had him tested. His entire life changed because of her interest in him.

CANFIELD

I'm on the board of advisors of the Dyslexic Awareness Resource Center here in Santa Barbara. The reason is because I taught high school and had a lot of kids who were called "at-risk"—kids who would end up in gangs and so forth.

What we found over and over was that about 78 percent of all the kids in the juvenile detention centers in Chicago were kids who had learning disabilities—primarily dyslexia—but there were others as well. They were never diagnosed and they weren't doing well in school so they'd drop out. As soon as a student drops out of school he or she becomes subject to the influence of gangs and other kinds of criminal and drug linked activities. If these kids had been diagnosed earlier we'd have been able to get rid of a large amount of the juvenile crime in America because there are a lot of really good programs that can teach dyslexics to read and excel in school.

WRIGHT

My wife is a teacher and she brings home stories that are heartbreaking about parents not being as concerned with their children as they used to be, or at least not as helpful as they used to be. Did you find that to be a problem when you were teaching?

CANFIELD

It depends on what kind of district you're in. If it's a poor district the parents could be on drugs, alcoholics, and basically just not available. If you're in a really high rent district the parents are not available because they're both working, coming home tired, they're jet-setters, or they're working late at the office because they're workaholics. Sometimes it just legitimately takes two paychecks to pay the rent anymore.

I find that the majority of parents care but often they don't know what to do. They don't know how to discipline their children. They don't know how to help them with their homework. They can't pass on skills that they never acquired themselves.

Unfortunately, the trend tends to be like a chain letter. The people with the least amount of skills tend to have the most number of children. The other thing is that you get crack babies (infants born addicted to crack cocaine because of the mother's addiction). As of this writing, in Los Angeles one out of every ten babies born is a crack baby.

WRIGHT

That's unbelievable.

CANFIELD

Yes, and another statistic is that by the time 50 percent of the kids are twelve years old they have started experimenting with alcohol. I see a lot of that in the Bible belt. The problem is not the big city, urban designer drugs, but alcoholism.

Another thing you get, unfortunately, is a lot of let's call it "familial violence"—kids getting beat up, parents who drink and then explode, child abuse, and sexual abuse. You see a lot of that.

Wright

Most people are fascinated by these television shows about being a survivor. What has been the greatest comeback that you have made from adversity in your career or in your life?

CANFIELD

You know, it's funny, I don't think I've had a lot of major failures and setbacks where I had to start over. My life's been on an intentional curve. But I do have a lot of challenges. Mark and I are always setting goals that challenge us. We always say, "The purpose of setting a really big goal is not so that you can achieve it so much, but it's who you become in the process of achieving it." A friend of mine, Jim Rohn, says, "You want to set goals big enough so that in the process of achieving them you become someone worth being."

I think that to be a millionaire is nice but so what? People make the money and then they lose it. People get the big houses and then they burn down or Silicon Valley goes belly up and all of a sudden they don't have a big house anymore. But who you became in the process of learning how to be successful can never be taken away from you. So what we do is constantly put big challenges in front of us.

We have a book called *Chicken Soup for the Teacher's Soul*. (You'll have to make sure to get a copy for your wife.) I was a teacher and a teacher trainer for years. But because of the success of the *Chicken Soup* books I haven't been in the education world that much. I've got to go out and relearn how I market to that world. I met with a Superintendent of Schools. I met with a guy named Jason Dorsey who's one of the number one consultants in the world in that area. I found out who has the bestselling book in that area. I sat down with his wife for a day and talked about her marketing approaches.

I believe that if you face any kind of adversity, whether it's losing your job, your spouse dies, you get divorced, you're in an accident like Christopher Reeve and become paralyzed, or whatever, you simply do what you have to do. You find out who's already handled the problem and how did they've handled it. Then you get the support you need to get through it by their example. Whether it's a counselor in your church or you go on a retreat or you read the Bible, you do something that gives you the support you need to get to the other end.

You also have to know what the end is that you want to have. Do you want to be remarried? Do you just want to have a job and be a single mom? What is it? If you reach out and ask for support I think you'll get help. People really like to help other people. They're not always available because sometimes they're going through problems also; but there's always someone with a helping hand.

Often I think we let our pride get in the way. We let our stubbornness get in the way. We let our belief in how the world should be interfere and get in our way instead of dealing with how the world is. When we get that out of that way then we can start doing that which we need to do to get where we need to go.

WRIGHT

If you could have a platform and tell our audience something you feel that would help or encourage them, what would you say?

70

CANFIELD

I'd say number one is to believe in yourself, believe in your dreams, and trust your feelings. I think too many people are trained wrong when they're little kids. For example, when kids are mad at their daddy they're told, "You're not mad at your Daddy."

They say, "Gee, I thought I was."

Or the kid says, "That's going to hurt," and the doctor says, "No it's not." Then they give you the shot and it hurts. They say, "See that didn't hurt, did it?" When that happened to you as a kid, you started to not trust yourself.

You may have asked your mom, "Are you upset?" and she says, "No," but she really was. So you stop learning to trust your perception.

I tell this story over and over. There are hundreds of people I've met who've come from upper class families where they make big incomes and the dad's a doctor. The kid wants to be a mechanic and work in an auto shop because that's what he loves. The family says, "That's beneath us. You can't do that." So the kid ends up being an anesthesiologist killing three people because he's not paying attention. What he really wants to do is tinker with cars.

I tell people you've got to trust your own feelings, your own motivations, what turns you on, what you want to do, what makes you feel good, and quit worrying about what other people say, think, and want for you. Decide what you want for yourself and then do what you need to do to go about getting it. It takes work.

I read a book a week minimum and at the end of the year I've read fifty-two books. We're talking about professional books—books on self-help, finances, psychology, parenting, and so forth. At the end of ten years I've read 520 books. That puts me in the top 1 percent of people knowing important information in this country. But most people are spending their time watching television.

When I went to work for W. Clement Stone, he told me, "I want you to cut out one hour a day of television."

"Okay," I said, "what do I do with it?"

"Read," he said.

He told me what kind of books to read. He said, "At the end of a year you'll have spent 365 hours reading. Divide that by a forty-hour work week and that's nine and a half weeks of education every year."

I thought, "Wow, that's two months." It was like going back to summer school.

As a result of his advice I have close to 8,000 books in my library. The reason I'm involved in this book project instead of someone else is that people like me, Jim Rohn, Les Brown, and you read a lot. We listen to tapes and we go to seminars. That's why we're the people with the information.

I always say that your raise becomes effective when you do. You'll become more effective as you gain more skills, more insight, and more knowledge.

WRIGHT

Jack, I have watched your career for a long time and your accomplishments are just outstanding. But your humanitarian efforts are really what impress me. I think that you're doing great things not only in California, but all over the country.

CANFIELD

It's true. In addition to all of the work we do, we pick one to three charities and we've given away over six million dollars in the last eight years, along with our publisher who matches every penny we give away. We've planted over a million trees in Yosemite National Park. We've bought hundreds of thousands of cataract operations in third world countries. We've contributed to the Red Cross, the Humane Society, and on it goes. It feels like a real blessing to be able to make that kind of a contribution to the world.

WRIGHT

Today we have been talking with Jack Canfield, founder and co-creator of the *Chicken Soup for the Soul* book series. Chicken Soup for the Soul reaches people well beyond the bookstore, with CD and DVD collections, company-sponsored samplers, greeting cards, children's entertainment products, pet food, flowers, and many other products in line with Chicken Soup for the Soul's purpose. Chicken Soup for the Soul is currently implementing a plan to expand into all media by working with television networks on several shows and developing a major Internet presence dedicated to life improvement, emotional support, and inspiration.

CANFIELD

Another book I've written is *The Success Principles*. In it I share sixty-four principles that other people and I have utilized to achieve great levels of success.

WRIGHT

I will stand in line to get one of those. Thank you so much being with us.

ABOUT THE AUTHOR

JACK CANFIELD is one of America's leading experts on developing self-esteem and peak performance. A dynamic and entertaining speaker, as well as a highly sought-after trainer, he has a wonderful ability to inform and inspire audiences toward developing their own human potential and personal effectiveness.

Jack Canfield is most well-known for the *Chicken Soup for the Soul* series, which he co-authored with Mark Victor Hansen, and for his audio programs about building high self-esteem. Jack is the founder of Self-Esteem Seminars, located in Santa Barbara, California, which trains entrepreneurs, educators, corporate leaders, and employees how to accelerate the achievement of their personal and professional goals. Jack is also founder of The Foundation for Self Esteem, located in Culver City, California, which provides self-esteem resources and training to social workers, welfare recipients, and human resource professionals.

Jack graduated from Harvard in 1966, received his ME degree at the University of Massachusetts in 1973, and earned an Honorary Doctorate from the University of Santa Monica. He has been a high school and university teacher, a workshop facilitator, a psychotherapist, and a leading authority in the area of self-esteem and personal development.

As a result of his work with prisoners, welfare recipients, and inner-city youth, Jack was appointed by the State Legislature to the California Task Force to Promote Self-Esteem and Personal and Social Responsibility. He also served on the Board of Trustees of the National Council for Self-Esteem.

JACK CANFIELD
The Jack Canfield Companies

P.O. Box 30880
Santa Barbara, CA 93130
Phone: 805.563.2935
Fax: 805.563.2945
www.jackcanfield.com

CHAPTER FIVE

Live Your Dream

An Interview with . . . **Minh Pham**

DAVID WRIGHT (WRIGHT)
Today we're talking with Minh Pham. Minh, welcome to *Stepping Stones to Success.*

MINH PHAM (PHAM)
Thank you, David.

WRIGHT
So what is *Walking on Water* all about?

PHAM
Walking on Water is a nonprofit, approved 501(c) organization that came about from my background of service and my passion for helping individuals

actualize their true potential. *Walking on Water* holds retreats, workshops, and training on empowering individuals to live their dream lives now.

How we do this is we get to the root of a person's problem and identify a solution for that problem. We know that every problem has a solution and we can get to that solution by a process we use in our workshops and retreats. The other aspect of *Walking on Water* helps individuals get on their feet by allowing them to live in our transitional housing and by teaching them life skills, financial skills, and other career skills.

Here in this interview we'll focus more on the former objective of *Walking on Water* because *Walking on Water* is a non-profit that has two different objectives—transitional housing and life empowerment retreats and workshops.

WRIGHT

So would you tell our readers why you started *Walking on Water*?

PHAM

I had a spiritual experience that changed my life forever. I believe it was God talking to me, not in words like you're hearing here, David, but right to my soul—right to my heart. I imagined a beautiful cathedral with ceilings that were sixty to eighty feet high, angels singing in the background, and then a big light at the altar. As I opened the doors to this cathedral, the thought came into my mind, "Do you want it?" I heard the question again, "Do you want it?" Then, one last time, as I got to the front of the cathedral and the bright light, the question resonated in my soul, not in words, "Do you want it?" I said, "Yes" all three times.

I guess the question meant, "Do you want this journey that I'm about to put you on?" I had no idea what that was all about. This actually happened over ten years ago. I knew it was powerful and I knew it was something I had never experienced in my life before. The experience helped me understand certain important things about my life. One of those is that I need to help people in the world realize their true dreams and calling. It's a great passion for me to help others because I love people.

I felt as though that experience I had was to "awaken" me to share my abundance and knowledge with individuals. I've achieved wonderful success for myself through applying the principles of being "conscious" that we'll talk about here. I realized that it was time to give back by sharing what I know. I've been blessed with the gift to communicate, to understand certain life-changing concepts, and I like to share that with individuals. I know it helps them because I see their lives change and it's very rewarding.

WRIGHT

So what aspects of a person's life can you help?

PHAM

We can help individuals with many things, such as money, health, relationships, and peace of mind. We provide techniques, analyze people's thought patterns, and stay in touch with them to ensure they are practicing the habits we have trained them in during our retreats, conferences, and workshops. The strange thing is that often a person comes to our program for one thing that they want to make better in their life. They come out of our program with other benefits because when they change their core beliefs, their entire life changes.

WRIGHT

So how is it different from any other coaching seminar retreat out there?

PHAM

That's a great question. The biggest difference in what we do is that we figuratively clean house before we bring in new furniture, and move in. To give you an example of that, imagine a house that needs renovation. It also has a lot of stuff in there—junk, trash, garbage, almost to the point of where you can't even walk through the house. Underneath all that stuff is a house that needs to be renovated.

Then imagine an eighteen-wheeler truck full of brand new furniture and fixtures; everything in there is new. The movers are then going to unload all of that new furniture and fixtures into the existing "stuff-ridden" house. It doesn't make sense. Most people say, "Well, that's stupid." Yes, it is, but that's what most people do.

When they go to a workshop or a conference, they have existing baggage—fears, doubts, anxiety, and accumulated programming—that holds them back. It gets mixed in there with all these new, fresh ideas and content. Although this does work for a minority of the people—I would say less than 5 or 10 percent—for the majority of people it doesn't work because they may be motivated for a day or two, maybe a month or two, but then they get back into their old habits; that's where it loses effectiveness. We really take a different approach than that of other motivational programs.

At our retreats and workshops, we must get rid of the fears, the negativity, and the anxiety before we can start to live our dream life. In our typical two-day retreats, day one is about cleaning house and day two is about rebuilding the new program—that dream life that people envision for themselves. It's a process and it doesn't take one weekend for most people. We teach you techniques to use on a practical basis, every day of your life; the retreat begins the process. Through time, lasting changes can occur.

WRIGHT

So in your experience, does it work?

PHAM

Yes, absolutely, our techniques do work and we have a lot of success stories. You can watch "View the Testimonies" on our Web site to see people who have had life-changing experiences at our workshops, and who now experience joy and freedom after attending our program.

WRIGHT

Will you give our readers some examples of how this works?

PHAM

Yes. For example, if you are overcome with fear, doubt, and negativity, it's you're thinking; it's the makeup of who you are. You've heard the maxim, "You are who you think you are," meaning you are what you think about. Unless you change your thoughts, you can't change your life. You've heard people say, "think before you act," but when it comes to changing your life, you have to "act before you think" because often people "think" themselves out of it.

Let's go back to the reference of cleaning house. When you are present in the moment, you can act on an idea. Where people go wrong, in the sense of living a peaceful life, is that they dig into their past experiences and take the negativity, judgments, and other reasons why something was not successful and apply them to the current idea; therefore, their past experiences ruin the current opportunity.

In life, you have to try new ideas and take new actions in order to get a different result. People go back to the junk in their heads to make decisions. That old junk is fear and negative programming—the programming that is destructive and not constructive. "Cleaning the house" is being present in the moment, and not referencing either the past or the future in order to make your decisions.

Another example is you may have a business. You're new, anxious, and maybe even fearful. You know you need to make some phone calls. You know you need to set appointments to meet with prospects, to tell them about your ideas, services, or products, but for whatever reason, you don't go or you don't make those phone calls to get those precious appointments. Why?

The only thing that happens is that your thoughts control your actions because your thoughts are telling you, "Don't call; don't pick up that phone; you're going to get rejected; you're not good enough; you're not smart enough," and so on. Therefore, thoughts come into play; you are thinking of the future.

You wonder, "What will others think? What will happen when I get turned down? What if it doesn't work and I don't make money and I become poor and then homeless?" These and hundreds of other unconstructive and negative thoughts stop you right in your tracks. They destroy your action of calling the prospects to get your appointments. Those thoughts kill the idea of action even before you make the calls. Thinking negative thoughts is a real dream-killer. This goes back to cleaning house again—if you are not present in the moment when making your decisions, you are worried about the future; therefore, your decision is not to take action and your thoughts kill the idea before you can act upon it.

Take an example of relationships. I have a client who is going through a divorce, and it is really tainting his perception of finding companionship with another person. He keeps telling me about how nasty the divorce is and how he's taking it slow and not getting into relationships because he doesn't want to get hurt again. So, when it comes to making a decision to meet a new person or trying a new relationship, he refers back to his junk—his past. He is afraid of how the relationship may turn sour like his divorce. If he would be more present in the moment and not be influenced by his past, then his decision would be one of possibility. This is a repetitive drain on his relationships—or lack of relationships—with women. Thoughts of his divorce that are playing over and over again are destroying every opportunity to date or meet new women.

If you agree that your thoughts could be junk that are holding you back from living a stress-free and happy life, let's talk about how you can change your thoughts. When are your thoughts who you are? That's the magic question.

We can't change peoples' thoughts because it's hard, but they can change their own actions. Going back again to what we mentioned earlier, the key is to act first, before you think. We have exercises, tools, and tips that show people how to catch their thoughts and allow themselves to change because unless they do that, their thoughts continue to consume them and their new ideas for a better life. Being in the moment and acting with full consciousness is the key.

In our retreats, one of the exercises we do allows one to physically change one's thoughts. Here's how it works: If thoughts come through, we have our clients write them down and then we analyze them. We ask them, "Where is this thought coming from? Is this thought fear-based?" The exercises could be physical exercises that basically allow them to bring awareness and consciousness to what they're thinking, by writing their thoughts down on a piece of paper. The act of doing something changes their thought process. We have hundreds of thoughts, sometime thousands per day, and this exercise allows them to take inventory of their thinking by taking action.

Essentially, there are things we can do and there are a lot of different techniques we can use. Of course, it's hard to cover all of that in an interview like this; however, once people experience what works for them, they'll get the hang of it and they can begin to actually apply it in their daily lives. This is part of the cleaning house we refer to in our workshops and retreats. Our attendees also benefit from the wonderful support they receive from fellow participants in the retreats and workshops. They help each other to facilitate consciousness and change.

WRIGHT

Well, it is different from other seminars and retreats. Everybody I've ever talked to says you need to think before you act.

PHAM

Sure, you do need to think before you act, but they mean it in another context. In the context of changing one's life, the only way to do so is to act before you think. In reversing this paradigm you have a new experience because you are not thinking yourself out of it.

You may have heard of people with too much "analysis paralysis." They think too much. Just like our examples above, those individuals start to eliminate the action before the action ever takes place. What they are doing is conjuring up junk—the old or negative thoughts that rule their current situation and actions.

We teach people to be present in the moment, and that is the essential concept. A "clean house" is a person who is both present and conscious. As thoughts come up—whether they are in the past or the future—if they don't serve your life, it is junk. Before you can clear that programming, you have to be present and in the moment.

It's really odd, but if you ask a person in distress or who is unhappy with his or her life, "Do you want your life to go well, and do you want your life to be successful?" most people would say, "Yes." If you asked them inversely, "Do you enjoy the pain; do you enjoy the misery, the fear, the scarcity, and the stress?" most people would say, "Are you crazy? Why would I enjoy that?"

What they fail to acknowledge is that a lot of things that they don't enjoy, they are creating unconsciously. Underneath their thoughts is a subconscious creation built by fear, scarcity, anxiety, and past programming. It's unconscious junk in the head that is a projection of either the past or the future.

Here's another example that will help you understand the concept. Think of your unconsciousness (past and future projections of your mind) as a little mouse. Imagine that there is a mouse hiding underneath a table. If we lift up the table, what do you think the mouse is going to do? It would run because it's not used to the light. It's exposed.

You have brought light into a dark (past and future projection) situation. That's what you're doing when you bring in a new awareness. It is like that light—it shines upon the scary things you want to change in your life, which is the culprit behind your creations (your regular destructive programming). By exposing the things that ruin your life, such as negativity, doubt, fear, and pain, you can become aware of those things you create and bring change into your life. You're cleaning house brings in light, as though you lift up that table and expose the mouse. You are forcing yourself to change, consciously.

WRIGHT

So why should people try your service?

PHAM

People are tired and they are stressed; they want to change and they have tried a lot of things that may not have worked for them, so they try us. We're different in the sense that no one else out there is doing exactly what we're doing. Obviously, if they were, I wouldn't have started Walking on Water.

WRIGHT

So you're saying that your program works. How so?

PHAM

Our clients and attendees say so. They go through our process and they realize that the mind and thoughts create reality. There are two levels of how our minds create reality. There is a conscious level, for example—what you are wearing today and what you ate for lunch. You chose that. You chose exactly those articles of clothing and you chose what you ate for lunch today. People constantly make decisions and for the most part, they know how to make those choices.

The other type of creation is the unconscious, the things that people are not aware of that they create, such as unhappiness, pain, stress, misery, and even poverty. How do they do that? Again, there is something in all of us called the "junk mind." We bring awareness to our unconscious thoughts, as I mentioned earlier when exposing the mouse. This is also another form of creation, yet individuals who are not conscious of this don't know they are creating these manifestations in their lives. Once they realize they are hurting themselves, they can begin to change that and stop hurting themselves.

For the most part, it is dormant. It becomes active and takes over when there is an argument, a fight, or a drama. In some people, that "junk mind" is very, very strong; it controls them and creates the reality in their life. We bring this to our clients' consciousness. We bring awareness to all the fears and negativity in their mind, enabling them to be aware of the drama that they create in their lives and show them that they can do something about it.

We are talking about it again because it's so important and we like to emphasize that the real power is the conscious awareness that gives individuals control of their lives. You can be conscious of your unconsciousness. When you are, you can totally create what you desire in your life, rather than reacting to unconscious creations. The unconsciousness is the junk in our heads, whether from the past or the future, and we teach attendees how to live and to be conscious of the "now."

WRIGHT

So what gives you the credibility to do what you do?

PHAM

People ask me this question. I believe that my experiences have led me to great knowledge and wisdom and I've been able to share that knowledge with others. And more importantly, the results give me credibility. You can view people online who have benefited from what we do, so people can judge for themselves if this is effective and true.

Recently, we had Dr. Glenn B. attend one of our retreats and afterward he shared with us his experience in comparison to various workshops and programs he's attended. He noticed that after attending our program, he is beginning to experience balance in his life. After only one week, he has started to see real changes in his life. You can see on our Web site other examples of people with various backgrounds and situations in their lives whom we have helped. The bottom line is that we get results and that is the biggest reward for our clients, our attendees, as well as for us, so it justifies our efforts.

WRIGHT

So who can you help?

PHAM

We can help anyone who wants to change his or her life and is ready for change. Most people need change but they either don't believe it or they are not ready. One needs to believe one can change and must be ready to make changes. We believe that when the "student" is ready, the "teacher" appears. Change doesn't happen by accident; it is by conscious choice that one can change one's life.

WRIGHT

Thanks for your time today.

PHAM

Absolutely; you are welcome. We are passionate about what we do, how we can help individuals, and this interview allowed us to further our cause. Our program is different from all others because we help individuals make lasting changes by showing them a process that works for them. It's more than self-help—it can change a person's habits and life forever. The key question for anyone interested is: will you want it to work for you? Some programs help people on the surface but they really don't help people at the core, root level, and we have a program that does.

WRIGHT

Well, Minh, I really appreciate all the time you've taken with me today to answer these questions. I've learned a lot and I think our readers are going to learn a lot, as well.

Today, we've been talking with Minh Pham, founder of Walking on Water. He is passionately dedicated to inspiring and empowering individuals to live their dream lives right now.

Minh, thank you so much for being with us today on *Stepping Stones to Success*.

PHAM

Thank you so much, David, I really enjoyed it.

ABOUT THE AUTHOR

MINH PHAM is referred to as a "consciousness advocator," especially in regard to interpersonal consciousness. For twelve years, Minh has been a professional speaker, investor, revolutionary idealist, author, and the founder of Walking on Water.

Minh is passionately dedicated to inspiring and empowering individuals to live their dream lives now. Minh is a passionate believer that life is to be lived and experienced completely, every day. For more than twelve years, he has been teaching a network of students and listeners in the United States and overseas. Minh is recognized for coaching CEOs, business owners, investors, and individuals, helping them learn to lead themselves in order to lead others.

Minh has an extensive background in human development, which has not been through the traditional institutional trainings that one may go through to be a spiritual teacher, but rather through his personal experiences and his relationships with his clients. His methods emphasize progressive consciousness and spiritual practices. Minh has had several spiritual awakenings in his personal and business life that have motivated him to explore the possibilities for profound personal experiences that he can relate to other individuals to help them in their lives.

Minh Pham

Founder, *Walking on Water*
'Live Your Dream'
888-83-HOUSE
Fax: 1-202-315-5830
www.Walking-on-Water.org
Minh@Walking-on-Water.org

1718 M Street, NW # 298
Washington, DC 20036
or
2655 Ulmerton Rd. #131
Clearwater, FL 33762

CHAPTER SIX

Growing and Empowering Future Leaders
An Interview with . . . **Dr. Amicitia Maloon-Gibson**

DAVID WRIGHT (WRIGHT)

Today we're talking with Dr. Amicitia Maloon-Gibson who is President and Chief Executive Officer of ATIC and MG Center for Excellence, and MGAA. She is an executive life coach and professional speaker with an emphasis in the areas of leadership, management, women's careers, and youth issues. She is known as the "Empowerment Doc" and her friends call her "Cita." Her expertise is supported by thirty-three years of combined experience of military service, federal government, and private industry. She has provided keynote presentations, workshops, and seminars for federal agencies, universities, and nonprofits. She was recently featured in the *NAFE Magazine* (National Association of Female Executives) as one of the authors with the Professional Women's Network. She conducts workshops and seminars for professional development, growth, and empowerment of leaders. She has numerous military, civic, and community awards for leadership and service. She has received national recognition by receiving the Department of

Defense Woman of Color Award for Leadership in Diversity and Affirmative Action, a first for the agency.

She was nominated for The 2009 Woman of Excellence in Business in Melbourne, Florida. Her company, ATIC & MG Center For Excellence & MGAA, was nominated through the Cocoa Beach Chambers of Commerce for Nonprofit Small Business under one hundred employees, for business of the year, 2009. She is an active member of the Women's Army Corps Veterans Association, Military Officers Association of America, Disabled American Veterans, and Associate Member of the Tuskegee Airmen Inc., just to name a few of her professional memberships and affiliations.

She is a native of St. Thomas, U.S. Virgin Islands. She retired at the rank of Lieutenant Colonial in the United States Army (regimental affiliation with the Corps of Engineers) and is a highly decorated veteran who served for almost thirty years with honorable service to the nation. She is a five-time author and co-author. She is a professional speaker who is available for keynote addresses, executive retreats, and seminars locally, nationally, and internationally. She is an executive life/career coach and confidante to senior executives and military leaders.

Cita, welcome to *Stepping Stones to Success*.

DR. AMICITIA MALOON-GIBSON

Thank you, David; it is a pleasure to be here.

WRIGHT

I know you've heard many, many definitions of success, but how do you define success?

MALOON-GIBSON

Success is a direct result of failure; that's the way I look at it. Our journey in life teaches us this because success is a result of getting back up each time we fall. In using this philosophy, you can condition your mind to be successful. Success is overcoming the barriers to reaching your goals from where you are to where you want to be in your season of life. Success is when you can be what you want to be, do what you want to do, live where you want to live, and experience what you want to experience. Success is about living life without limits and helping others to be successful. It is your opportunity to be on stage and be your authentic self. It applies to the whole life cycle. For me that includes the spiritual, physical, emotional, financial, and social phases of life.

WRIGHT

So what would you say would be the biggest contribution to your professional success?

MALOON-GIBSON

I would have to say that it's my upbringing and my socialization process during my early childhood years. I believe having a sound, loving extended family contributed to who I am today. Knowing who I am and knowing my purpose for life, and knowing whose child I am contributed to my professional success.

I enjoyed reading the book by Rick Warren, *A Purpose Driven Life,* because that had something to do with some of the steps I have taken in recent years. I also like John Maxwell's, *21 Irrefutable Laws of Leadership.* His book is what helped me to refine my leadership skills.

Having great mentors, role models, and "sponsors" were equally important to my professional success. My education, my values, and my beliefs formulated my foundational base for the person I am today.

My biggest success secret is continuous learning. Living is about continuous learning, about discovering new things, and growing. Successful people don't think they know everything—they are open to new ideas, change, and they are willing to find other ways to a better solution. That's why they're successful. A closed mind gets you nowhere. Be open to learning and trying new things. If you wish to achieve more, grow more, and to be successful at what you want, learning strategies must have a place in your life.

I would have to say also that one of the biggest contributions to being a successful professional is when you are no longer your own hostage in your prison of life. This means that you are released to experience your highest joy and your highest potential. You can experience this when you break away from the mediocrity that exists all around you. It is when you stand tall and reject negativity and social conformity. You are then free to soar with eagles and experience greater validity, and greater joy. For me, I felt peace in knowing that the joy of the Lord is my strength. It is when you can work smarter because you understand the rules and you won't be intimidated by others' success. When you're in control of yourself and not hostage to what other people think or say of you, you are successful. Don't let other people control you and your mind. It's about getting out of your own way most of the time and enjoying a life full of unspeakable joy. It's about freedom to enjoy the wealth that we so richly deserve. I look forward daily to life, hope, love, and joy instead of fear, stress, and anxiety.

WRIGHT

So what do you think are the biggest obstacles people face in trying to become successful?

MALOON-GIBSON

I would have to echo Shakespeare and say, "to thy own self be true"—you must take yourself out of your own way. You can be your biggest hindrance, especially if you have low self-esteem and self-worth. Overcoming negativism is a challenge for some people. As a man or woman thinketh so, is he or she. I remember Napoleon Hill once said that whatever the mind can conceive and believe you can achieve.

At the crossroads of life, when we get to the lane of making a decision, the greatest and biggest obstacle is people. You and I will encounter a lot of situations and circumstances that surround us, and influence the cognitive process—the way we think, which will affect our minds. I remember reading one of Bishop Noel Jones' books. He wrote a powerful and a wonderful book titled *The Battle for the Mind*. In his book he spoke about the raging war in our mind between opposing forces and the challenges that we encounter as we do a self-assessment of ourselves. In simple terminology, we tend toward "self-condemnation." I truly believe that the biggest obstacle in my life was myself.

Whatever you are taught and whatever your thought patterns are will determine the outcome of any new project or endeavor, whether it's in a business relationship, a change in your personal relationship, dietary habits, or other habits such as smoking, sex, or alcohol consumption. You will inevitably fall back into your old ways of thinking that will make you look in the rear mirror into your own lifestyle. You must stay focused and keep your eyes forward on your purpose and calling in life. I call this stage your Next Level Blessings.

When invoking changes in our life we should consider our cognitive process foremost. Our minds are better than computers. We can reprogram our minds and our thoughts to override the old patterns. You might be wondering how this can be done. You can do it through positive affirmations. A powerful quote that I use most of the time is "For as he [or she] thinketh in his [her] heart, so is he [she] . . ." Proverbs 23:7, KJV. If anyone wants to change his or her way of thinking I believe it is possible. People can change their thinking but they will have to be patient, diligent and resourceful. Resourceful literally means "self empowerment" because it will not happen within the twinkling of an eye. Change in our cognitive process is a process that requires time, effort, and commitment. Yes, you can change and it's going to be your choice—your decision.

There are three areas that changed my mindset and launched me from failure to success. The three principles below can change your mindset from failure to success:

1. The first principle is to put God first and learn about His higher thoughts. The most powerful way of changing our mindset is by acquiring the one that God has by reading the master strategic plan for life. It's the greatest book and is the number one bestseller that instructs us—the Bible. Read about His way of thinking; let it constantly flow through your eyes by reading it, into your ears by hearing, and into your mind by understanding His teaching. The prophet Isaiah wrote, "so is my word that goes out from my mouth: it will not return to me empty, but will accomplish what I desire and achieve the purpose for which I sent it." That's the first principle" (Isaiah 55:11, NIV).
2. The second principle is empowerment—now. Empower, empower, empower. Read biographies of successful men and women. The human capital is full of greatness and successes. We are surrounded by great leaders—managers, entrepreneurs, educators, political leaders, religious leaders, and community leaders. What a tremendous influence upon us and an unlimited network of resources at the touch of our fingertips or within our communities. It is critical for us to grow as leaders and future leaders. It is important to surround yourself with people who are

successful, positive, and who have elevated themselves to where you want to be. I call this exposure and networking, empowering yourself.

3. The third principle is that "quitting is not an option." This means that changing your mindset will be a challenge and you must resolve not to quit. Historically, humans believed that man could not go to the moon. Well, the United States is the pacesetter in the space program globally. I keep the faith and remember these words that James Bridges, a friend of mine, told me. He said, "Short-term pain repositions you for long-term gain." So in any good success formula, quitting is excluded as an option.

WRIGHT

Would you tell our readers a little bit about what drives you to be successful?

MALOON-GIBSON

Absolutely, yes I can. I am just living life without limits, which includes my faith, family, friends, and of course my finances. As previously stated, a biblical strategy of mine is to seek God first in whatever I do. I consider myself a God-fearing woman and a Proverbs 31 woman. The strategy that drives me to be successful comes from Proverbs 31:29–30 (NIV). It says, "Charm is deceptive, and beauty is fleeting; but a woman who fears the Lord is to be praised." My drive is to live a life of excellence and not of mediocrity. I would like to leave a legacy for others who come after me because of my passion in growing and empowering future leaders. My drive for success also comes from the opportunity to serve others, whether in a volunteer, mentor, or coaching capacity.

I'm not tooting my own horn, but I am a skilled, highly professional woman who is multitalented and diverse in several career tracks. I am living the dream of my life. That is the title of a workshop that I conducted and a future book project for me. Today's societal therapists would probably call me the superwoman of the Baby Boomers era.

Got options? Yes I do. Recently, at The National Training Conference for Blacks in Government, I held a workshop addressing the importance of repositioning for the future. I explained to the attendees that before making the leap (i.e., before changing directions in careers or personal goals), they must back up their backup plans. In these challenging economic times, for some people the only sure things are paying taxes and death. Here are some options and suggestions that helped me and can help you, too:

Think and act in ways that are different from most people.

Create a product or information or residual income that your clients will want to buy, and stay focused. Staying focused makes your options work. Each of us has gifts and talents within and God has given us the ability to produce wealth through which we can create and develop products and resources easier than ever now in the twenty-first century.

To succeed at anything, I believe that we must possess or develop these six key traits:

1. Be steadfast and unmovable, which is being focused in our goals.
2. Develop passion and enthusiasm for what we are working to create; we definitely must be committed to our goals.
3. Start achieving your goals one bite at a time. Each goal is actually comprised of smaller multiple goals. Each lesser goal is as important as all the other goals, for only when achieved together is the big goal reached. Usually some hard work is called for.
4. Next I would say that working toward your dream isn't hard. If you're enjoying what you're working for or what you're doing, it can be fun. Change is important because you learn to be flexible, adaptable, open, and willing to learn new things and new ways. You can let go of the old luggage and the old baggage and get a light attaché.
5. Attitude is everything, be patient and persistent; anything worth having takes time. Enjoy the seasons and cycles of life in business, your family, and your community. There is a time and season for everything. It's what I call the farmer's philosophy, and it's also a biblical principle. There is a time for seed—planting. There is a time for time—watering. There is also a time for harvest—the rewards and gains. Your dreams and goals are no different.
6. Last, I say that the use of empowering and encouraging self-talk and phrases of affirmation are very critical. You must make a choice and decision that success is your goal. So that when obstacles come your way—and they will—be determined to succeed and decide to be a success.

WRIGHT

Is it important to balance your success in life? If so, how do you balance your success with your life?

MALOON-GIBSON

It is extremely important to balance success and life. The way I do that is to use the holistic approach to balancing life and success. Unfortunately, we can't control how many hours are in a day. However, we must try to control how we spend the hours we have in each day.

I like to look at life as a wheel. In the center of that wheel—the nucleus or the core—is everything I do. I look at it as a gift of love. You must love your work, you must love your family and friends, the environment you're in, yourself—your health and your body. You must love to learn and you must have the love to achieve. I don't want to say that you must have the love for finances, but you must love the process you're doing to be able to have your finances work for you. Last but not least, you must love to have a lot of fun. I love to have fun. I like to balance my work and what I call my playground with travel.

WRIGHT

So what is the message that you want people to hear to learn from your success?

MALOON-GIBSON

The message I want people to hear is that success doesn't just drop into your life—you must position yourself for success. Try to live life without limits. This requires preparation, preparation, preparation; it requires education, education, education, and it requires networking and good sound relationships.

Life is about living and it is also about giving. Volunteering and giving back is part of being successful. Get mentors, a life coach, or an executive coach like myself.

WRIGHT

Explain what a transitional life coach is.

MALOON-GIBSON

A transitional life coach is a coach who works or intervenes with other customers who are going through transitional periods in life. Life transitions and challenges for most people include facing a new career, retirement, job loss, a new marriage or ending one, a new member to your family or losing one, disease or death of a friend or loved one. You may be preparing for something new or completing something old. Life transitions all create stress. These types of stressors can be strengthened or depleted. A transitional life coach can assist you to adapt to the changes you are facing through assisting you to identify and access your internal strength and give you new skills to help you continue with your life.

Most people lose the eye or "sight" of life when they become weak. Rebuilding a relationship with yourself after a loss is paramount to going on with life in joy. A coach can assist you in moving through the stages of rebuilding a relationship with yourself and can help you to develop a new vision and new goals.

Health is another area where a transitional life coach can help you. If you're facing a health related challenge, be it your own or that of a loved one, stress and worry can decrease your energy and make it difficult for you to be proactive in the healing process. Many have difficulty getting accurate information from their healthcare providers. A coach can assist you in clarifying what is most important to you and to teach you skills to communicate clearly with your family and the medical community.

Those are just a few of the areas that a transition life coach can help people prepare to reposition themselves in life, relationships, and business.

WRIGHT

You speak about passion being a compass for your life and how it is the main factor in accomplishing success. Is passion alone truly enough?

MALOON-GIBSON

I would like to say passion alone is not truly enough. We can have passion to do a whole lot of things. I say passion without work is just an idea. It's just like the fact that faith without works (demonstrating our faith by what we do) is dead. We have to prepare ourselves.

If you have a passion, you have to prepare and propel yourself to do the work to maintain that passion. You can have a passion to do something, but if you don't put action behind that passion, it is just an idea—a dead idea.

Now, when I talk about my passion, people tell me, "Give me the thirty-second definition of what you do, Cita." I will say, "I am Cita Gibson, C-I-T-A. The C stands for coaching and consulting. The I stands for inspiring and "Incouraging" individuals. The T is for transforming and teaching and the A stands for being an advocate and also stands for Agape, the Greek word for unconditional love. My goal and passion is to have a positive effect on each person I meet or greet. So, I must continuously be passionate about being the best me. In order to do that, I have to continue to improve myself and my situation so that I can give my best to others. I am blessed (meaning successful) to be a blessing (having the ability to help others).

WRIGHT

We all know what the dictionary definition of empowerment, but how do you define it?

MALOON-GIBSON

The definition from Wikipedia says, "Empowerment refers to increasing the spiritual, political, social, or economic strength of individuals and communities. It often involves an empowered developing confidence in their own capacities." The term Human Empowerment covers a vast landscape of meaning, interpretations and disciplines ranging from psychology to the highly commercialized Self-Help industry and Motivational sciences. Sociological empowerment often addresses members of groups that social discrimination processes have excluded from decision-making processes through—for example—discrimination based on disability, race, ethnicity, religion, or gender.

WRIGHT

So how did you begin speaking and why did you choose passion and empowerment as your main topics?

MALOON-GIBSON

Many years ago I had the distinct honor of reading *Empowering Yourself: The Organizational Game Revealed* by Harvey J. Coleman. Then several years later, I had the opportunity to meet him at a workshop when I was studying at the Command and General Staff College in Leavenworth, Kansas. He talked about what is called the "PIE," an acronym for Performance/Professionalism, Image, and Exposure. For me, Empowerment is about improving yourself and helping others to get to their purpose.

1. *Performance/Professionalism*—We must have the performance and the professionalism that people want to hear from us and that we can share with others. We must also have the image and the information. (I added information and professionalism onto his formula.)
2. *Image*—We must have the image and the information that we can share with others.
3. *Exposure*—In order to share with others, we must have exposure.

So you cannot be someone who has a passion for empowerment if you don't have the PIE, all together. If you don't have your performance and professionalism, if you don't have the image and the information, and if you don't have the exposure (network effectively), you won't have the clients or meet their needs. Networking is a great component of empowerment.

I have a series of empowerment topics that I share with women and youth; I talk in general areas of management and leadership. I talk in the areas of diversity and inclusiveness and in the areas of living a healthier lifestyle.

I challenge people by daring them to dream and to live the dream of their lives. I challenge individuals to empower themselves and manage their own careers. I challenge them by asking them the question: "Have you got options? If you don't have options, you need to make sound decisions before you leap. Then, and only then, can you have a backup plan to back up your backup. In these challenging days, if you don't have that backup plan and take some risks but aren't successful with those risks, you are going to lose a whole lot of different things. So you have to think about backing up your backup plans, too.

It used to be that we had retirement pensions and savings plans, but now you have to look beyond retirement plans. You have to back up your retirement plans or your investment plans for the future. So the empowerment and passion that I have is not only for myself, it's about empowerment of others and seeing them succeed.

One of my friends said to me, "You share too much of your knowledge with others—you give too much. Why don't you sell all of this?" I didn't think about selling—I just have a desire to help people who can't help themselves. I want to motivate people to be their best. I concluded that speaking was my passion when I became a senior military officer and I had to empower people. Others came to me and sought me out for mentoring, for coaching, for advice, and for counseling. Senior leaders asked me to be their confidante and their sounding board. This is when I decided this was my "niche" and my passion. Then one of my girlfriends said, "You talk too much." In reply, I said, "I get paid to speak a lot!"

WRIGHT

So would you say that when people follow their passion and excels at it, does the passion bring the success, or does the success bring more passion?

MALOON-GIBSON

I think they're intertwined. It's like a rope its strands weave together. The passion brings success because if you don't like what you're doing, you're not going to be successful at it. My passion brings my success. I have a passion for working with youth and working with women. I have a passion for developing and growing individuals or people into future leaders. I have that passion because I am a forward thinker; I am looking at the future and I want to be a part of the solution in my community rather than to be the one sitting there twiddling my thumbs asking what's next. I want to be a change agent.

WRIGHT

Well, what a great conversation. I really appreciate all the time you've spent with me answering all these questions. I have learned a lot and I'm sure our readers will also learn quite a bit.

MALOON-GIBSON

Well, David, I thank you so much for having me. I thank you for indulging with me as I share some of my success strategies in leadership, business, and community. I do hope that the readers will at least find one nugget of information that can help them step up to success or one stone that can help them in their journey to be successful.

WRIGHT

Today we've been talking with Dr. Amicitia (Cita) Maloon-Gibson. She is an executive life coach, professional speaker, and author/co-author of five books. She conducts workshops and seminars for professional development, growth, and empowerment of leaders.

Cita, thank you so much for being with us today on *Stepping Stones to Success*.

MALOON-GIBSON

Thank you very much, David, for inviting me. I hope you have a wonderful day.

ABOUT THE AUTHOR

DR. AMICITIA (CITA) MALOON-GIBSON is President/CEO of the ATIC & MG Center for Excellence & MGAA. She conducts workshops and seminars that are presented throughout the United States and abroad. Dr. Maloon-Gibson has been a senior executive in the federal government and is a professional diversity and inclusion leader with special emphasis in civil rights and women's issues. Dr. Maloon-Gibson recently appeared in the National Association of Female Executives magazine (spring issue), Military Officer (*The Official Magazine* fall issue), *Space Coast Magazine*, and on several radio shows such as, *National Federal Talk Radio, The BIG Experience,* and the PBS local NBC television show. Her topics are: "Stepping Stones to Success," "Living the Dreams of Your Life," "Overcoming Negativism," "The Browning and Aging of the Workforce," "Got Options: Back up Your Backup Before Making the Leap," "Can you Hear Me Now?" and "The Super Woman Syndrome." She has written numerous articles such as "Playing the Organizational Game: Empowerment Now," "Becoming a Career Woman in the Federal Sector," "Inculcating a Successful EEO Program: Living a Balanced & Healthier Lifestyle," "Strategies for Getting the Promotion You Deserve," and "Women as Leaders." These articles have appeared in local newspapers, business journals, federal magazines, and on various Web sites. Dr. Maloon-Gibson's workshop on "Leadership Strategies for Women" is requested and conducted for federal, state, and private industry businesses (including nonprofits).

Additionally, Cita brings thirty years of experience working with government and private organizations in the areas of leadership, training, motivation, team-building, employee recruitment and succession planning, and organizational development. She has a bachelor's degree in Psychology/Sociology, a master's degree in Management, a master's degree in Human Resources Development, and a doctorate in Social Psychology.

She has professional memberships and is affiliated with the Society of Human Resource Management, American Association of Christian Counselors (AACC), the Black African-American Christian Counselors (BAACC), and the Marriage and Family Network (AACC). She is a certified Mediator/Life Coach.

She is a charter member of the Brevard County Business and Professional Women/USA/FL, the National Association of Female Executives, the Association for Conflict Resolution, Veterans Association of Women Army Corps, and Disabled Veteran of America. She has membership in several Speakers' Bureaus. She is a Veteran of the U.S. Army (Lieutenant Colonel Retired), with honorable and distinguished service to the nation of almost thirty years. She is a Board of Director member of Christian Services Charities and Neighbor to Nations (2008–2010), home-based in the Washington/Virginia area. She also serves as Professional Women's Network Advisory Board Member and Advisory Board member to the Orlando Diversity Council. She is recognized in communities where she serves and throughout the United States for selfless service and commitment to leading women and youth. She received the Department of Defense Woman of Color Award for Leadership in Diversity/Affirmative Actions, a first for the agency.

Dr. Maloon-Gibson delivers exceptional seminars and keynotes, and is available for regional, national, and international travel engagements. Her international travels include the British Virgin Islands, U.S. Virgin Islands, England, Germany, Prague, France, Belgium, Puerto Rico, Hawaii, Aruba, Bahamas, and Costa Rica.

DR. AMICITIA CITA MALOON-GIBSON
P.O. Box 411482
Melbourne, Florida 32941-1482
321.537.5002
www.citagibson.com
www.mgc4e.org

CHAPTER SEVEN

Stepping Stones to Ethical Leadership

An Interview with . . . **Gael O'Brien**

DAVID WRIGHT (WRIGHT)

Today we're talking with Gael O'Brien. Gael is a consultant and executive coach with an extensive corporate background, who has been working with leaders to create successful outcomes for more than twenty-five years. Her focus includes ethical leadership, building trust and reputation, and communications. Her client list includes Rand, The Conference Board, The Ethics and Compliance Officer Association, Bain & Company, and several dozen other companies and nonprofit associations. She is President of Strategic Opportunities Group, and President of the Professional Coaches, Mentors, and Advisors (PCMA) association in Orange County, California. Certified in business ethics, she is an author and presenter on topics including leadership, values and ethics, and strategic communications. Her blog, The Week in Ethics, is widely referenced on leadership and reputation websites. Gael is also a columnist for Business Ethics Magazine.

Ms. O'Brien welcome to *Stepping Stones to Success*.

GAEL O'BRIEN (O'BRIEN)

Thank you.

WRIGHT

Is the subject of ethical leadership moving to the front burner in light of headlines about the economic meltdown and all the scandals, frauds, and ongoing investigations, as well as polls showing less confidence in business?

O'BRIEN

Absolutely. The unthinkable happened to the world's economy, and the meltdown's many causes will require many solutions to address. One of which is to consider the way in which we do business, particularly the role of leadership. This is a global discussion.

One outcome is a campaign that started last year to enroll graduating MBA students in the "MBA Oath," written by students and intended to be like a Hippocratic Oath for business. Those signing the Oath pledge, among other things, agree to "accept the duty to act with utmost integrity." By April 2010 nearly two thousand MBA students from more than three hundred business schools had signed and numbers continue to climb.

Crises have many causes but they aren't inevitable. I've seen too many situations in business and life where crises happened because people looked only at the information they wanted to see, or forgot what they stood for and made decisions they would later deeply regret. We've all watched circumstances like that; maybe we've even been involved in them. It doesn't turn out well.

Ethical leadership isn't a magic wand that protects all who have it from any problems; it is a way of conducting oneself that reduces the likelihood that problems will spiral out of control. And, given the enormous financial burden and human energy needed to try and restore reputation once credibility is lost—if it even can be—ethical leadership has no downside.

It is easy to argue that leadership should encompass being ethical so the term "ethical leadership" isn't needed. However, "leadership" is a word that can include or exclude a number of qualities. Executive recruiters I've interviewed agreed that ethical leadership was not something boards of directors traditionally flagged as being important in recruiting a CEO. It was a presumption that the selected candidate would be ethical, so the screening focused on business competencies. While we might agree that being a leader means acting with integrity—determining the right thing to do, and doing it—there is a big gap between intentions and actions. It is a gap we see played out all too often in stories of corporate, government, or civic leaders who've gained notoriety for lying, committing fraud, or conduct that ruins reputations.

In my experience, leaders drawn to making a difference are motivated by seeing what is possible for an organization and working with others to do more than just return record profits. They believe the organization should stand for something. Making a difference is really how we find our voice. Leadership is about how we use our voice.

Talking about ethical leadership is important because it makes us more aware of what we stand for and who we are as leaders in our field, organization, or community. And in doing so, we become more intentional about what our voice can mean.

WRIGHT

How do leaders find their voice?

O'BRIEN

Every leader has a story about how he or she has developed a leadership point of view and expression. Because he had been so successful building Alcoa into a highly profitable company and using core values to shape the culture, I wanted to know former chairman Paul O'Neill's story. It started with his ideas about worker safety.

Paul O'Neill was very clear about the impact he wanted his leadership to have and it went far beyond ensuring a high rate of return for shareholders. He came to Alcoa with the belief that it should be a place where people are never hurt at work. He brought with him a handwritten piece of paper on which he'd written "What is the Agenda?" followed by his answer, a list of fifteen items. His first four items were: "Safety, Quality, Respect for each individual, and Rethinking everything we do without restrictions to see if there is a better way." His list also included "setting some symbols that every person can believe in" (like no one ever being hurt at work) and several specifics for addressing growth and profitability.

Leadership, he explained to me, began with an idea that great organizations always have three propositions that every person can say yes to every day without reservations. His ideal when he went to Alcoa in 1987 was that "I was going to work in such a way that I could create an organization where everyone could say yes to these propositions every day." His propositions are:

1. I am treated with dignity and respect every day by everyone I encounter.
2. I am given the things I need—education, training, encouragement—so I can make a contribution that gives meaning to my life.
3. People whom I respect recognize me for what I do.

There were bosses earlier in his career he didn't want to be like. "I remembered what it was like to be a low level employee and feel the lack of direction and a lack of caring from people who were above me in the chain of command," he said. He was a fan of employee surveys and was able to track the progress of the culture he sought to build. "I didn't think it was possible to achieve greatness in an organization where the people didn't know that there was a values-based culture and where we not only espoused values but we lived by them."

He indicated that, "There were those who argued early on when I started pushing workplace safety that we couldn't afford to be perfectly safe." The legal team argued that he was inviting litigation by developing a comprehensive, global Internet system of real-time reporting of workplace injuries that had an analysis of what went wrong, what in process or training should change, and what would prevent a reoccurrence. "In the thirteen years I was at Alcoa, we never had a single lawsuit about workplace injuries," he added. During his tenure, the company also had record profits and growth.

"If you are elected to be the CEO of an organization," he asks, "why wouldn't you begin immediately with a vision for the organization and the people in it? Why wouldn't your leadership be about creating a wonderful, fulfilling organization that is not about money? Money is a consequence, not an object."

Paul O'Neill served in four presidential administrations, primarily in the Office of Management and Budget, had several roles at International Paper including president, and in 2000 he retired as Alcoa's chairman; he was U.S. Treasury Secretary in 2001–2002 and continues to be involved in current economic policy, health care, and other issues.

WRIGHT

What is the disconnect between intentions and actions that trips leaders up?

O'BRIEN

We don't get credit for intentions—how we'd like to act if nothing gets in the way.

There is an irony that leaders seek additional executive training in change management strategies, brand marketing, or finance, for example, as professional development to enhance their skills as the demands of their job intensify. However, as most people consider themselves ethical, there can seem a stigma about intentionally talking through a problem from the perspective of "is this ethical, is this the right thing for us to do based on who we are"?

Two illustrations come to mind of what happens when the values of a culture are at loggerheads with leaders' decisions: when what the organization stands for on its Web site is not ingrained in the criteria used in the board room as well as part of everyday discussions in offices, conference rooms, and lunch rooms.

Hewlett Packard (HP) paid a very high price for a disconnect. Its "Global Master Privacy Policy" spells out the privacy and data protection principles it says it follows to earn trust in HP and its business practices. However, this policy was not top of mind when HP's former board chair, unable to find the source of leaks of confidential information to the media, gained approval to hire outside security experts who used pretext to spy on board members and reporters. HP's spying scandal, and subsequent congressional and criminal investigations, cost millions of dollars in fines and months of bad press internationally, derailed careers, and required re-establishing credibility internally and externally.

Last year, *The Washington Post* apologized for a pay-to-play ethics scandal, made more embarrassing because of its reputation for exposing influence peddling, and the paper's own strict conflict of interest policy. The publisher and executive editor approved a plan to sell sponsorships of up to $25,000 each for access to government decision-makers and business leaders and others at dinners (dubbed "salons") hosted by them and at least one *Post* reporter at the publisher's house. Several senior editors were asked to give feedback and the idea was shared with about two hundred managers, with no one raising red flags then. Later, when the "salons" became public and the *Post* was lambasted externally, several said they'd had some concerns but felt they would be worked out in the details. "I wish I had the perspective I now have of understanding how people would perceive an event like this," said Katherine Weymouth, *Post* Publisher and President in a July 12, 2009, *Post* column about the scandal. "I didn't perceive it. It's my responsibility."

WRIGHT

What is an example of something relatively simple that people can do to help prevent ethical issues from blowing up in their face?

O'BRIEN

Sometimes it is as simple as stopping the rush of activity around an idea long enough to ask yourself, "Does this really makes sense?" As silly as a reminder to breathe may sound, it is astonishing how many bright and talented type A people get caught up in adrenaline surges as they multitask. Not a good context for making important decisions.

The "do no harm" principle in medicine is also applicable to business ethics. There are a number of questions we should ask ourselves when faced with a challenge to get at what may be the ethical dimension. Ultimately, the decisions we make define the reality in which we will live.

I like the simplicity of the questions Texas Instruments had at one time on its Web site to help employees in decision-making. Called the Ethics Quiz, it asked:

- Is the action legal?
- Does it comply with our values?
- If you do it will you feel bad?
- How will it look in the newspapers?

The last question is often mentioned as a means of judging would you feel the same way about a decision if everyone you knew, knew that you made it, if it were published in a story on the front page of *The New York Times*. Or, if your teenager were to learn what you did, would you be able to look her (or him) in the eye? This brings home that we own our decisions and don't have the luxury of only feeling okay with a decision as long as no one knows we were the ones who made it.

WRIGHT

A lot of companies would have benefited from asking those questions to avoid a crisis. Mitsubishi Motor Manufacturing of America was involved in a crisis of epic proportions when the Equal Employment Opportunity Commission (EEOC) filed against them in what was then the largest sexual harassment lawsuit in 1996. Mitsubishi also was dealing with a national boycott led by Reverend Jesse Jackson's organization and the National Organization for Women. And yet, with all that going on, you were recruited and accepted a job to help lead Mitsubishi's model workplace initiative. Why did you take on those challenges?

O'BRIEN

I believed I could make a difference. I could visualize the company it could become, and my work in strategic communications, vision articulation, and organizational change gave me a lot to draw on. Former U. S. Secretary of Labor Lynn Martin had been retained to help the company in the initial stages of the culture change and I knew it was a once-in-a-lifetime chance to test myself and put into practice what I believed in the most challenging of environments.

The company had lost credibility internally and internationally and my role as head of corporate and community communications overlapped several areas. While I didn't agree with the decisions made before I got there, I quickly came

113

to respect my boss because he wanted the best thinking as he weighed possible solutions to a very complex situation. When I found myself on shaky ground from pushing too hard, he respected that my motive was to help the company do the right thing. The hours and pressure were horrific, especially during the first two years before the EEOC suit was settled. But one experience kept me going, making me feel it was worth it.

Seven months after I arrived, Mitsubishi Motors and Rev. Jackson reached an agreement to end the national boycott. My boss was to represent the company at Rev. Jackson's press conference. Before my boss and I left for New York, the company's legal advisors read his remarks and were adamantly opposed to his following my counsel, and that of others, to apologize to the women employees involved in the lawsuit. In response to their opposition, my boss took the apology out. We had a tense flight to New York because independent of the legal process underway, if the company couldn't apologize I believed we couldn't advance the healing needed in our workforce.

The next morning at the press conference my boss added an apology back in his remarks. Those few words in an audience of critics shifted the entire energy of the room. I asked later what had changed his mind. He had listened not to others' voices, but to his own. Then he knew the right thing to do.

WRIGHT

You mentioned the importance of a company having a vision and values. How did both impact Mitsubishi Motors' culture change?

O'BRIEN

Mitsubishi Motors' vision was to become a model workplace, setting a very high bar. The company agreed to develop a mission statement and guiding values that would help define the workplace being created. I had the opportunity to lead the values process with four thousand employees. A colleague and I compiled a list of twenty-two values from reading the annual reports of several dozen most admired companies. We created a workbook for group leaders and supervisors to use in special employee meetings, including a process for facilitating discussions with their group on the twenty-two values so each group could vote on the three values they felt most important to the company.

Employees' top five vote-getters—honesty, respect, fairness, teamwork, and quality—were presented to senior management as the guiding principles. By prior agreement, senior management added proactive to the guiding values. The values supported the mission statement, which was to build world class vehicles. During the next year, each group in each department developed action steps to relate the values to the work of their area. The values were also incorporated into performance appraisals for nonunion employees.

It is my experience that people select values that are not sufficiently present that they want to be more evident. For example, at Mitsubishi Motors, safety didn't draw a place in the top five because there was already a big push for safety throughout the organization. But respect, fairness, honesty—these are values essential in changing a culture and they were at the top of the list.

This was another turning point, taken seriously and reinforced. It took more than eighteen months before the first positive media stories began to break indicating that the culture of the company was changing, and among the sources for the stories were the employees themselves. The workplace had effective programs and a number of best practices in place, the lawsuit settled, and during the next few years, the company successfully completed global certification for both ISO 9002 Quality Management System and ISO 14001 Environmental Management System. The vision and the values were steppingstones that made a critical difference.

WRIGHT

What is your experience with how stories about leaders gain traction in companies and what does that mean?

O'BRIEN

A workplace culture is defined by the stories that employees tell and see as the truth. They observe the CEO, draw their own conclusions, and that snapshot becomes part of the lens through which the company is viewed. Leaders aren't successful in orchestrating the stories told about them.

Mitsubishi Motors got a new leader about the time the sexual harassment litigation was resolved and the company's mission and values statements were taking hold. The new guy was very visible, spending many hours each week walking around the plant asking associates questions. When he ran into employees at church, the movies, the mall, or restaurants, he would introduce his wife and spend time talking to the families. In the summer, second shift employees would often meet spouses for their dinner break at picnic tables near the parking lot. Inevitably at 7:00 PM or 7:30 PM, after a work day that started at 5:30 AM, the president would bypass his car and go the picnic tables for a quick chat with whoever was there. It wasn't long before the stories began to circulate about what a straight shooter and nice guy he was. In the tough business challenges that were ahead, he was able to use the credibility he'd earned to keep the momentum strong and the vision of what the manufacturing company could become a rallying point.

At another company, a CEO and an employee were headed to a meeting. The CEO told her at the airport that as the boss, he couldn't, as a matter of principle, sit in first class while any employee he travelled with sat in coach. He indicated he would either go back to coach with her or use his miles to upgrade her. When a mileage upgrade on her ticket wasn't possible, he bought her a several-hundred-dollar upgrade, telling her he was personally paying for it, not the company. He suggested that two years hence, that story of what he had just done would be part of the stories defining the company culture. The stories circulating in company corridors then were focused on why the CEO's secretaries kept quitting and the overall high attrition. Whether the CEO's message at the airport was one of the stories defining the culture two years later is unknown; the employee with whom he'd shared it had long since joined the ranks of those who'd left.

WRIGHT

Leaders are by nature fallible and mistakes of judgment are made often. How does that reconcile with raising the bar to talk about ethical leaders? Isn't the term "ethical leader" almost a set up for failure?

O'BRIEN

Absolutely not; striving to be an ethical leader is about fully coming into your own as a trustworthy person, connected to your core beliefs and acting out of them. You are in a rhythm that is congruent not conflicted.

The term "ethical leader" actually sets you up for success because it is about deciding how you want to show up in the world and what you need to do to support yourself and gain support from others in achieving goals and making a difference.

It is certainly true that some have touted themselves as ethical leaders and been felled by their own demons. People like Jim Bakker, Ted Haggard, Jerry Swaggart, pedophile priests, and Ponzi predators like Bernie Madoff never travelled in the league of authentic leaders. There are also sad examples of conflicted self-saboteurs like former New York Governor Elliot Spitzer and former Boeing CEO Harry Stonecipher. Stonecipher, recruited to help Boeing move beyond an ethics scandal, was forced to resign because his affair with a subordinate was inconsistent with the ethics code he helped write. In the case of Spitzer, his post-resignation soul-searching may yield another chapter in his leadership.

Business leaders, like any of us, stumble. The ones who have taken responsibility, dealt with the problem they created, expressed genuine regret, and kept the confidence of their boards have been able to become more self-aware and perhaps even better able to serve as leaders.

Ethical leadership involves knowing yourself and what you stand for, being authentic and consistent, and honoring what you value by congruent actions in your life and work. It is about taking responsibility, seeing a greater purpose and inspiring others to be part of making that purpose happen.

"Ethical leadership does not imply that the leader dictates moral direction to the led," according to Dr. Michael Hoffman, Executive Director, Center for Business Ethics and Hieken Professor of Business and Professional Ethics, Bentley University. "The true mark of leadership is the ability to create opportunities for others to morally lead themselves."

WRIGHT

What are ways those running organizations, both companies and nonprofits, can be more effective leaders utilizing values and purpose to accomplish their goals?

O'BRIEN

It starts with the right questions. A fundamental question for leaders to ask themselves is "will this decision or action be consistent with what I stand for or what the organization stands for?"

I worked with the officers of a family business creating a plan for their first-ever layoffs. Outside legal counsel had approved the plan for eliminating a few positions as part of cost measures needed as sales faltered. The officers wanted to think through what implementing the plan might mean to the organization. They told stories from their perspective about the parties they'd hosted to celebrate employee achievements and how the officers had been intentional about cultivating a family atmosphere. While the company's values weren't written down, the officers were aligned on the importance of the company, like a family, caring about each other and working well together to create products that earned the praise of customers.

The challenge, the officers agreed as we talked, was to act consistent with what they said they stood for. While employees knew there were budget cuts coming, they had no hint that some positions would be eliminated. Therefore, there was more work to be done around creating honest and transparent communications, valuing the employees who'd leave, and how, after they left, leaders and employees would work together to build the future.

Being "like a family" puts a lot of pressure on leaders to make and carry out decisions that are consistent with a caring, functional, environment-supportive group of people doing their best work. The challenge is that if you have core values, whatever they are, they need to reflect what you are committed to creating with your teams. The rewards and benefits are commensurate with that commitment and alignment. Inevitably, there will be disconnects and mistakes, the severity of which will depend on how far out of alignment a leader or organization is. The danger isn't standing for something and being found lacking, because there is always room to grow. The real danger is not aiming high enough because then we will only get the little we believed was possible.

WRIGHT

What are things that leaders can do to strengthen the credibility of their leadership and minimize the potential for ethical lapses?

O'BRIEN

There are a number of things that leaders and organizations can do to create increased trust and credibility in ordinary and extraordinary times. These ten I consider especially important for leaders when faced with challenges:

1. Own what the organization stands for, its mission, vision, and values.
2. Listen to what is alleged, even if it is inconsistent with what you believe to be true.
3. Resist the reflex to defend, explain, or justify.
4. Make it safe for people to talk to you by your attitude, body language, and emotions.
5. Seek out facts through unbiased, independent channels.
6. Convene smart people with relevant expertise to discuss and disagree and learn all you can.
7. Focus on whether the right questions are being asked.
8. Ensure a credible process for arriving at decisions that would withstand public scrutiny.
9. Believe in and utilize the value of two-way, transparent communications.
10. Understand that employees overhear and see leaders handling potentially ethical issues and learn more from watching than they do from any code of conduct on the wall or Web page. The way you show up as a leader defines employees' stories, not the words you use.

I call these Stepping Stones to Ethical Leadership.

WRIGHT

What a great list.

Well what an interesting and timely conversation. These are some extremely important subjects you have brought to mind. It is daunting to think what can happen when leaders are unethical. This has really been a great conversation. I have learned a lot and I am sure that our readers will also.

O'BRIEN

Thank you very much.

WRIGHT

Today we've been talking with Gael O'Brien who is a consultant and executive coach focusing on ethical leadership, building trust and reputation, strategic planning, and communications. After listening to her today, I think she knows what she's talking about.

ABOUT THE AUTHOR

GAEL O'BRIEN is a consultant and executive coach with an extensive corporate background who has been working with leaders to create successful outcomes for more than twenty-five years. Her focus includes ethical leadership, building trust and reputation, and communications. Her client list includes Rand, The Conference Board, The Ethics and Compliance Officer Association, Bain & Company, and several dozen companies and nonprofit associations. She is President of Strategic Opportunities Group and President of the Professional Coaches, Mentors, and Advisors (PCMA) association in Orange County, California. Certified in business ethics, she is an author and presenter on topics including leadership, values and ethics, and strategic communications. She writes a weekly blog on ethics and leadership at http://theweekinethics.wordpress.com and is also a columnist for Business Ethics Magazine

GAEL O'BRIEN
Huntington Beach, CA 92648

strategy@fgi.net

www.strategicopportunitiesgroup.com

CHAPTER EIGHT

Awaken To The Power Within!

An Interview with . . . **Renée McRae**

DAVID WRIGHT (WRIGHT)

Today we are talking with Renée McRae, Author, Personal Development Trainer, and Performance Poet. Her empowering book of transformational poetry is titled *Truth In Rhyme* and is an approved textbook with the New York City Department of Education. Ms. McRae is also the Founder of Poetic Motivations, LLC, which is a personal and professional development training company. Uniquely utilizing writing exercises, role play, and the art of writing poetry, Renée has developed Life-Alignment Workshops focusing on leadership, self-sufficiency, conflict resolution, and career path choices. Some of Renée's clients include colleges, homeless shelters, public schools, domestic violence shelters, juvenile detention centers, mental health facilities, and substance abuse recovery centers. Her award-winning transformational poetry has been published in several magazines, nine anthologies, and is also available on her newly released CD titled *Truth Be Told!*

Renée, welcome to *Stepping Stones to Success*.

RENÉE MCRAE (MCRAE)

Thank you so much, David. It's great to be here.

WRIGHT

Renée, you train on a variety of topics and to diverse audiences. If you had to encapsulate your message to the world into one sentence, what would it be?

MCRAE

I would say: *you will have or be anything you choose.*

WRIGHT

I noticed you used the word *"will"* and not *"can."* Most often I've heard motivators say, "You *can* have or be anything you choose." Using "will" actually changes the meaning a little bit, doesn't it?

MCRAE

Yes, it does change the meaning, and I deliberately said you *will* have or be anything you choose. You see, David, having or being anything we choose is not something we *can* do, it's something we *will* do. It's so important to understand that we live the consequences of our own choosing; and please note that we are choosing in *every* moment.

I'll give you a small example. I was talking with a woman just yesterday. She told me she's been going through a divorce for the past two years. What she did not realize was that her statement was (and is) a choice—a choice that is keeping her in the state of going through a divorce. As a matter of fact, she will continue going through a divorce until she changes that statement to something like: "I *went* through a divorce two years ago" or "I've been going through a divorce for the past two years, and I sure am glad *that's* over!" All too often we do not realize that we are making choices that imprison us in situations, and then we wonder why we can't get out of the situation or why we are repeating the same experiences over and over again. We are calling it, claiming it, stating it, creating it, and then living it.

"By the thoughts we think and the words we say,

We're creating our worlds every day.

What are the thoughts that we don't see

That hold us in this misery?

Once we know we're writing the script

Maybe we'll change the language a bit.

You see, words like *try* and words like *fate,*

They keep us living in the same old state.

Words like *could* and words like *should*

They keep us living in the same neighborhood.

Then we want to search the clouds,

And yell and scream and pray out loud,

And responsibility we deny;

But we're the ones speaking the lie." [1]

WRIGHT

Well, your poetry definitely says it all. Will you tell us a little about your Life-Alignment Workshops? What are they, and what does the term Life-Alignment mean?

MCRAE

Life-Alignment is a term I use to describe the process of bringing people's reality into alignment with who they really are and what they are here (on Earth) to do.

Unfortunately, many of us are living in the world in an unconscious way. We very often have no direction or purpose. Because we haven't been taught and we don't understand how to utilize the laws of the universe and/or creation, we find ourselves living an existence of mediocrity as opposed to a life of splendor, focusing on survival as opposed to enjoyment.

Life-Alignment Workshops are designed to assist people in awakening or coming into the awareness of who they are at the core of their being and bringing

---

[1]"Creation" originally published in *Truth In Rhyme* and *Truth Be Told* by Renée McRae

the *expression* of their lives into alignment with this new understanding, thereby fulfilling their destiny and living life on purpose.

WRIGHT

Wow, that's a tall order, Renée. How does poetry fit into this equation and when did you get into poetry?

MCRAE

You know, David, it's a funny thing—I never did get into poetry, poetry just got into me one day. Poetry became the vehicle by which I would receive these life-changing messages. I know it sounds amazing, but I had absolutely no interest in poetry and you could not have told me at any given point before 1983 that I would ever write poetry and *certainly* not any that would assist me in bettering my life.

To answer your question, I was driving home one day contemplating the misery of my life and, for lack of better words, my frustration with it (what I like to call *"living in the question"*) when out of the blue, these words came:

"What is this thing we call life—
Hustle, bustle, struggle, and strife?
Where do we come from
And where does it end?
I mean, are we in control
Or at the mercy of the wind?
Where are we going?
Is anyone sure?
I mean, what the heck is this?
Is there a cure? . . ."[2]

---

[2] Excerpt from the poem "Give Me A Break" published in *Truth In Rhyme* and *Truth Be Told* by Renée McRae.

This poem went on for about another twelve lines, and by the time I arrived home I had memorized it. I wrote it down immediately. This scenario repeated itself time and time again for years.

I did not understand the significance of these events until much later, but I did get the answers to my pending questions by the end of each poem. It didn't matter whether I was in chaos, confused, dealing with personal relationship issues, finances, professional decisions, seeking direction or even purpose, I would receive another poem, and my answer would be right there by the time it was finished.

Since these poems would always come at times when I couldn't write them down, I would be forced to memorize them. Before I knew it, I was reciting poetry for different events. The memorized poems and inherent messages became ingrained in me, and I began to change—and my life began to change, also.

WRIGHT

Now, how did you begin to combine your poetry with the life skills workshops and use it as a life-alignment tool?

MCRAE

One day I had what you would call an epiphany. You've probably heard the question, "What's wrong with this picture?" Well, I asked myself that question and realized—it was me! I quit my job as a marketing director in North Carolina immediately and moved back to New York with no plan or purpose (and a kid in tow). My mom thought I had lost or, at the very least, was losing my mind. I guess that's what one might think when you give up your only means of support and arrive on their doorstep with no plan, purpose, or direction that you can explain to anyone's satisfaction.

One night, though, about six months later I awoke from a dream in which I was teaching in a classroom, but not math or history, mind you. I was teaching personal development and life skills—through poetry! David, to this day I have never felt anything more right. At that time I was temping as a legal secretary, and had it not been for the *feeling*, I would never have *imagined* myself teaching. Soon thereafter, however, opportunities began popping up, and before I knew it I was speaking at events and facilitating poetry writing workshops in schools! As I became trained in different other topics such as leadership, HIV prevention, conflict resolution, and domestic violence, I began to integrate the subject matter with the art of writing poetry.

I knew I was on to something when I facilitated a series of workshops for a program within the New York City Department of Mental Health. This program assists their clients who have histories of substance abuse and mental illness with obtaining jobs and housing. Following the series, I received a thank you letter from the director stating, "Your ability to engage and motivate often hard to reach clients, combined with your capacity to create a safe, non-threatening environment, resulted in poetry that revealed more about some individuals than I was able to elicit in traditional settings over the past year."

WRIGHT

Wow. What a unique ability.

Going back a little to the story of how you left North Carolina, what courage it must have taken to drop everything and move to another state without a plan.

MCRAE

You know, David, I was listening to Les Brown recently and he quoted Ambrose Redmoon:

"Courage is not the absence of fear, but rather the judgment that something else is more important than fear."

128

How cool is that? We all have fear, but once we focus on the thing we want to do, we accomplish it. Anthony Robbins says we are all motivated by our fears. Actually, I was more afraid of staying where I was than moving into the unknown.

I remember one day sitting on the edge of a swimming pool at a friend's home. I'm one of those people who resists getting into the pool all at once because I fear the water will be too cold. Consequently, I inch into the pool a little at a time. Some people just jump right in—but not me. Well, my girlfriend, Linda, and I were sitting on the first step watching our friends diving off the board and casually talking as we did our inching into the pool. Meanwhile, a three-year-old got away from her mom and with no fear (and no life vest) she just ran right past me stepping down one step, two steps, and under she went. At first I thought she could swim but then I saw little bubbles coming up from her lips to the surface and she was just standing underwater!

In a split second, and without thought, I sprang into action. As I jumped in and put my hands underneath her armpits, I heard someone say, "Get the baby!" I promptly lifted her up and delivered her poolside to her frantic mom. She seemed to not even be phased by the ordeal. She didn't even cough. I, on the other hand, was a wreck. It was about five minutes later by the time I realized I had fully submerged my body in the water and I wasn't cold at all. I never even felt the cold water. In my total focus on saving this little girl's life I hadn't stopped to consider the water being cold or my fear of it—". . . the judgment that something else is more important than fear."

It's almost like you have to create an escape velocity to overcome the pull of habitual thought or behavior. In this instance, my total focus on getting to this little girl and pulling her out of the water outweighed any fear I had about getting wet or cold. I know it wasn't a major fear, but the concept is still the same. We have to determine how important is the thing we want to accomplish? How important is success?

WRIGHT

Speaking of success, I know you have a unique way of looking at success. How do you define success?

MCRAE

Well, I'm not sure how unique it is, but I would say success is relative. Like beauty, it is truly in the eye of the beholder. On the one hand, success is an opinion. Opinions stem from judgments. We often deem a person successful or not based on the judgments we, ourselves, hold about our own achievement or lack thereof and our own ability to acquire or desire to acquire material possessions.

For example, many may feel that one is successful based on how they interpret what they see—a luxury car, a big house in a secluded area, what appears to be a loving relationship, a prominent position in society—all the things we may have been taught equal success. What we often don't take into consideration or overlook, is the idea that what we are seeing or interpreting may not even be true. The person we've determined to be successful could, in fact, be six months behind in the mortgage on that very same house in a secluded area or perhaps he or she is suffering abuse in the relationship we thought was so peachy or experiencing any number of other unseen calamities. Additionally, there still remains the possibility that people we think are successful may or may not consider themselves successful at all simply because they never wanted any of those things. They could have wanted to live alone in a small apartment in downtown Manhattan with no children and go to the park and photograph birds all day. "Ah, now that would have been success!" someone might say.

In any event, the fact still remains that regardless of what we *think* is going on and what is *really* going on—objective or subjective—success is still relative and changes from person to person depending on who is interpreting it.

WRIGHT

So, on the one hand success is relative to a person's opinion. I see what you mean. What about on the other hand?

MCRAE

Now, on the other hand, success is a fact. It either is or it isn't. You either did or you didn't. Truly, success is nothing more than the receipt of a desired outcome. Success is an indicator of the completion of a goal, whether it was a written goal, a planned-out goal, an acknowledged goal, a long-term goal, a short-term goal, a fleeting thought you had one time or something you thought about many, times. Success indicates achievement.

Here's an example. Both of my daughters have *successfully* graduated from prestigious universities. They are not successful because of that. They succeeded because they achieved their desired outcomes. I have just today successfully traveled from Virginia to New York. This morning I was in Virginia and my plan was this evening I would be in New York. Now I am in New York—success! I wanted to live in a house with a Jacuzzi in the master bath, and then I lived in it. Success! I wanted a glass of water, and now I'm drinking a glass of water. Success!

Success can be as small as a glass of water (or smaller) or as large as anyone's imagination will allow. Success is receiving the desired outcome, nothing more, nothing less. So the question then becomes, "Do you want success or do you want the desired outcome?" Understand this: success is not attainable. When you receive the desired outcome, you have already succeeded.

WRIGHT

So, assuming a person might want to receive a desired outcome, as you say, and change a desire to a simple fact, how would one go about accomplishing that?

MCRAE

Well, first and foremost, people have to know that success is even possible for them *and* that they already possess the power to achieve it. In short, we have to recognize and realize who we are. You see, when we know who we are, we already know that success is possible and that the power to achieve it lies within us. Unfortunately, for a great many of us, however, we have not been taught the skills to go inside and see what lies waiting there. It is we, ourselves, who possess the great genie in the fabled story of Aladdin's lamp.

I'd like you to think about something. I usually ask this question in my workshops: "Have you ever thought about someone you haven't seen in a long time and wondered what ever happened to him or her?" Of course, everyone has. And then I ask, "What happens next?" Simultaneously, everyone begins to convey how the person just *coincidentally* showed up in a grocery store, a bank, on a bus or train or any number of other locations. Sometimes he or she shows up in a place we typically go every day or any day at that same time. Sometimes the person shows up at a place we would *never* have been on that particular day of the week or in that particular doctor's office or wherever. Sometimes the person we're thinking of will just call us on the phone, and tells you that he or she *accidentally* ran into a mutual friend who had our phone number. Either way, the person showed up after we thought about him or her. Why? Synergy? Coincidence? Happenstance?

What gets me is the amount of people this has happened to. It is generally an overwhelming majority of people in the room. Could it possibly be that what we think about we bring about? There's an old saying, "Be careful what you ask for because you just might get it."

When I was growing up, it was not uncommon for me to hear my grandmother on the phone saying, "You are going to live a long time. We were just talking about you the other day." As a matter of fact, this very thing just happened to me about two months ago. I was in New York and I remember wondering whatever happened to my old friend, Joanne. I hadn't seen or heard from her in about seven years or so. About a week later, while in Virginia, I received a phone call from my mom. "Renée," she said, "someone named Joanne called for you and left her number." I was shocked. She now lives in Tampa, Florida. I would never have found her. Joanne said she had run across my mother's telephone number in an old phone book.

But why do we take these things for granted? Why do we write them off as coincidences? More importantly, why don't we investigate the possibility that we create our own worlds? That reminds me of late night talk show host, Arsenio Hall. He used to talk about "Things that make you go, *hmmm*."

Here is an interesting thought—could it be that we don't want the responsibility? Could it be that it's easier to be the victim because then we can always blame someone else for the perceived mess we've made of our lives. *Hmmm.*

WRIGHT

That is an interesting thought. I noticed you said "perceived." Isn't it either a mess or not?

MCRAE

Actually, no it's not. What seems like a mess could actually be the catalyst for learning. The "mess" could be exactly what we need to move to the next level in our growth and understanding. An "unwanted mess" can often point us in the direction of satisfaction, peace, and the tranquility we desire.

I once heard a story about a man who went to the edge of the city every day. Standing at the ocean's edge he would gaze at the distant tropical island and yearn to be there, lying under the one lone palm tree he could see. He would come to this spot every day and envision that he was no longer living in the city with its tall buildings and concrete sidewalks but living in that tropical paradise he could barely see. He longed to be away from the rush hour traffic and scores of people.

One day, as he stood at the water's edge, a large wave swallowed him whole. He couldn't breathe. He was frightened. He was drowning! He was in a "mess." He tried like crazy to get back to the city, back to the safety of the place he had been standing—the only place he really knew—and back to some *air*! He struggled and fought but, alas, he lost consciousness. When he came to, choking and coughing, he looked around. To his surprise and amazement, he had washed up on that very island he had looked at every day—and he was lying right under that very same palm tree he had yearned for.

There are so many points in this story but the one I want to make here is how much of a "mess" was he really in? His perceived *mess* in actuality proved to be *transition*, didn't it? He was, in reality, being delivered to the place he had visualized every day, wasn't he? I mean, he could have assumed the victim role, blamed the wave, and totally missed the blessing.

WRIGHT

Yes, that's true. You mentioned his visualization. How important do you think visualization is in determining success or receiving a desired outcome?

MCRAE

Without a doubt, visualization is very important. Have you heard the quote "without vision, the people perish"? How about, "If you can conceive it, you can achieve it"? You have to be able to see it as a possibility for yourself. Knowing, as we spoke about previously, is the preface to vision and vision is the preface to the action. Vision gives us our direction. If you cannot envision yourself doing something, you will not attempt to do it. Many athletes have said that they visualize themselves achieving the feat before they actually do it.

> "I never hit a shot, not even in practice, without having a very sharp, in-focus picture of it in my head. First I see the ball where I want it to finish, nice and white and sitting up high on the bright green grass. Then the scene quickly changes, and I see the ball going there: its path, trajectory, and shape, even its behavior on landing. Then there is a sort of fade-out, and the next scene shows me making the kind of swing that will turn the previous images into reality" —Jack Nicklaus.

I remember when I was fourteen years old and my family had reason to go into an attorney's office on Court Street in Brooklyn. I can still remember the feeling when I saw his secretary sitting at her desk. Her back was erect in her chair with her hair pulled back into a little neat bun, reading glasses on the bridge of her nose, typing away. Every few seconds the little bell would ring signaling that she had reached the end of a line or the margin, and she would seemingly unconsciously grab the silver handle on the left-hand side of the carriage and shove it back to the right side of the little black typewriter and go right back to pecking away at the keys, not once looking up.

I was struck with awe at how she never even looked at the keys as her fingers flew effortlessly over them. I remember the intensity with which I wanted to do that. Of course, the rest is history. Being a legal secretary became my first profession. Whether it's gymnastics, golf, hitting a home run, or becoming a legal secretary, the process is the same—visualization is the preface to the action.

WRIGHT

Now, what about beliefs? I heard that you liken beliefs to railroad tracks?

MCRAE

It's interesting that you brought that up, David. Belief is a tricky thing. It's like my interpretation of success. On the one hand, belief indicates uncertainty. When you believe something, you don't really know for sure. For example, if someone asks me what my name is, I wouldn't say, "I believe it is Renee." I would say my name with certainty, not because I *believe* it, but because I *know* it. Then on the other hand, you could believe something that is not even true but it *will* be your truth. An example of this is if you were convinced by someone or a group of people that you were locked in a room, in your mind the door is locked. If you wanted to escape, you might try the windows, the ceiling, pick at a hole in the wall, but the one thing you would not try to do is escape through the door. But the door could actually be unlocked, and the only door that kept you imprisoned would be the belief in your mind that the door was locked.

Much like a train runs on railroad tracks, you have to know that your life runs on tracks, too. They're called beliefs. Think about where you see trains. A train will not run down the middle of your street unless there are railroad tracks down the middle of your street. Otherwise, you will not see a train running in front of your

135

home. If you see a moving train, you can rest assured with certainty that there are tracks beneath it. Belief systems are the tracks that our lives run on. Whatever it is that we believe is what we will be able to visualize and/or achieve. If a woman believes it is a man's world and women can't succeed or make as much money or be promoted or make decisions that matter the universe will grant her that reality because:

> "What we think and what we feel
> Form our beliefs and will be real.
> It's all in your attitude—
> What you believe will be true for *You*."

The other thing about beliefs is that they are very often invisible and rarely stand alone. What I mean by that is belief systems are comprised of connected thoughts like the branches of a tree extending from the trunk.

For example, let's take the time I was stuck alone in a parking garage elevator. I could have a belief system like this: "This elevator is stuck, therefore, every elevator will get stuck." That's one. Then there's, "This elevator got stuck, therefore, every elevator will get stuck and every time I'm alone in an elevator, it will probably get stuck." That's two. How about, "Bad things always happen to me!" That's three, and we can go on and on. I could even develop a phobia about parking my car in parking garages. Now, it doesn't matter if it's true or false, it's my belief system, and it's in effect. It becomes my truth mentally, and it most likely will control my behavior physically.

Additionally, we have not even *touched* the concept of the universe or God providing me with the reality that I focus on. Regardless of that, we now have the situation of my repeating the same experience over and over and then justifying it by saying, "See, I told you this would happen," without my realizing or recognizing the fact that I am the one creating or *re*-creating the situation myself. I am not the victim, I am the creator. We all know people who experience the same thing repeatedly. They explain it away as a coincidence. Here's a belief for you: I don't believe in coincidences.

WRIGHT

You mentioned that beliefs are very often invisible. Would you explain that, please?

MCRAE

Well, most often beliefs *are* invisible, at least until you know how or where to look for them. Most of us don't even know we *have* beliefs or how important they really are. Belief systems are formed from our interpretations of the experiences we have. Once we have the experience, we develop a judgment or an opinion about it, and *voila!* the belief system is born. After that there is no reason to think about it again. Under the guise of learning, it becomes a failsafe or an idea structure that is in place to protect us in the future. What it really is, however, is a boundary or a limitation—a line that keeps us on one side and away from the other side. That's where the expression "think outside of the box" comes from. It's the box designed from the limitations within which we think (and live). It's no one's fault really, we just haven't been taught how to figure this stuff out. In any event, one thing is for certain, regardless of whether or not a belief is visible or invisible your life *will* be governed by it. But the good thing is: beliefs are like a ball of yarn. Once you find that loose string, you can unravel the whole thing.

WRIGHT

Do you have an exercise or a way to find a particular belief?

MCRAE

Sure. Let's say you are dealing with finances and wondering why you never have any money or enough money or something similar. One of the activities I use in my workshop is to have the participants write the answer to this question: "What do you believe is the reason why you don't have any money?" A person might write any number of reasons ranging from, *"I was raised in an impoverished home and I didn't have any rich role models"* to *"I was never taught about finances in school"* to *"I can't get a good paying job."* Now, whatever the answer is, know this: in that answer is your loose string, because the key phrase in the question was "What, *you believe,* is the reason . . ." The answer is going to contain the person's *belief.*

Let's take the first answer. Let's pretend it's you and you answered, "I was raised in an impoverished home and I didn't have any rich role models." Your *belief* is that you cannot get rich because you never had any rich role models when you were growing up. Is it the truth? No. There are countless rich people who never had any rich role models when they were growing up. That didn't stop them from becoming rich or having enough money to pay their bills. But it stopped *you.* Why? Because it is *your* belief that you cannot get rich without having a rich role model in *your* life. Simple!

WRIGHT

Wow. Can you do this with anything?

MCRAE

You can do this with everything. Just ask the right questions and you will uncover the belief or belief systems you hold about that issue. The answers will give you the reasons you use to justify not having enough money or not having a rewarding personal relationship or not being able to travel or not having the right job or whatever the topic of dissatisfaction might be.

Another way to find a belief is to search your past for your defining moments. Any event that made a difference in your life is a defining moment, and every defining moment contains a belief system.

WRIGHT

Thank you. Now, we know the steps we overlook are just as important in obtaining a desired outcome as the ones we pay attention to. So, from your perspective, what is something most people might overlook on their quest for success?

MCRAE

Well, from my experience, one of the most overlooked steps in this process of successfully achieving a desired outcome is gratitude—being thankful in our everyday lives—thankful for where we are, thankful for the things we have, for the air we breathe, the family members who love us and support us, the clothing on our backs, being able to read, having toilet paper, *whatever*—just being thankful. We can always find *something* to be thankful for, no matter how dismal we perceive our situations to be.

I like to look at life as an ever-unfolding imaginary staircase. Wherever we are in life is the step we are standing on, and this is the only step that will take us to the next one—above it or below it. But get this: it is only in placing our weight fully and firmly on the *current* step that we can get the leverage we need to catapult us to the *next* step. How do we place our weight fully and firmly on it? By being thankful. You see, every one of us is on our own step, and every step is equal. Remember, there is no good or bad, no higher or lower, no right or wrong. There is only learning, growing, and accepting. It is only in our judgment that it appears there are levels—levels of intelligence, levels of accomplishment, levels of ability.

But, as we accept, enjoy, and are thankful for where we are, our realities change! We move to the next place. It's like in the Harry Potter series where the staircases move and the place you once thought you were moving toward actually changes to a another reality altogether. Remember this: we live in a magnificent, marvelous, majestic universe and when we change on the inside, the outside automatically changes, too.

Sometimes we want to be in what we perceive to be a better place in our lives so much so that we curse the place where we are or the situation we are in. Please know this: when we curse anything, it becomes a curse in our lives. The more energy you give a thing in your life, the more solidity that thing has in your life.

What is important to understand is that thoughts become things. When we state, we create. When we restate, we recreate. Thoughts manifest into things.

We can be *Creators by Nature* or *Creatures of Habit,* but *Create,* we will. When we are thankful for something, we actually get more of it.

When I stopped cursing my bills and became consciously more thankful for my income, I started receiving more income! Gratitude opens up the pathway to receiving more simply because what you place your attention on begins to take up more space. So, what we need to understand is this: the thing we are thankful for will manifest into physical form and will be bigger in our lives.

WRIGHT

How can one go about giving thanks? Is it as simple as thinking it?

MCRAE

It can be. A person could think about it, but I don't recommend that method when first getting started. When we are new to this concept, most of us are a little too scattered to maintain the level of focus necessary to bring enough attention to the thought or thoughts we would like to manifest. If you did want to just think your thanks (so to speak), you might want to set aside a time dedicated to just thinking. Every morning, for instance, or just before going to sleep would suffice— any time you can remember consistently to do it. It's like going to church every Sunday at 11:00 AM. One of my daughters uses the numbers of her birthday as a reminder on the clock. So, for instance, if your birthday was November 23 (11/23), you could deliberately give thanks at 11:23 every morning and again at 11:23 every evening. You would do this, not because it's your birthday as much as it is a consistent time when you can remember and from which you can form a habit. Consistency is imperative to make the impression on the subconscious mind that this particular thought is really important. Remember, we have thousands of thoughts daily. What makes one thought more important than another? Repetition. And writing down the thing you are grateful for is important because it will isolate the idea from the rest of the mind-chatter and habitual thoughts occupying your mind space.

"Think about the life you're living
And what you want it to be.
Write it down, believe in it,
And just you wait and see.
The day will come when you'll be shocked,
For as you look around,
Everywhere you turn you'll see,
The thing that you wrote down.
You don't have to understand it,
You don't have to think it's true.
Just try it out and you will find,
That you're in charge of you."[3]

I write down everything I'm thankful for. But I write down plenty of other things, too, such as: the grocery list, a letter to a friend, my to-do list, a telephone number—tons of stuff. So, what makes this thing I'm grateful for stand out from another thing? "Focus, energy, and consistency" is the answer. By using a special book such as a gratitude journal or a separate section in a notebook, by deliberately giving thanks every night or every morning or some other designated time, and last, but certainly not least, by the energy I feel when I write "I am thankful for this thing or that."

Energy is the fuel that ignites the idea, like striking a match. If you do not add energy, you may as well be trying to strike a wet match. Where can we get the energy? You must know that not only do we have energy, but we are energy. Imagination can be a pump, however. Visualize yourself with that car, achieving that goal, passing that test, walking down that aisle. That vision and the image of yourself in that vision should bring up all the energy you need, provided, of course, that it is truly what you desire.

---

[3] Excerpt from the poem "Truth Be Told" published on the CD *Truth Be Told* by Renée McRae.

I heard one time that *"why"* is where your energy lies. *Why* you want to do a thing is what primes your energy. So to recap: we have to write down the things, people, places, situations, etc. that we are grateful for *consistently* and add the most important ingredient—*energy*.

WRIGHT

Well, we've covered quite a bit. Is there anything else you feel would be necessary in creating or manifesting a successful outcome?

MCRAE

My mom says that until you make a decision you will experience discomfort, stress, and/or turmoil. I think that bit of wisdom bears sharing since I, too, have found it to be true. Until a decision is made there will be no forward movement, and stagnation is not a fun place to be. You can decide to move your pinky finger or you can decide to run for President; either way, nothing happens until a decision is made.

Now, why people don't make decisions is another matter entirely. But understand this: even when we don't make a decision, we are still making a decision.

Let me give you an example: a man is contemplating whether or not to leave his wife or his job. Until he decides to leave, he has already decided to stay.

Here's another example: a woman is vacillating about whether to take the two o'clock bus or the four o'clock bus. At 2:05 there is no more decision to be made—she has decided not to take the two o'clock bus. It is an unconscious decision, of course, but a decision nonetheless.

The above two examples demonstrate what I meant earlier when I said that very often we are living in the world in an unconscious way. But the good news is this: just as we have been unconsciously creating what we don't necessarily want, we can *consciously* create what we do want, as well.

WRIGHT

What about commitment? Some say commitment is the bottom line to getting *anything* done.

MCRAE

And I concur. Commitment is one of the most *important* of all steppingstones, and I'll tell you why. Without commitment, providence cannot move. You see, providence is the universal assistance we receive when we become committed to something. In a world of cause and effect, manifestation is the effect and commitment is the cause. But you must understand the equation: burning desire births intention, and intention births commitment. So the question becomes, how strong is your burning desire? Burning desire is the energy that fuels and will determine your level of commitment.

We've all heard the story about the hen and the pig and their level of commitment to the breakfast. If you have not heard it, however, the bottom line is this: considering a breakfast of ham and eggs, the hen contributed an egg and the pig contributed his life. Obviously, the pig had a higher level of commitment to the breakfast. How much of a commitment do you have to your dreams? How much are you willing to sacrifice for the thing you say you want? How badly do you want it? We have to have a commitment as strong as the pig's (or at least the person who killed the pig).

> "Think the thought and hold the vision.
> See with your third eye.
> Face your fears, walk through the door.
> You must only be *willing* to die."[4]

We have to have an *"I will have this or die trying"* attitude. It doesn't mean you have to actually die. What it does mean is that in some cases you have to be *willing* to die. You may have to want it that badly. Your desire may have to be that strong.

---

[4] Excerpt from the poem "Behold" published in *Truth In Rhyme* and *Truth Be Told* by Renée McRae

The reason is that sometimes we have so much to mentally overcome or compensate for.

Based upon the aforesaid interpretations of experiences and habitual ways of thinking, we sometimes have so much energy and focus in the opposite direction of the goal, we will only create in the opposite direction of the goal. That is when your commitment gets tested. How long can you hold your breath? How long can you tread water? How *strong* is your commitment to have the thing you say you want? You see, the law is the law is the law, period. It works without judgment and without prejudice. The Law of Creation assists us by producing the manifestation or physical reality of the strongest energy we provide it. If we think about the bills with anger (and anger is energy), we create more bills. If we think with forceful energy about the traits we don't like or want in a mate, we get more of the traits we don't like or want in our mate. So the nature of your commitment has to be that there is no turning back.

My daughters, for instance, have had an easier time consciously manifesting than I did at their ages. The main reason for this is because they didn't have to overcome the habitual patterns of negative thought, necessarily. (And by negative I only mean minus-goal thought just as positive is plus-goal thought or thinking that is toward the direction of the goal.) I made a point of teaching them very early that poverty or prosperity begins in your mind. They think about what they want and they get it—habitually.

Now, on the other hand, I was quite the opposite. I remember my dad asking us if we thought money grew on trees whenever we wanted to go to the ice cream truck. I remember having to go back upstairs to turn off the bedroom light or the bathroom light because "we don't have stock in the electric company," he would say. The list goes on and by the time I was a teen, I had developed such a solid pattern of what I would call a "mentality of lack" that I had to overcompensate in the opposite direction in order to get the desired outcome. I guess that's why it was easy for me to pack up and leave North Carolina with no plan and a kid in tow. I've developed a habit of going to an extreme in the opposite direction. It's the only way I was able to overcome the fear of failure or success or lack or rejection or death or not being good enough or whatever.

Nevertheless, without the energy—that burning desire—there will be no commitment and consequently, the desired outcome will continue to be elusive.

WRIGHT

Renée, you have been just great. In conclusion, is there anything else you would like to leave our readers with?

MCRAE

Thank you very much. I'll leave you with the concept of never accepting less. As I see it, we have to know what we want and not accept less. Of course, it's easier said than done, but the concept is absolutely simple. And it has everything to do with focus and faith. We've all experienced it. Getting distracted can show up in a way as minute as going on the computer to get driving directions and wind up checking e-mails and veering off onto search engines and answering the telephone, shutting the computer down, and never getting back to the directions we first went on the computer to get.

It can also show up in a larger way like wanting to marry a religious man but accepting the first man who comes along in a nightclub or wanting to have a Jaguar but shopping at the Hyundai dealership for a new car. When you couple getting distracted with fear and lack of faith (and not understanding belief systems) it is no wonder we accept less. The good news is if you put it out there, it's coming to you, so don't accept less!

"What idea has died in me,
And brought about this poverty?
And what is the thought remaining intact
That brings about this life of lack?
When something dies it also gives;
The message is—that something lives.
There is no one without the other,

There is no child lest there be a mother.
If you see and if you hear,
You can learn the thoughts held dear
For thoughts held deep within your mind;
They come about with passing time.
When will the thought of poverty die,
And shine the light upon the lie?
Receiving more lives in the death
Of wanting more, yet accepting less."[5]

WRIGHT

Today we've been talking with Renee McRae, personal development trainer, coach, and performance poet whose Life-Alignment Workshops and poetic performances help people live more fulfilled and self-determined lives.

Renée, thank you so much for being with us today in *Stepping Stones to Success*.

MCRAE

Thank you, David. It was my pleasure.

---

[5] "Receiving More" originally published in *Truth In Rhyme* and *Truth Be Told* by Renée McRae

ABOUT THE AUTHOR

RENÉE MCRAE is the founder of Poetic Motivations, LLC, a personal and professional development training company. She is a performance poet and personal development trainer with nineteen years of experience facilitating life skills and leadership workshops in shelters, colleges, public/private schools, substance abuse clinics, as well as other venues. Additionally, Renée is the author of *Truth In Rhyme,* which is an approved textbook with the New York City Department of Education, and *Truth Be Told,* a compilation of change-your-life poetry recently released on CD. Free samples of both are available on her Web site, www.reneemcrae.com.

One of Renée's greatest joys is to see clients and workshop participants experience "A-ha!" moments.

RENÉE MCRAE

Poetic Motivations, LLC

8808/C Woodyard Road
Clinton, MD 20735
646-898-7907
info@reneemcrae.com
www.reneemcrae.com

CHAPTER NINE

Choose the Right Steppingstones:
The Subtle Elements of Success
An Interview with . . . Dr. Ethel Drayton-Craig

DAVID WRIGHT (WRIGHT)

Today we're talking with Dr. Ethel Drayton-Craig. She is a dynamic, inspirational mentor and success motivator. She received national exposure through the private sector in the area of executive development as well as through television, radio, and print media. She provides telephone consultations to individuals to facilitate them in achieving their goals and turning their visions into reality. She also provides one-on-one customized retreats to enable individual executives, entrepreneurs, healers, artists, athletes, and performers to function at their peak with respect to creativity, clarity, balance, and producing results.

Dr. Drayton-Craig, welcome to *Stepping Stones to Success*.

ETHEL DRAYTON-CRAIG (DRAYTON-CRAIG)

Thank you. Thank you for having me.

WRIGHT

What are your thoughts about success?

DRAYTON-CRAIG

The American scenario for success is primarily a measure of career and money related advances and acquisitions. Typically, parents and educators want their young to complete high school, go to college, receive a degree, receive an advanced degree perhaps, and get a job so that they can be self-sufficient. As Life progresses, they settle into the job that becomes a fast acceleration of promotions and pay increases, otherwise known as a career.

Somewhere along the line, parents hope that their children will get married, buy a house, have children, furnish the house, and later embellish the house so that it adds to their status. Automobiles, vacations, busyness 24/7, on-call 24/7, cosmetic surgery, and perfectly sized bodies with sculpted abs are additional popular culture indicators of disposable income and lifestyles of success.

What one decides about how he or she will live is a personal matter. Surely, the acquisition of material things is a personal desire. When you are young you are definitely drawn to work in order to have things—pretty things, shiny things, sharp looking things, and the most modern of things. It is in our younger years when, typically, the energy needed and the desire to acquire is at its greatest. I can say that is how it was for me in my early Life.

However, almost thirty years ago I was struck by something that a personal mentor said that had an immediate influence on me. She said that her goal in Life was to embody the Christ Consciousness in such a way that wherever she was— just walking down the street, for example—people around her would be affected positively without her saying a word to anyone. Further, she hoped that whatever was going on with people in that moment, got better because she passed by.

I knew that when I heard this, it was a powerful thought. To this day, I can remember the moment she said that and how I began to think about what my Life could be like if I cultivated that sense of being as my nature.

Today, when I talk to groups of people about success, I tell them that it is fine to set goals and to achieve the desires they want. By all means, think *big*. What you think you can achieve and believe you can achieve, you can.

However, I offer a different perspective on success: Success is living in such a way that people are blessed by your presence whether you interact with them or not; whether you are in their physical space or not. I ask, "If you drive by a car parked on the side of the highway with the driver looking under the hood of the disabled vehicle or next to its flat tire, will just your passing by ameliorate the situation? Whether you stop or not, does help or assistance come to that driver because you passed by? When you hear a siren in the distance, is the situation getting better because you are attuned to it? Is healing taking place? Is comfort and necessary help being administered for the well-being of all concerned, even though you are not there? If you pass by a commotion or argument between people on the street, has ease and calm entered into the situation as you go by? Do people come up to you and ask you for directions or help? Do they smile, nod, or say, "Hello" in a public area as they approach you? In other words, is your state of being in the world such that it brings ease, wholeness, comfort, peace, light, love, and healing to others by your sheer presence? If your answer is "yes," that is how I define success.

This provides a context or backdrop for how one leads his or her Life—how one develops his or her personal spiritual journey. It is cultivated over time, and it becomes a way of Life.

WRIGHT

With respect to achieving personal and business goals, where does a person start?

DRAYTON-CRAIG

To commence the act of creation, put God first. Get centered, be still, and know the presence of God directing your path.

Usually, when a person takes on a new vision, project, or undertaking, it is not something that is completed in one hour or one day. I am talking about the creation of a new endeavor that will require a major commitment on your behalf. You would want to start out having laid the proper foundation.

I am reminded of two important Bible verses that give the keys to creation and manifestation. The first is found in Luke 12:31, "But rather seek ye the kingdom of God and all these things shall be added unto you." The first place to start is with God—always. In the quietness of your soul, you can listen for the guidance you need. You may just say, "God, please show me how to create this project" or "Please give me the idea that I need" or "I would like to accomplish this goal and I want it to be aligned with my Life purpose. God, please guide me."

The ideas may flow immediately. They may take a while. Every time you take time to sit still for a few minutes to clear your mind and center yourself, you are cultivating the soil in which you plant your seeds for what you desire. Sow in fertile ground. The best soil to bring a good harvest is the soil aligned with your purpose for being. Your actions and projects should come from the reason you are here. Those quiet times reveal the way. So, quiet time and stillness needs to be a daily practice.

The second Bible verse that is essential to know is John 1:1, "In the beginning was the Word, and the Word was with God, and the Word was God."

Your word is critical. It can be a silent declaration or an audible statement that you make to yourself. Declare your vision of what you plan to create, even if you do not know the answers as to how it will come about. Put things into action by declaring it to be so and holding that thought in your mind—for years if need be. Your word binds you to the outcome of your desire. It is not to be taken lightly. For, in your world, it is the seed out of which your desires are manifested. That is the given model in the Bible.

WRIGHT

How important is it to crystallize your goals, or vision and to declare it?

DRAYTON-CRAIG

Let us say that you are unhappy in a particular job and you would like to do something else. However, you do not seem to know exactly what the next career move should be and nothing piques your interest. A simple prayer can get things moving: "Lord, show me what other work you would want me to do." You can also affirm the declaration: "I am now in my right place of employment where I experience fulfillment." Hold that thought.

Things can shift for you quickly or it can take years. When you put it in God's hands, you can be assured that the outworking is occurring, but timeliness is God's time, not yours. You see, other things may need to be in place for your ideal job to come along, such as when there would be the least upheaval for your family or when you have the breadth of expertise to handle what is next. Therefore, I am saying that even when you are unsure of the exact details of the outcome you want, you set things in motion by a declarative thought in its most simplistic form. That moves you toward the ultimate outcome.

The manifestation of your desire begins from the thought—the word.

WRIGHT

You mentioned sowing in fertile ground. How do you tend to that soil and cultivate your dream?

DRAYTON-CRAIG

You create Best Practices as your daily habits. These keep you attuned to your project in a positive frame of mind, with optimal enthusiasm. They enable you to meet challenges head-on and to find balance so that other areas of your Life work. Especially during the period in which you are creating something, be intentional in your thinking and speaking. Try to see possibility when faced with difficult situations involving people—where is there an opening for a way to get what you need?

Do not go into mental agreement with anything you hear that limits, minimizes, or invokes a negative outcome for what you desire for yourself or know to be true of yourself.

You may find that people around you in social conversation, whether they are speaking to you or to others, make general statements about Life that are indicative of a belief in hardship, illness, financial strain, and difficult times. When you hear or overhear such statements, in the quiet of your own mind, you can cancel the suggestion and rebuke it as not being true for you or your Life. The more you do this, the more discerning you become to magnetize the type of experiences that you do want to see as part of your Life. You will grow keen in flexing your intentionality muscle.

Remember that even if the attainment of your goal is well into the future, act within yourself now as though you had been successful in achieving it already. For example, it is likely that when you attain the goal, your schedule, activities, demeanor, dress, tastes, and confidence might shift. Make those changes now. Envision how the attainment of the goal will affect your Life. What new responsibilities will you incur as a result? What time will be freed? What time will be encumbered? What will the new activities be? What kinds of new things will you be able to do, if there is a shift in your finances? It is important, if there are financial goals, that you act as though you have what you want now.

Perhaps you cannot purchase the new automobile or new home yet. However, you can visit showrooms and view magazine pictures of what you desire. You certainly can handle your record-keeping and bookkeeping in a manner that will be required for the income change that you anticipate. If it is a vacation abroad that you have as a goal, you can indulge yourself in a meal featuring the cuisine of the country that you want to visit. If you are seeking to enter a certain profession in the future, become knowledgeable about what people in that profession do. Read what they read. Familiarize yourself with the issues, the vocabulary, and trends in that field now. In other words, you are what you want to be already. All of the ingredients are inside you. Act the part until the time that your education and work experience are complete and you reach the level you seek.

Keep your plans to yourself. Loved ones and friends can raise your doubts by their concerns that you could risk failure, hurt, or disappointment. People can also be jealous of your lofty aspirations and therefore, knowingly or unknowingly, make comments to ridicule, scare, and create apprehension. If you want to share your ideas or goals, be sure you choose to do so with friends who you know will be objective and helpful, yet champion you forward. You can share them with a professional who has the expertise you seek.

Surround yourself with positive images in your home and place of work, such as art, photos, and objects that are pleasing to your eye and make you feel good. Place photos of yourself that you like in your physical space. They help you envision yourself happy and feeling good. Be sure to engage in appropriate exercise for your body. Also, walk or spend time outside in nature.

Remind yourself that you deserve what you desire, and that you are able and capable. Demonstrate that you find yourself deserving and worthy by doing something kind and nice for yourself at least once a week. Find something that does not cost money or that is inexpensive, yet that will bring a smile to your face.

The important thing is to create a timeline/to-do list for the project with projected completion dates that you value and will act upon. View this timeline/to-do list frequently in the week and keep it current by checking off what is completed. Add new things that need to be completed and modify any items when necessary.

WRIGHT

How do you deal with the human conditions of doubt and fear?

DRAYTON-CRAIG

When doubt and fear creep into the mind they hold you back. You certainly want to explore your project well and know issues that may be challenges. You want to understand those things for which you need to plan. You want to ensure the integrity of your well-being (physical and other) in any undertaking. You want to be compliant with essentials such as legalities.

You also need to understand that many undertakings do not have clearly marked road signs ahead alerting you to blocks, adversity, challenges, or pitfalls. Embarking on the path with the unfolding of Life itself takes us to these places. They can be troublesome, daunting, overwhelming, and they could also be exhilarating. Yet, moving through, over, under, and around these situations make the journey one of exceptional value. In times of trouble or seemingly insurmountable challenges, what is required in a very big way is *trust*. It is a critical factor. It is something that the individual has to cultivate on an individual basis. Trust in something bigger than yourself.

A soothing reminder that comforts the soul is a Bible quote, Isaiah 26:3: "Thou wilt keep him in perfect peace, whose mind is stayed on thee: because he trusteth in thee."

Visualization of the project completed as you would like it to be gives you a mental space to which you can retreat for encouragement. Think about what you will look like the day the project is complete. With whom will you be? What will make the time special? Keep your eye on your vision when the going gets rough. When doubt and fear enter your mind, assess the situation and modify anything that can truly be of danger. Move forward by holding your vision, find the thoughts that bring you comfort and inspiration and work yourself through it. Pause if necessary.

Assess your exposure to negative messages. It is difficult enough to manage a buoyant heart and optimism when you run into snags, delays, opposition, and no results after you have embarked on a new quest. You do not need negative input from elsewhere to add to your concerns. Are these additional strains from the outside? How can you cease the input? Are you under personal and family challenges that place greater demands on your time or compromise your well being? If so, how can you minimize these demands or handle them?

It is ever important to be mindful of one's thoughts and speech. Avoid at all costs thoughts that describe your Life as, "not working," "poor," or "unsuccessful." Rather, it is imperative to assess the situation, re-strategize, but do so from the context that things are working out for the best for all concerned. In other words, affirm the results that you do want to see. Give power to that. Do not give power to the conditions that you do not want to see.

WRIGHT

So, what do you do when you have challenges—when things do not seem to be working?

DRAYTON-CRAIG

There is always room to assess, to learn, to ask questions, to strategize, and give more of oneself to one's work. However, the basic thing to remember is the Bible verse, "Judge not according to the appearance" (John 7:24). This means that while you have the presence of a problem, or the absence of a solution related to some aspect of a project on which you are working, how you contextualize the situation has bearing on the outcome. A rational mind can help at times. However, it can also limit you. There are other levels and dimensions to knowing. What you see before you is the situation as you think it is. Do not be so sure that it is the way you observe it to be because you are viewing the situation from your perspective with the limitations of your humanness. God's point of view is quite different—one of perfection. If you could hold to the perfect picture of your situation, even though the evidence looks contrary, you might see resolution, movement, and positive results.

Also, play full out. Do everything you can to make results happen. Make requests of people. Tell people what you need. Ask for help. Get beyond objections. Pursue excellence in every aspect of how you do what you do. Keep your word, even to yourself. Remember the power is in the word. I often observe people who are beset with setbacks and problems. Two things they have in common: first, they can rattle off reasons why they cannot do something that you ask them to do. Second, they cannot be counted on to do what they say they will do. They always have an excuse for why they did not show up or did not do something. Rarely do they initiate a call to alert you that they will not keep the appointment. In all of the cases I have observed, the quality of their personal lives suffer and they do not flourish. When you do not have integrity in your word, you have no power in the Universe to create.

Have gratitude every day, more and more. Build fun into your Life for balance. If everything has been done and you have given 100 percent of yourself, 150 percent of yourself, 200 percent of yourself, and you have put yourself out there again and again—you have verbalized your needs in telling people about the project and you have made modifications and improvements to it, then that is the time to "let go and let God." Surrender. Surrender, not in resignation; but rather, in anticipation—wait and see what happens next.

Own any disappointments and make peace with them. But, find the good in the things that you were able to accomplish with the project and let it go. Time may bring about what you desire. Surrender is not giving up on your desires; rather, it is letting go. It is like turning the intensity knob way down, real low, because you trust that things are working out for the good of all concerned and you know that at whatever point you have reached, there is nothing further you can do.

WRIGHT

What do you do when you are really in an adversarial situation?

DRAYTON-CRAIG

We are talking about doing battle. As much as we do not like it, we may be called upon to develop our warrior spirit. Before you go into battle, you need to develop methods for protecting yourself. This might include prayer, pronouncing a blessing on yourself, and a blessing on your physical space and on your opponent(s). The battle can take place in an office, a courtroom, or a public forum. The Bible details the armor with which you should clad yourself (Eph. 6:11–18). Read it over and mentally dress yourself with the armor. For example, many of our work environments are emotionally and mentally toxic environments. If that is the case, then I would read this passage to myself every day as I start work.

I have found that the most calming and affirming words of inspiration for times of feeling defeated when entering a battle situation in which the opposition represents a mighty force, are the biblical words, "Be not afraid nor dismayed by reason of this great multitude: for the battle is not yours, but God's. Tomorrow go ye down against them: behold, they come up by the cliff of Ziz; and ye shall find them at the end of the brook, before the wilderness of Jeruel. Ye shall not need to fight in this battle: set yourselves, stand ye still, and see the salvation of the Lord with you, O Judah and Jerusalem: fear not, nor be dismayed; tomorrow go out against them: for the Lord will be with you" (2 Chron. 20:15–17).

This passage is telling you to prepare yourself well. Do your work. Dot your I's and cross your T's. Prepare your documents. Prepare your presentation. Do what your lawyer tells you to do, if you are being represented by a lawyer. Suit up. Go in to face your opponent and watch how God moves through you in that room. Go with confidence!

WRIGHT

What if you have done all that you think you can do and things are still not resolved or what you desire does not come to pass?

DRAYTON-CRAIG

Give. Make sure that you tithe 10 percent from the top of income, gifts, or unexpected money—even if you are struggling financially. You have to prime the pump. Tithing is giving back to the Source of your spiritual nourishment. This is not to be confused with charity giving. Wherever you get your spiritual sustenance, you are giving to that source when you tithe.

Give yourself away. Volunteer. Be of service.

Surrender. Let go. Let God.

WRIGHT

What is the role of nature in the process?

DRAYTON-CRAIG

We are inextricably linked to nature. As natural beings, we are in our element when we are among natural landscapes, trees, under sky, and near birds, insects, and animals. When we can stand, walk, and sit on the earth, we can allow the Earth's rhythms to vibrate through us. Spending time outside clears the mind and often lifts the spirit. It can give us a new perspective on aspects of Life.

It can be surprising to pose a question to an audience of trees, let's say, and wait until you sense an answer back inside your being. This is the synchrony we have in being at one with the Universe. You can develop keen insight by observing natural settings—light, insects, water, and animal behavior. I find that nature is essential to well-being. Our existence is sustained by the Earth and the air.

WRIGHT

Isn't it all just about hard work?

DRAYTON-CRAIG

Effort is required. I use the word "effort" because I do not want to program things to be hard, as in hard work. Remember intentional thoughts. Do we often toil or work hard? Yes. Is that all there is that is necessary for success? No. There are nuts and bolts types of things that you have to do—study, learn, plan, execute, and communicate in order to do business. However, it is not all work. There must be balance.

Joy should also be a critical element. We forget that. Joy should be found every day. If there is no joy in the work you are doing, or in the goals that you have set for yourself, then you need to ask yourself, why are you doing it? Really, why? For how much longer are you willing to do it?

Love should be essential—love what you do because where there is love there is joy.

WRIGHT

What are the other critical elements that a successful person needs to include in his or her Life?

DRAYTON-CRAIG

A support system is essential, such as friends, who are objective. You want friends who will listen but not buy into your drama. They should not be co-workers. You do not need a lot of friends.

Discern who can fulfill these requirements. Select one to three people. Be discreet. Do not tell everyone your goals until you are well on your way. You do not need naysayers.

If you do not have a good friend who can be a person of support to champion you onward, then it is all the more necessary for you to be strong in faith and in developing a spiritual walk with a Power and Presence greater than you are. For me, that is God.

WRIGHT

Well, what an interesting conversation! You have presented a different take on success.

DRAYTON-CRAIG

A different take—*indeed!*

WRIGHT

But one that makes more sense.

I really do appreciate all the time you've taken with me today to answer these questions. You have made me more introspective here today and I'm going to think about what you have talked about. Hopefully our readers will do the same.

DRAYTON-CRAIG

Thank you so much, David.

WRIGHT

Today we've been talking with Dr. Ethel Drayton-Craig. She is a dynamic inspirational mentor and success motivator. She provides consultations to individuals to facilitate them in achieving their goals and turning their visions into reality, as well as one-on-one customized retreats to enable executives, entrepreneurs, healers, artists, athletes, and performers to function at their peak with respect to creativity, clarity, balance, and producing results.

Dr. Drayton-Craig, I really do appreciate this time and I thank you so much for being with us on *Stepping Stones to Success*.

DRAYTON-CRAIG

You are quite welcome.

ABOUT THE AUTHOR

DR. ETHEL DRAYTON-CRAIG provides telephone consultations and customized individual retreats to assist people in turning their visions into reality.

She has been an independent consultant to corporations and individuals in Career Center Development, Employee Selection, Stress Management, Success Motivation and Effective Presentations. She was a program planner with implementation, training, and individual counseling for large-scale corporate outplacement projects. Clients included Chemical Bank, Chase Bank, American-Express, Hoffman-La Roche, and Eastman Kodak, among others.

Prior to that, she was a vice president for the gold standard of the Human Resources/Outplacement Counseling industry, Drake Beam Morin, Inc., New York, where she created its Pre-Retirement Planning product in 1980.

She practiced as a school psychologist for the Newark, New Jersey, Board of Education and she has been a college administrator in the area of diversity.

She earned her BA at the State University of New York at Stony Brook, an MS and Professional Diploma in School Psychology at Queens College of the City University of New York, and a PhD in Urban School Psychology at Fordham University.

ETHEL DRAYTON-CRAIG, PHD

3440 Lehigh Street, Ste. 238
Allentown, PA 18103
484-695-1453
Zebragrace@msn.com
www.etheldrayton-craig.com

CHAPTER TEN

Discover Your Inner Resource

*An Interview with...***Dr. Deepak Chopra**

DAVID WRIGHT (WRIGHT)

Today we are talking to Dr. Deepak Chopra, founder of the Chopra Center for Well Being in Carlsbad, California. More than a decade ago, Dr. Chopra became the foremost pioneer in integrated medicine. His insights have redefined our definition of health to embrace body, mind and spirit. His books, which include, *Quantum Healing, Perfect Health, Ageless Body Timeless Mind*, and *The Seven Spiritual Laws of Success,* have become international bestsellers and are established classics.

Dr. Chopra, welcome to *Stepping Stones to Success*.

DR. DEEPAK CHOPRA (CHOPRA)

Thank you. How are you?

WRIGHT

I am doing just fine. It's great weather here in Tennessee.

CHOPRA

Great.

WRIGHT

Dr. Chopra, you stated in your book, *Grow Younger, Live Longer: 10 Steps to Reverse Aging,* that it is possible to reset your biostats up to fifteen years younger than your chronological age. Is that really possible?

CHOPRA

Yes. There are several examples of this. The literature on aging really began to become interesting in the 1980s when people showed that it was possible to reverse the biological marks of aging. This included things like blood pressure, bone density, body temperature, regulation of the metabolic rate, and other things like cardiovascular conditioning, cholesterol levels, muscle mass and strength of muscles, and even things like hearing, vision, sex hormone levels, and immune function.

One of the things that came out of those studies was that psychological age had a great influence on biological age. So you have three kinds of aging: chronological age is when you were born, biological age is what your biomarker shows, and psychological age is what your biostat says.

WRIGHT

You call our prior conditioning a prison. What do you mean?

CHOPRA

We have certain expectations about the aging process. Women expect to become menopausal in their early forties. People think they should retire at the age of sixty-five and then go Florida and spend the rest of their life in so-called retirement. These expectations actually influence the very biology of aging. What we call normal aging is actually the hypnosis of our social conditioning. If you can bypass that social conditioning, then you're free to reset your own biological clock.

WRIGHT

Everyone told me that I was supposed to retire at sixty-five. I'm somewhat older than that and as a matter of fact, today is my birthday.

CHOPRA

Well happy birthday. You know, the fact is that you should be having fun all the time and always feel youthful. You should always feel that you are contributing to society. It's not the retirement, but it's the passion with which you're involved in the well being of your society, your community, or the world at large.

WRIGHT

Great things keep happening to me. I have two daughters; one was born when I was fifty. That has changed my life quite a bit. I feel a lot younger than I am.

CHOPRA

The more you associate with young people, the more you will respond to that biological expression.

WRIGHT

Dr. Chopra, you suggest viewing our bodies from the perspective of quantum physics. That seems somewhat technical. Will you tell us a little bit more about that?

CHOPRA

You see, on one level, your body is made up of flesh and bone. That's the material level but we know today that everything we consider matter is born of energy and information. By starting to think of our bodies as networks of energy information and even intelligence, we begin to shift our perspective. We don't think of our bodies so much as dense matter, but as vibrations of consciousness. Even though it sounds technical, everyone has had an experience with this so-called quantum body. After, for example, you do an intense workout, you feel a sense of energy in your body—a tingling sensation. You're actually experiencing what ancient wisdom traditions call the "vital force." The more you pay attention to this vital force inside your body, the more you will experience it as energy, information, and intelligence, and the more control you will have over its expressions.

WRIGHT

Does DNA have anything to do with that?

CHOPRA

DNA is the source of everything in our body. DNA is like the language that creates the molecules of our bodies. DNA is like a protein-making factory, but DNA doesn't give us the blueprint. When I build a house, I have to go to the factory to find the bricks, but having the bricks is not enough. I need to get an architect, who in his or her consciousness can create that blueprint. And that blueprint exists only in your spirit and consciousness—in your soul.

WRIGHT

I was interested in a statement from your book. You said that perceptions create reality. What perceptions must we change in order to reverse our biological image?

CHOPRA

You have to change three perceptions. First you have to get rid of the perceptions of aging itself. Most people believe that aging means disease and infirmities. You have to change that. You have to regard aging as an opportunity for personal growth and spiritual growth. You also have to regard it as an opportunity to express the wisdom of your experience and an opportunity to help others and lift them from ordinary and mundane experience to the kind of experiences you are capable of because you have much more experience than they do.

The second thing you have to change your perception of is your physical body. You have to start to experience it as information and energy—as a network of information and intelligence.

The third thing you have to change your perception on is the experience of dying. If you are the kind of person who is constantly running out of time, you will continue to run out of time. On the other hand, if you have a lot of time, and if you do everything with gusto and love and passion, then you will lose track of time. When you lose track of time, your body does not metabolize that experience.

WRIGHT

That is interesting. People who teach time management don't really teach the passion.

CHOPRA

No, no. Time management is such a restriction of time. Your biological clock starts to age much more rapidly. I think what you have to really do is live your life with passion so that time doesn't mean anything to you.

WRIGHT

That's a concept I've never heard.

CHOPRA

Well, there you are.

WRIGHT

You spend an entire chapter of your book on deep rest as an important part of the reversal of the aging process. What is "deep rest"?

CHOPRA

One of the most important mechanisms for renewal and survival is sleep. If you deprive an animal of sleep, then it ages very fast and dies prematurely. We live in a culture where most of our population has to resort to sleeping pills and tranquilizers in order to sleep. That doesn't bring natural rejuvenation and renewal. You know that you have had a good night's sleep when you wake up in the morning, feeling renewed, invigorated, and refreshed—like a baby does. So that's one kind of deep rest. That comes from deep sleep and from natural sleep. In the book I talk about how you go about making sure you get that.

The second deep rest comes from the experience of meditation, which is the ability to quiet your mind so you still your internal dialogue. When your internal dialogue is still, then you enter into a stage of deep rest. When your mind is agitated, your body is unable to rest.

WRIGHT

I have always heard of people who had bad eyesight and really didn't realize it until they went to the doctor and were fitted for lenses. I had that same experience some years ago. For several years I had not really enjoyed the deep sleep you're talking about. The doctor diagnosed me with sleep apnea. Now I sleep like a baby, and it makes a tremendous difference.

CHOPRA

Of course it does. You now have energy and the ability to concentrate and do things.

WRIGHT

Dr. Chopra, how much do eating habits have to do with aging? Can we change and reverse our biological age by what we eat?

CHOPRA

Yes, you can. One of the most important things to remember is that certain types of foods actually contain anti-aging compounds. There are many chemicals that are contained in certain foods that have an anti-aging effect. Most of these chemicals are derived from light. There's no way to bottle them—there are no pills you can take that will give you these chemicals. But they're contained in plants that are rich in color and derived from photosynthesis. Anything that is yellow, green, and red or has a lot of color, such as fruits and vegetables, contain a lot of these very powerful anti-aging chemicals.

In addition, you have to be careful not to put food in your body that is dead or has no life energy. So anything that comes in a can or has a label, qualifies for that.

You have to expose your body to six tastes: sweet, sour, salt, bitter, pungent, and astringent because those are the codes of intelligence that allow us to access the deep intelligence of nature. Nature and what she gives to us in bounty is actually experienced through the sense of taste. In fact, the light chemicals—the anti-aging substances in food—create the six tastes.

WRIGHT

Some time ago, I was talking to one of the ladies in your office and she sent me an invitation to a symposium that you had in California. I was really interested. The title was *Exploring the Reality of Soul*.

CHOPRA

Well, I conducted the symposium, but we had some of the world's scientists, physicists, and biologists who were doing research in what is called, non-local intelligence—the intelligence of soul or spirit. You could say it is the intelligence that orchestrates the activity of the universe—God, for example. Science and spirituality are now meeting together because by understanding how nature works and how the laws of nature work, we're beginning to get a glimpse of a deeper intelligence that people in spiritual traditions call divine, or God. I think this is a wonderful time to explore spirituality through science.

WRIGHT

She also sent me biographical information of the seven scientists that were with you. I have never read a list of seven more noted people in their industry.

CHOPRA

They are. The director of the Max Planck Institute, in Berlin, Germany, where quantum physics was discovered was there. Dr. Grossam was a professor of physics at the University of Oregon, and he talked about the quantum creativity of death and the survival of conscious after death. It was an extraordinary group of people.

WRIGHT

Dr. Chopra, with our *Stepping Stones to Success* book we're trying to encourage people to be better, live better, and be more fulfilled by listening to the examples of our guest authors. Is there anything or anyone in your life who has made a difference for you and has helped you to become a better person?

CHOPRA

The most important person in my life was my father. Every day he asked himself, "What can I do in thought, word, and deed to nurture every relationship I encounter just for today?" That has lived with me for my entire life.

WRIGHT

What do you think makes up a great mentor? Are there characteristics mentors seem to have in common?

CHOPRA

I think the most important attribute of a great mentor is that he or she teaches by example and not necessarily through words.

WRIGHT

When you consider the choices you've made down through the years, has faith played an important role?

CHOPRA

I think more than faith, curiosity, wonder, a sense of reference, and humility has. Now, if you want to call that faith, then, yes it has.

WRIGHT

In a divine being?

CHOPRA

In a greater intelligence—intelligence that is supreme, infinite, unbounded, and too mysterious for the finite mind to comprehend.

WRIGHT

If you could have a platform and tell our audience something you feel would help them and encourage them, what would you say?

CHOPRA

I would say that there are many techniques that come to us from ancient wisdom and tradition that allow us to tap into our inner resources and allow us to become beings who have intuition, creativity, vision, and a connection to that which is sacred. Finding that within ourselves, we have the means to enhance our well-being. Whether it's physical, emotional, or environmental, we have the means to resolve conflicts and get rid of war. We have the means to be really healthy. We have the means for being economically uplifted. That knowledge is the most important knowledge that exists.

WRIGHT

I have seen you on several primetime television shows down through the years where you have had the time to explain your theories and beliefs. How does someone like me experience this? Do we get it out of books?

CHOPRA

Books are tools that offer you a road map. Sit down every day, close your eyes, put your attention in your heart, and ask yourself two questions: who am I and what do I want? Then maintain a short period of stillness in body and mind as in prayer or meditation, and the door will open.

WRIGHT

So, you think that the intelligence comes from within. Do all of us have that capacity?

CHOPRA

Every child born has that capacity.

WRIGHT

That's fascinating. So, it doesn't take trickery or anything like that?

CHOPRA

No, it says in the Bible in the book of Psalms, "Be still and know that I am God"—Psalm 46:10.

WRIGHT

That's great advice.

I really do appreciate your being with us today. You are fascinating. I wish I could talk with you for the rest of the afternoon. I'm certain I am one of millions who would like to do that!

CHOPRA

Thank you, sir. It was a pleasure to talk with you!

WRIGHT

Today we have been talking with Dr. Deepak Chopra, founder of The Chopra Center. He has become the foremost pioneer in integrated medicine. We have found today that he really knows what he's talking about. After reading his book, *Grow Younger, Live Longer: 10 Steps to Reverse Aging*, I can tell you that I highly recommend it. I certainly hope you'll go out to your favorite book store and buy a copy.

Dr. Chopra, thank you so much for being with us today on *Stepping Stones to Success*.

CHOPRA

Thank you for having me, David.

ABOUT THE AUTHOR

DEEPAK CHOPRA has written more than fifty books, which have been translated into many languages. He is also featured on many audio and videotape series, including five critically acclaimed programs on public television. He has also written novels and edited collections of spiritual poetry from India and Persia. In 1999, *Time* magazine selected Dr. Chopra as one of the Top 100 Icons and Heroes of the Century, describing him and "the poet-prophet of alternative medicine."

DR. DEEPAK CHOPRA
The Chopra Center

2013 Costa del Mar Rd.
Carlsbad, CA 92009
info@chopra.com
www.chopra.com

CHAPTER ELEVEN

Spiritual Leadership I
An Interview with . . . **Dr. Bonnie Howell**

DAVID WRIGHT (WRIGHT)

Today we're talking with Dr. Bonnie Howell. Dr. Howell has twenty years' experience in the healthcare field. She was the President and CEO of a major regional medical center, chair of the Healthcare Association of New York State, served on committees of the New York State Department of Health, and is a Fellow of the American College of Healthcare Executives. Dr. Howell holds two degrees from Cornell University, a BS in Organizational Behavior from the College of Human Ecology and an MPA from the Johnson School of Business, and a doctorate in Healthcare Administration from the Medical University of South Carolina. She is a certified spiritual counselor with a degree in Divinity from the University of Metaphysical Sciences. Dr. Howell has taught leadership at both Cornell University and New York University. She served as a director of a community bank in Ithaca, New York, for over twenty years and has lectured for healthcare, financial, and corporate clients across the Northeast. She specializes in private, one-on-one leadership and team coaching for administrative and physician executives in healthcare organizations across the country. Dr. Howell has three daughters and resides in Jersey City, New Jersey.

Dr. Howell, welcome to *Stepping Stones to Success*.

BONNIE HOWELL (HOWELL)

Thank you, I'm delighted to participate in this wonderful project.

WRIGHT

So many people I have interviewed have said that the difference between a manager and a leader is vision. You have said that a true leader promotes vision. How does a leader promote vision?

HOWELL

The first step in making the transition from manager to leader and to spiritual leadership is an internal job. The leader must set aside time for contemplation, for thinking about the big picture and the leader's place in it. Contemplation time can take many forms. For some it's through prayer, if they have an acknowledged higher power, or through meditation or other forms of alone "thinking" time. In this contemplative space, we look for direction and meaning for ourselves and for the organizations we lead. Of course the vision must be consistent with moral values and the company's existing mission. Though each company's mission is a little different, I've found that most are based in the same kinds of contemplative or spiritual traditions.

I also believe that the vision needs to be communicated to staff along with an explanation of why it's important to the company and to them. The best way to promote and communicate a vision *is to live it* as the CEO and as a senior leadership team member. It's spoken and unspoken, it's written and unwritten. In other words, it's consistent through word and deed.

WRIGHT

So how can a leader communicate how a company vision will benefit its employees directly and then measurably?

HOWELL

That's a very good question and an important one because it's certainly not just words on paper. If it's only on the shelf, then it can't be a living, guiding document for the organization.

David, let me give you a couple of examples about how we communicated the vision at the medical center that I led for many years. Part of my vision, as expressed in the medical center's mission statement, was that all would be treated fairly. I said very early on in my career that I would not lay off staff except as a very last resort, and for more than twenty years I was able to keep my commitment to our employees and that part of the hospital's vision and mission. It was through the employees themselves that I was able to fulfill this promise. We weren't overstaffed; we were well within industry standards—neither too many nor too few. When we went through financially difficult times, the vision wasn't compromised because our employees had so many great ideas for ways we could save money and other resources.

Another way we demonstrated that the vision was a living, breathing document was through the compensation system. We tied our pay increases to realizing our goals, which were based on the mission and vision. If employees were participating in the vision, they were participating in the pay increase program. They understood ahead of time how the vision and compensation tied together. They knew at the beginning of the fiscal year, for instance, what the individual percentage increases would be for each category on the performance evaluation and that their score was directly tied to the percentage of their pay increase. We all essentially marched to the same drummer and we were able to use that system year after year. It was a consistent, predictable program grounded in the organization's vision and mission statements.

WRIGHT

You have also stated that a true leader will always follow the ethic of reciprocity. Will you explain to our readers what you mean?

HOWELL

Yes, that's one that, again, is very central to the whole idea of spiritual leadership. It's better known as the Golden Rule, one of the oldest guiding principles of ethical behavior upon which human interaction is based. Specifically, "do unto others as you would have them do unto you." In other words, envision your followers as though "you were following you." Put yourself in their shoes and walk in them for a while and really appreciate and feel how happy or unhappy you are as a result. Are you treating others the way you enjoy being treated? Do you meditate or spend time contemplating the decisions that affect them, or do you jump to conclusions and follow prejudices?

A spiritual leader, in my mind, will always investigate thoroughly and objectively before making those hard decisions. There will be no unpleasant surprises for the people whose leadership he or she provides, and that holds especially true in things like performance evaluations. I believe that every person under my leadership should know how I'm doing, how they're doing, and what we both expect and that we should communicate this as early and as often as possible.

WRIGHT

Reading some of your work, I've concluded that you're really not a fan of saving things up for evaluation time, so how do you suggest a leader communicate with their employees regarding areas that need improvement?

HOWELL

I don't mean to be flip about it, but my one-word answer regarding how to communicate is "constantly." The old system usually dictated a yearly evaluation. Typically managers wouldn't address their concerns with employees between evaluations, or if they did, it was not specifically behaviorally oriented. So, once a year the employee would sit down in the supervisor's office and the supervisor would pull out a paper from under her pile someplace. At that point, the supervisor would list all the ways the employee didn't have the kind of performance that they had both hoped the employee would have and this would come as a complete surprise to the employee. So, David, that's the way it *shouldn't* be done.

Let me hasten to add that I'm not against annual evaluations. Remember, in my own organization, pay increases were tied to these yearly assessments.

However, what I said to my employees was that "if in the annual performance evaluation you hear something that you have never heard before, you will automatically get the next higher level of pay increase". So I tried to put my proverbial money, or the organization's money, where my mouth was by communicating throughout the year. This was an example of consistency in values, vision, and execution.

Putting the annual evaluation aside for a moment - as far as those things that happen along the way, it's best to communicate them as immediately as possible. It's about acknowledging the positive and the negative. At the time, right then, it's catching a person doing something right and letting him or her know. It's also acknowledging that sometimes we do things incorrectly or short of our potential. If you mention it right away, then people can begin new behavior before the old behavior gets cast in concrete.

I also believe that employees should have an opportunity for self-evaluation and they should have plenty of time to complete that self-evaluation. As their leader, you should encourage and thoroughly read these self-introspections. You, as the leader, should be prepared to comment on what your employees think about their performance and take it into consideration in the overall formal performance appraisal.

I also believe in the 360-degree evaluation. In other words, as a part of our self-evaluation form there was a section where employees could evaluate me and note what had transpired organizationally from their perspective over the past year. I learned a lot over the years and made changes in my own leadership style based on this feedback.

WRIGHT

Many people try to build themselves up by tearing other people down. Will you discuss some positive ways to share the credit for company and personal successes in an effort to build people up?

HOWELL

Well, to start, always give away positive outcomes and keep the negative ones for yourself. What I mean by this is that if something goes right in the organization, very seldom is any one person be able to take credit for the entire outcome. As a matter of fact, that's never been my experience, so it's not only a good thing to share credit, but it's honest. To be able to say, this wonderful thing happened in our company, this great outcome came to pass, and here's how you contributed to it is a rewarding experience as a leader.

On the other hand, if something negative happens, whether it's a result of individual behavior or the company as a whole, you take responsibility— you own it. Even if it means taking credit for something negative that you had nothing particularly or directly to do with, it's still the right thing to do. You will gain a lot of respect from your employees because essentially you're backing them up. You are acknowledging this bad thing happened, "we'll talk about it later, but right now, yes, I'm out front on this one. I'm in it with you".

WRIGHT

You talk about encouraging, developing, and empowering people. How do you do that in practical ways to ensure that they will know you really are personally interested in their career advancement?

HOWELL

David, you asked about developing and empowering a work force. I like to start by saying "early and often." "Try this and let me know how it works out" or "Gee, is there anything I can do to help to make your job a little easier?" or, "Do you have an idea of how we can do things differently, something that you think would work out better for our employees or for our clients?" By being out there and asking these questions and respectfully listening to the answers, you have a good start.

The next step, of course, is to follow up on the feedback, because if you never follow up on it, and employees never hear anything about their ideas or concerns again, then your credibility won't outlast the next calendar year.

To summarize this point on a positive note, the spiritual leader shares the employee's goals and is invested in each employee's success as his or her own. A leader openly and honestly listens to those who follow, for that is where the truest information will come from and because nothing makes a person feel more important than to be heard by a leader who truly cares. The leader gives employees what they need to accomplished their jobs as easily and as effectively as possible. Encourage employees in all ways possible, but especially encourage their continuing growth with your time, good counsel, and equitable compensation. This is the best way to show that you are as interested in their happiness and well-being as in the company's. In short, that's what is meant by developing and empowering people.

Now a little on the "how to", or putting the tenets developed above into action. Visibility is the number one rule of spiritual leadership. Visit employee work areas to personally share positive feedback; don't use email to send congratulatory notes. E-mail or even a written memo is not the best way to communicate almost anything within the workplace. These forms of communication often encourage a leader to hide in his or her office. That is the worst possible place from which to provide spiritual leadership. In any case, take the time to visit with an employee in his her work area to say, "Hey, I had a really nice letter from one of your clients [patients, whatever it might be] and I wanted to come and to personally let you know how much I appreciate the work you did." This is even more meaning for an employee when said in front of as many people as possible, unlike negative feedback, which should only be communicated in private.

Also a word about recognition events: I prefer "recognition moments" rather than "recognition events," but recognition events are another positive way to motivate and empower staff, and make celebration a part of the organization's culture. These are opportunities to get everyone together and celebrate individual and collective successes. Again, it reinforces the vision and values in a real and tangible way.

WRIGHT

A lot is written and spoken about the importance of trust in relationships. How do you create and sustain trust with your employees?

HOWELL

Well, trust develops in the process of always keeping your word. That's the most important thing, and I touched on it a little bit earlier. As I mentioned in the earlier example, I was able to complete my career at the medical center without ever having to ask for a staff layoff. I was able to make sure that pay increases weren't the first thing sacrificed when we had to downsize because times were tough. Like most other hospitals at the time, we needed to cut costs and we did. However, we didn't lay off staff or ask for wage reductions because together we found better ways. Those are the actions that generate trust because the staff sees they're not going to be the "sacrificial lambs" when times become hard. Therefore, they'll be with you through thick and thin.

Sustain trust by backing employees and taking their side when they get in trouble with other members of the organization such as physicians, patients, or other customers. This is not to suggest, that they are always right, but you never undermine anyone publicly. You say simply, "We will investigate the situation and find the best outcome for all concerned." Then do so, and let everyone know the outcome without assigning public blame.

WRIGHT

So how does a leader keep cliques or in-crowd mentality from negatively affecting the organization?

HOWELL

Again, the central tenet of spiritual leadership is to lead by example. So start close to home by operating at the top in a spirit of inclusion. When you hire or add a new member to a senior leadership team, the biggest mistake you can make is to hire someone who looks, talks, or acts exactly like you do. That's sometimes an easy thing to let happen almost without thinking and it may be a comfortable thing initially, but it's a huge mistake. You want to bring people to the organization that offer different skills and perspectives than you do and who can reach out to different people than you can. So that's the first way to keep cliques from developing; by using the principle of inclusion in your hiring decisions, you're modeling inclusive behavior. Then, on an on-going basis ask yourself, "Is my senior leadership team a clique? Are we perceived by employees as a group of people in an ivory tower who never step out to interact and be with employees?" Does your leadership team lunch together, golf together, and are they always "in meetings" as a group? If you can answer no to all of these self-introspective questions, you are well on your way to keeping the "in-crowd" mentality out of the organization.

Another antidote for "clique behavior" is team-building with the whole organization being the team. We invented a team-building program at the Medical Center and though it was simple, it was very effective. One of our maintenance people found an old wheelchair, long forgotten in a storage area. He had it repaired, refinished, and polished up. We then put a plaque on it that read, "This chair is given to the department that contributed to the overall team effort through service to others."

We "awarded" the wheelchair on a quarterly basis. The department currently holding the chair had the opportunity to nominate another department, noting how the next department was making a contribution to the success of the organization. The awarding department couldn't nominate itself. The nominating department and the senior leadership team would all go en masse to surprise and present the wheelchair to the selected department. It was a wonderful process. The department members had their picture taken with the wheelchair and the picture was displayed in a central and public location. This was a way to encourage people to not just support their own area (their own potential clique), it was a way for them to look outward and find other departments that were also contributing to the success of the medical center. Wonderful stories developed about how critical care units nominated environmental services, and materials management nominated the accounting office. The goal was to demonstrate to employees how another's success was their success. We were trying to foster the idea that we were all in this together and no one does it alone.

WRIGHT

Most leadership trainers agree that criticizing employees in public is harmful to the employee and the organization, but most of us have trouble criticizing in private. How do you suggest leaders apply criticism?

HOWELL

Well, I suggest first of all getting rid of the word "criticism." The word has a negative connotation. No one likes to be criticized. On the other hand, positive feedback and negative feedback, if applied, are really the same. Both types of feedback have the same end point—the behavior we want to encourage. If you can give positive feedback in private, which most of us have no problem doing, then you can provide negative feedback in the same way. Your intention should never be to punish a person; you are not here to tell people they're idiots or bad people. Your intention is to convey that a certain behavior isn't the kind of behavior that will help the person in the organization or in life. If you can look at positive and negative feedback as the same kind of growth-producing opportunities, then it becomes a little easier to say what needs to be said.

WRIGHT

Keeping the company's vision foremost in the mind of employees is hard enough, so how does a leader create enthusiasm for the vision?

HOWELL

David, the short answer is by relating to your employees' personal vision and values in an authentic way. A leader needs to understand her employees well enough to know what their vision is for their work and then be able to relate the organization's vision in those terms. If you can't do it, then perhaps you need to rethink and rewrite your vision. Perhaps it's too complicated or esoteric if it doesn't meet this test. However, if you can relate it to their vision, then your employees are with you in a very fundamental way. Another way to approach these questions is to ask yourself what you want out of your own work experience and answer the question for yourself. Most people want basically the same things, and that's not really dependant on specifics of their particular position. Don't we all want to feel good about coming to work every day? Don't we want to feel as though we're valued, and to understand our contribution to the whole? Don't we want someone to understand and care about our struggles? By understanding these things about the people who work with you, you can then frame the company's vision in words they can relate to.

So for instance, if part of the patient care vision is that every patient will be treated with dignity, with respect, and with an understanding of what the patient brings to the experience, then how do you "teach" that value to employees? I used to say to my staff, "Perhaps this is just another day for us—we come to work, and do our job. Yes, we deal with life and death and that's not the same as making widgets, but this is what we do and our routine protects us from the constant stress of dealing with difficult issues. However, for this patient, this family, our routine day may be a once in a lifetime experience. It may be the first of many stress-filled days; it may be the last of many, but for them it's not just another day. This day may change their life as they know it, so we need to come to work every day remembering that this is really the business we are in and this is what we're dealing with."

Now, if you put together the example with the tenet that the leader is essentially asking employees what they want out of work and then the employee's answer will likely be something like this: "I want recognition, I want understanding, and I want to feel good about what I do." From that point, the leader's job is to point out that our customers want the same kind of treatment Out of that comes the vision for patient care (or for making widgets). We want our customer to feel good about coming to see us. We want our patients to know that we are trying to understand them and that we want it to be as good an experience as it can be. We are showing everyone entrusted to our care that no day is routinely the same for us, because they are in it.

So you see the company's values, the leader's values, and employees' values are never far apart. It just takes a little bit of working through the process together. Again, that's why I say leaders need contemplation time to work through these issues for themselves and from there it's a pretty straight line.

WRIGHT

Failure is a part of an individual's life as well as a part of an organization's life. How should an enlightened leader handle failure and then use it for good?

HOWELL

Yes, failure is an inevitable part of life because we are all human—no one is perfect—and by dealing with our mistakes or the things that could be considered failures, we have the opportunity to make mid-course adjustments. If you take the word "criticism" out of your organizational vocabulary and you give positive and negative feedback the same value within the same organization, then failure becomes a vital part of organizational life. We say, "Yes, this didn't go the way I thought it would. I take responsibility as your leader for the outcome and here's how I think it happened. Here's how I would do it over again. What do you think and what will we change because of this failure to make our organization better?" Failure then becomes a wonderful modeling opportunity because we are demonstrating that "if my leader can admit failures, then I don't have to cover anything up. If my leader not only accepts but embraces the failure that he, she, or we made, then I can bring my failure to the table and allow everyone to learn." So the culture then becomes a very open one and a very forgiving and celebratory culture even in its failure, because we learn from it. No one has to hide anything or cover up mistakes, and no one has to put the blame on someone else, because failure is part of our collective learning process.

WRIGHT

I always wished that I could have worked for an organization like that. It would have given me an opportunity to take more risk.

HOWELL

Yes, that's a wonderful insight David. It is through risk that we grow as an organization. In order to continue to meet the changing customer needs, the organization must change and anything that involves change, as you well know, involves risk. It's only through risk and change that the possibility for growth, or in some cases survival, comes to pass. Without risk, without change, the organization will wither and die because no organization, no civilization, can stay the same for all time and expect to survive. We talk and we laugh about those who do the same thing over and expect different results—some even use this as the definition of "crazy." This phenomenon tells us something in organizational behavior as well. Specifically, the world around our organization has changed, our customer has changed, but we kept doing the same things and expected to survive, even thrive. We all know conceptually that to not change is organizational suicide in the long haul. Yet over and over again we see organizations try not to change anything and maintain their success, usually with disastrous results.

WRIGHT

The number one complaint I've heard from leaders and company owners over the past few years is the lack of good prospective workers in the job market. Do you have any tips for hiring competent and capable employees?

HOWELL

Yes I surely do. The very best way to recruit staff is positive word-of-mouth through your current staff. Now, I was lucky enough (because I stayed in the same place for a long time) to manage a second generation of employees. The staff I had when I started eventually sent me their sons and daughters, nieces and nephews. People went into healthcare because the people who worked with me had a wonderful experience, had a great career, and loved the organization.

You can't recruit to any organization if the people who are already there aren't saying good things about it. If you go into a restaurant and the wait staff is telling you how horrible a place it is to work (and I did have that experience once), you probably don't want to eat there again and you certainly don't want to answer the "help wanted" sign on the front door.

It's the same thing with any organization. The current staff is going to be your best sales force for recruiting new employees. Without their active endorsement, if you can recruit at all, you're going to attract people who are just as unhappy as the people who are already there because you're just perpetuating the negative culture. Furthermore, the good people you have won't stay, so you have a downward spiral in terms of employee morale and the ability to recruit a good people to the organization.

I firmly believe that you must manage employee morale the way you manage any other important resource. You can't just expect to ignore what the staff is saying and feeling. To ignore it and think that morale is okay or it will come around with the next pay increase won't work anymore than materials will show up at your door if you don't order them. Patients won't come if the ones who are already being served aren't getting better or at least feeling good about the experience. So that's the important recruitment tool—making sure that the staff you have say good things because you're managing their morale and encouraging them to bring in their family, friends, and neighbors.

Sometimes organizations give bonuses to people who directly help recruit other people and that's good too, if that's what you need to do in times of real scarcity; but don't forget to ask the staff what you should do to get more people to apply for open positions in the organization. They'll tell you the real scoop. For example, I once was told, "My niece is going to community college and the community college doesn't really know very much about us. So I wonder if we might go to a job fair. I'd be happy to staff a table, Bonnie, if you want me to go and just tell the young people about what we offer here." You can't buy recruitment programs like that.

WRIGHT

So after doing the best job possible in the hiring process, how does a leader encourage collaboration among teams or coworkers in loyalty to the company's vision?

HOWELL

Well, first of all, make sure there are no losers and there are no winners in the organization. We all win or we all have a learning experience together. We do both but we emphasize reward, not so much individual effort, as contribution to the team. You have to carefully look at what you are rewarding because quite often it's not what you think, and then you wonder why you're not getting the outcomes that you were hoping for. So for instance, at the medical center, a major component of the individual employee's evaluation was their self-analysis as well as their supervisor's analysis of the contribution they were making to the team effort. We had the wheelchair, which wasn't awarded by senior management; it was awarded by the employees in other departments. To have the ability to reward each other for team effort, not only fosters loyalty from department to department, but overall to the whole company and its vision.

Another important way to encourage collaboration and another central tenet to spiritual leadership is to ask questions, ask more questions, and then ask some more. It's the most important activity a leader engages in and an absolute necessity before you engage in important activities like vision and value-setting, strategic or long-range planning, and other kinds of far reaching activities. Let's look at planning since we've talked about the rest.

In many organizations, often the senior management team gets together and does the strategic plan for the organization. Then the plan may or may not be presented to anyone except the board of directors. It's put on the shelf until it's time to do the next plan and then it's pulled out to use as a template. However, if the strategic plan is designed to be a living document, useful as a blueprint for all to use, then you need to start and finish your planning on the front lines of the organization.

We put together the medical center's strategic plan by starting with individual departments. I personally visited every single department for a strategic planning meeting with the entire departmental staff. I went in on nights and on weekends because we were a twenty-four-hour, seven-day-a-week operation. I told our employees: "We have to put a strategic plan together for the Board and we're looking for growth in order to improve and build on what we have. Will you give us your ideas?" I would provide a few very general examples or tell them what we had done, what similar organizations had done—just something to get them started. Then I would wait for them to give me ideas for the overall organization and ideas for their specific departments.

And the process worked. They suggested some wonderful ideas over the years that were developed and implemented as new programs and services. Before a lot of hospitals got into the wellness business, my facility was already in preventative care. We ended up with a full-service health and rehabilitation center. At the suggestion of staff, we put together ambulatory units away from the main campus in other parts of the community and thereby expanded our service area to support new services we wanted to offer. So a lot of the things that only very progressive organizations implemented, we were doing even before the trend began. This happened because I had bright and engaged people in all parts of the organization. Please remember that you never know where the next brilliant idea might come from, so be sure you include everybody. With this kind of effort and input your can present a plan to your board and staff that is truly the result of an organizational effort.

WRIGHT

Do you mind if I ask you the million-dollar question that most people back away from? How engaged should a good leader be in the personal lives of his or her employees?

HOWELL

Well, I laugh when I hear people say that "knowing your employees other than in a work context" is the number one management sin. On the contrary, I believe that you can't be a good leader, certainly not a spiritual leader, unless you are open to the employee as more than a company resource. Knowing them as people is important. Remember that they are not only a human resource but also human beings with families and other issues outside of their relationship with the organization. So I always listened when an employee wanted to talk. I made it clear that I had a role in the organization and I could only offer the expertise within the confines of my training. So if a person raised something clearly outside of my area of expertise, I would have a list of referrals to people I knew in the community who could help with a specific problem.

On the other hand, if the issue was within my area of expertise, then I tried to help. When applicable, I used examples from my own life. There is no reason not to say, "Yes it happened to me and this is what I did, and here's where I sought help."

There were other ways we showed interest in our employees as people. We ran support groups within the organization and we had an employee assistance fund. Let me digress and talk about that specific project. The interesting part about the employee assistance fund was that voluntary contributions were collected from employees (we were all included in this group) to be distributed to employees with a special financial need. The fund was managed by an employee committee that administered the distribution of the funds. Any employee who felt he or she needed monetary assistance for a one-time need could apply for the funds. Later, as the program grew and matured, the organization was able to match the contributions employees made.

We also tried to make sure that the benefits we offered were humanely designed as well as market competitive. I made sure that within our employee benefit package we had time off for people to do what they needed to do on a personal basis. These personal days allowed people to take the time they needed without forcing them to go through the process of calling in sick when they really needed to be off for a personal responsibility.

One example that comes to mind is an employee who is also a single parent and has three kids. If one of the kids got sick (before we made the change to our policy), the employee had to lie by calling in sick in order to take the child to the doctor. Why and for what purpose does an organization force an employee to violate what is most often a commonly held value of truth? The reason is because organizations don't acknowledge that the employee is a human being who has a life to be acknowledged and supported in a fair and equitable way. That is what occurs in a spiritual organization. So we developed a concept of plain personal time. This is another example of our being innovative and forward thinking. No one earned any more than anyone else because of personal circumstances, but everyone was able to use the time with a little more flexibility than having to call in sick.

WRIGHT

We all know that fixing problems outside the workplace is not expected of leaders, however, what can a good leader do to help employees who make us aware of their problems?

HOWELL

The spiritual leader should always start by knowing the community and the resources it has to offer. I think it's important to know your community anyway, but often we as leaders hole up in our ivory tower, so to speak, and interact with the community only as the organizational needs require. And if, heaven forbid, an employee comes to us for help, the usual response is, "Well, why don't you look that up in the yellow pages?" or "Gee, I think we have something like that. Why don't you go see human resources?" That is not spiritual leadership. It shouldn't be beneath the leader to be aware of resources available. It is much better to be able to say, "Yes, I know that's difficult. There is a community organization you might want to contact. Here's the phone number."

Here is an example from my own experience with an employee who was part of the sandwich generation. I told the person, "I know you're responsible for your elderly parents and it's hard for you when you're working forty hours a week here and raising your kids. Did you know about the Meals on Wheels program? We work with them. Here is a contact name."

Another time I had the occasion to say, "It certainly is difficult when you are going through a divorce and trying to help your kids with the changes. I know the school system has a program they call 'Banana Splits.' It's designed for kids who are going through divorces to support each other—my kids found it very helpful."

So knowing what's available in the community and not letting the employee feel isolated is a big part of the spiritual leader's role. You want to let them know that they're not the only ones who bring their problems to work or they're the only ones who have the problem. Feeling isolated and inferior is not good for the employee or the workplace. Employees' will not give their best creativity and their best day's work to an organization that doesn't see them and treat them as human beings with human problems. If employees are forced to lie about being sick, to cover up, to use their time in the workplace to talk about their problems to other people who aren't helping them, then you really haven't provided good leadership.

I tried never to cut people off when they brought up their personal life or to factor in personal problems with their job performance. What kind of person does that? What kind of humanness are you demonstrating to the outside world if you behave that way?

WRIGHT

Turning now to a more contemporary problem, how does one foster hope in the workforce in these troubling economic times?

HOWELL

That's certainly a timely question, though some may argue, economic times are almost always troubling with the ups and downs of our national and global economies. However, I think right now it's pretty hard economically for the whole country, therefore no one is exempt. We need to be communicating to our employees that we understand how it affects them. As the spiritual leader, we communicate our empathy. Hopefully you can say, "I know it's difficult for your family to make ends meet and it's scary for all of us. Here's what we're doing as an executive group to make sure that we continue to meet our mission and continue our responsibilities to our patients (or our customers). Here's what we, as the designated leaders, are doing to make sure that we don't sacrifice the future of the organization or the welfare of the staff in order to meet some financial obligation that a board of directors or someone outside the organization or even the economy has put on us. We'll work through it together." Then, it's not only okay, its desirable, to ask for their help. I'd say something like, "Hey, you guys are doing the same thing at home I have to do—you're trying to balance your family budget and pay your bills. I'm trying to balance the company's budget and pay the bills. What do you think—what can we do differently? Should we be using some different supplies? Is there anything you can think of that can save some money here and there?"

During an earlier economic down turn, after one of these conversations with staff, we ended up with one department saving soda bottles for the five cents deposit and giving the funds to the organization. Now you might argue that I must have engaged in communication overkill someplace along the way for people to start saving their nickels. Maybe so, but that gives you an idea what employees are willing to do to help the leader who is not afraid to say, "Look, I'm just one of the wounded heroes here. I'm not the perfect hero, I'm not invincible, and I don't know all the answers. I need your help. It's hard right now. Sometimes I don't know what's going to happen next but I'm always going to tell you the way it really is and I'm not going to throw you under the bus. So it's okay to collect pop bottles if that's what you can do, and I'll be grateful."

Keeping hope alive is a very important responsibility of the spiritual leader. Hope is second only to trust in the spiritual organization's culture (I call trust the earthly equivalent of faith). Be visible and remember that employees read your behavior. They will be more hopeful if you are not hidden away. Bear in mind, especially for those who might work in multiple locations and or have variable shifts that being visible to all may take some planning and logistics but it's worth it. Then, be positive in outlook, thought, word, and deed. Communicate decisions early and explain how they were made and why. Express your sincere regret if that's the appropriate emotion and *if* that's what you are feeling. Don't blame anything or anyone else—even the bad economy—it truly doesn't soften the blow.

WRIGHT

Following up on your answer, if things are not going well for the company, should a leader keep negative information away from their employees to protect them, or keep them informed of everything regardless of the possible outcome?

HOWELL

You should never try to keep negative information away from your employees because first of all, you won't be able to anyway. If you report to a board of directors or some sort of oversight committee, you're going to have to tell them. They're going to know the facts and they'll put their own spin on what they think they know. Then they'll tell someone else who tells someone else—you get the picture. The statistic in the field is that if there is a piece of negative information, it will be told twenty-five times on average, and if something is told twenty-five times, it's bound to get back to the employees, so who are we kidding? They're going to know and they're going to get the worst possible spin on it by the time it gets to them. So now they know what you didn't want to tell them and, in addition, they didn't hear it from you so they're not going to trust you again. I'm all in favor of telling staff the way it is, letting them see the same financial information that the board sees, letting them know if there have been either community or industry-wide negative events that are going to affect them.

But on the other hand, I also believe that communication should be well thought out, free of blaming, and as hopeful as possible. I don't believe in hit-and-run communication. Here's an example of this kind of communication faux pas. The leader goes out to the staff and says, "We have a lot of red ink and gee that's bad and the board is on my case and I don't know what to do next and everything is terrible and I'll be lucky if I don't get fired," and then the leader walks away. Doesn't that just make you want to say, "Oh, excuse me, but a little explanation and a little less self-pity might help." So don't hit them with information and run. Stay present as long as it takes, let your employees ask you question and let them share with you. Reassure them that you aren't the victim of bad news. In short, don't throw your hands up and run. Let your employees know that you intend to be there for the long haul. Tell them what you will do together to get through the difficulty.

Practice what you're going to say, try it on someone you trust. But absolutely do not try to keep bad news secret from the people who have an equal stake in the organization. You can't do it if you try, you're going to violate their trust, and you're not going to get it back any time soon. Remember, it takes a long time to develop trust, and it can be undermined and obliterated in a heartbeat through carelessness, callousness, or a false sense of importance. Secrets have no cash or organizational value, so don't hoard them.

WRIGHT

After much due diligence in thought and planning, a hard decision is made for the company. Who should communicate the decision and how should it be made?

HOWELL

Well, I always tried to communicate major decisions in person. If there is a newsletter or some other communication vehicle, then that's okay to use it as a follow-up, because you can't say anything important, whether it is positive or negative too often. Hopefully, whatever you have to say in the decision-making realm is coming back around the circle. This means that the decision is not coming out of left field. Remember that in a spiritually driven organization, the decision should have been made first by gathering input from everyone in the circle who wants to participate. It's important for the CEO to be out there again to report back to the decision-making circle. Try to align the decision to the extent possible with the dreams and the aspirations of your employees, as well as the company's. Then when the tough decision is made, you will have treated everyone with the fairness and respect that is due all of us. You want to be treated that way and not as the proverbial mushroom—kept in the basement in the dark, fed you-know-what, and then harvested when the time is right. You and your employees want to be in the light in all senses of that word. You then have an obligation and a responsibility to stand in that light and tell your employees how the decision was made, why it was made, and, if you're smart you will do so before it gets cast in concrete. That's key as far as I'm concerned.

WRIGHT

Can you give our readers a personal example of how you communicated or how you delivered what your employees considered to be bad news and how it was received?

HOWELL

Yes. I had to tell my staff that there was going to be a change in our corporate status. When I took over the organization, it was a county hospital and all of the employees were county employees. They were protected by civil service, belonged to the very generous state retirement program, and had an excellent benefit package. Each of them had accepted their position believing they had signed on to this structure for life. Now in truth, and from the Board's perspective, that happened to be a terrible way to run a hospital (or a railroad for that matter). I had tried to lead the hospital as a county facility and keep it financially viable and up to date, but I had come to believe it could not be done. It was also a very complex and cumbersome decision-making process.

For instance, if you wanted to add one staff member, you had to go through six separate county government committees. The Board and I wanted to keep the not-for-profit status, but make the hospital an independent community organization as opposed to a county organization. After many separate studies and consultant reports, we had come to the conclusion that the change in corporate status simply had to be done for a number of financial, strategic, and other reasons, which of course had to be communicated to the employees. I thought (no, I knew) that this was going to be a difficult, if not an impossible sell to employees because of the benefits and protections available in the status quo. To further complicate things, the employees (all employees) were represented by the Civil Service Employees Association that kept reminding them they were part of a state system—a system that would be very difficult to duplicate in the private sector. To say the least, the union was diametrically opposed to the change.

We held a meeting in every department and every shift, talking about the reasons why the decision was a good one and a right one for the long haul. We promised (and then delivered on that promise) to duplicate all the benefits they had, including the very rich retirement program, no matter how much it cost. I told them that if they wanted to be represented by a union, I would accept that decision and recognize their current union even though that union was primarily in the public sector.

The union was very vocal and invested a lot of money in a campaign to derail the transition. Partly through their efforts, the county governing board decided that before they would agree to the change they were going to hold a county referendum—a public referendum during the next general election. This was after the governing board had publicly supported the idea, in no small part due to the two million dollar deficit the hospital was running at a time when hospitals did not lose money. It became a long and nasty campaign with the staff and me being played against each other. Face time, in my opinion, won the day—being out there, answering questions, getting ideas—all the concepts we've talked about.

Not only did the vast majority of employees support the decision, they were out front talking to the public about why they should vote in favor of our change in corporate status.

We won the referendum and in the end I was presented with a petition signed by most of the hospital employees asking me not to recognize the Civil

Service Employees Association as the bargaining unit. The organization remained union free because we trusted one other.

David, let me digress to say, as I always do, that I have nothing against unions at all. Certainly when unions were developed and came to the fore in American history, they served a critical need. It included life and death protection for workers and addressed child labor and wage and benefit inequities. However, today I also say that employees don't unionize organizations, employers do. By that I mean that if employees feel they need to be protection from you, if they want a union steward to knock on your door instead of doing it themselves, then, my friend, you'd better look close to home for why they think so. I believe that a lot of money is spent fighting union-organizing attempts—money that could be better spent in treating employees fairly, openly, respectfully, and with an eye to their satisfaction in the workplace. If they aren't getting that from you then they have every right to seek it elsewhere.

WRIGHT

Tell me, Dr. Howell, do you have any other tips from your vast experience that might help our readers be more effective?

HOWELL

Your question brings to mind one of my favorite stories. Thomas Edison was interviewed by a young reporter who boldly asked if he felt like a failure and if he thought he should just give up. Edison replied, "Young man, why would I feel like a failure? And why would I ever give up? I now know definitively over nine thousand ways that an electric light bulb will not work. Success is almost in my grasp." And shortly after that, and after more than ten thousand attempts, Edison invented the light bulb. Sometimes I think I must have discovered 9,999 ways *not* to be a successful leader—and then I was an overnight success.

However, you asked me a closing question so let me answer with what I always say to my young VPs (and my not so young VPs, as they're coming up through the organization): "Trust your instincts. You're a good person; you want to do the right thing. Trust yourself, trust them, and you'll be fine."

Actually I say, "Trust your gut," and although that's maybe a little stronger than your readers will want to hear, it's an important and a quick way to remember that our inclination is usually on target. Usually leaders want to do the right thing, they want to be respected, and they want to treat others as they would wish to be treated. If you follow those gut instincts, you do the right thing. If it turns out to be a mistake, then back up, own it, learn from it, and move on.

The other caution I always give to new leaders is to remember that *no one ever does anything wrong*. The new leader will look at me and invariably say something like, "What? Of course people do wrong things. They do them all the time—they kill people, they rob corporations, they do all these wrong and bad things." I look at them, smile and say, "Yes, those are bad things; but remember, by the time people behave in that manner, they have convinced themselves that it's the right thing to do or that they had no choice." Our human brain has the capacity to view all good and bad as relative—and nothing the leader can say or do will override that capacity in the moment. If you approach your staff with that premise, when someone has done something you view as wrong, then you won't waste your time convincing the person to admit that he or she was wrong or that he or she was a bad person. You won't waste your time because you will walk into it knowing that by the time the person did whatever it is he or she did, the person felt there was no choice or that it was the right thing to do. Regardless of how it may look on the surface, the person was on his or her own higher road. If you begin the dialog with that understanding, then you are already on firmer ground in your role as leader. Model the behavior you are trying to produce. It's a better use of your time. With open constructive dialog, you may be surprised how often people come to the same analysis of the situation that you did.

My real final word is to translate all of this to our position as a country in global leadership. I'd like to discuss what I think global *spiritual* leadership could look like.

We're at a crossroads as a country in terms of our ability or desire to maintain the position of sole superpower or how do we move from being a superpower that dominates in order to protect and rescue other people and countries, to being only a part of the world's community. What road are we going to take?

Our values are still appropriate—we believe that all life is sacred and people have a right to self-determination with the maximum amount of freedom consistent with civilization. We add the premise that if left to their own design, people will want to do the right thing consistent with those principles common to world's organized religions, which is the basis upon which spirituality is built. We know that scarce resources must be shared to the betterment of humanity as a whole, and we know that we are all dependent on the future of the same planet, Earth. What we need to figure out is whether we can accept becoming only a productive part of the world community without dominating it, and that our democratic principles are based on respecting others, including their right to choose other forms of government unlike our own. Our principles should involve teaching our children an ethic of cooperation and harmony with children everywhere and let them grow together to make that better world we all hope for.

We must embrace a new set of principles - call them spiritual if you like, but ones that allow room for all to grow, to be flexible about world order, to be open to changing certain long-held beliefs, to be willing to give up some of what we have so that all can enjoy a decent life.

That's a difficult thing for a society to go through and other great civilizations have fallen rather than accept the inevitable pain of making those hard decisions. But I believe that if we use President Obama's campaign mantra, "Yes We Can," we have a very good place to start. "Yes we can" give the rest of the world this chance. "Yes we can" learn to be passionately logical, objective, and rational without having to know all the answers. "Yes we can" have a spiritually-based set of ethics that we don't want or need to go to war over. "Yes we can" live in a world where starvation is not tolerated, where abundance is meant for everyone and not at someone else's expense. Perhaps this is all a dream, but it's not a bad blueprint for our collective well-being.

David, I want to raise just one more controversial point and I'll leave it for future discussion. I think that as we've moved away from our great religious traditions, we haven't replaced them with anything else. I believe we need to give that fact some serious consideration. Our children need something to believe in, something to guide their behavior, something to count on in a world that grows ever more uncertain. I'd like to see that be a future theme for steppingstones.

WRIGHT

Well, what a great conversation.

HOWELL

I enjoyed it very much and look forward to the next one.

CHAPTER TWELVE

Spiritual Leadership II

An Interview with . . . **Dr. Bonnie Howell**

DAVID WRIGHT (WRIGHT)

So you mentioned that one should use spiritual principles at home and that you have some regrets around that issue. Would you elaborate?

BONNIE HOWELL (HOWELL)

Yes David, I have spent quite a lot of time thinking about this because my three daughters are now grown, gone from my home, involved in individual careers or education, and starting their own families. I remember coming home from work, having, of course, worked very hard all day to use good management and spiritual leadership skills. But often I would walk into a somewhat hectic household with three girls, bringing homework to me all at once, or fighting among themselves. The natural inclination was to just start yelling and telling everyone to sit down, and to stop fighting—all of the things I would never do at work.

203

Although they seem none the worse for wear, looking back now on the reality of working and raising the girls, I do have some regrets about coming home from work and having that transition at times be less smooth, or as loving as I would have liked. So I'd just like to remind our *Stepping Stone* readers to take a few minutes to transition from work to home, to think through what you'll probably be faced with when you arrived home and to remember, you are a key figure in the household. Inevitably there will be days when your children, spouse, or your partner's difficult day will hit you as you come through the door. If you can focus on the need to be a good leader and to practice spiritual principles at home, everyone will fare better for your efforts.

WRIGHT

A lot of readers and managers would like a better balance between their work and their home lives. Would you tell us how you went about achieving that balance if you did?

HOWELL

Well, it's interesting, people always use balance between home and work as something we should aspire to and focus on. We talk about the work-life balance; the marriage balancing with the organizational needs, and yet as I think about it, balance, by its very nature, is an unstable state. I think about the concept of balance in this way: My younger brother and I always loved going to the playground and getting on the teeter-totter and striving for that perfect balance where we were evenly distributed our weight so that the teeter-totter hung in midair. I love that image because it is easy to feel how unstable that balance was; it never lasted. It was never the same from one day to the next, or one week to the next. In many ways balance is not really a state we can achieve for the long haul. Balance is a nice concept but it speaks to the idea of separate and very unstable compartments in your life that you try to balance as in the example of the teeter-totter.

Instead, we should think of our lives as coherent or whole. Some days, or some moments, one particular area will need more emphasis or more attention, and another day something else will require our focus. Balance is never a distinct

204

separation between what's going on in our work life, home life, or that third area we often lose sight of—what's going on inside of us emotionally, physically and spiritually. None of those things can be ignored. Striving for perfect balance is perhaps not only out of reach, but a faulty goal to begin with.

Striving for a perfect life in perfect balance is just not achievable. I can remember thinking that no matter where I was, I felt as though I should be someplace else. If I was at work—working late doing the things that a CEO needed to do—I would think, "Oh, I should be home with my children. I'm missing their school play or recital or just time with them." If I was at home or if I volunteered to do some of the school activities as their mom, I would think, "Oh boy, I should be at the office." In short, maybe the real question is whether or not the quest for perfect work-life balance is more of a guilt trip than a desired state to which we should all aspire.

WRIGHT

You've talked about the ATM of spiritual life. I'm not sure what you mean by that, but it does sound intriguing. Will you spend some time developing that concept for us?

HOWELL

Yes, of course. It's one of my favorites because it's such a vivid image for me and for those of us who like to define leadership in terms of transactional analysis.

However, before I start, I'd like to give credit where it's due. The ATM concept is actually an outgrowth of the conversation I had with a dear friend who is a banker. In discussing these concepts with her over coffee one day, she likened the process of organizational spiritual leadership to an organizational or emotional ATM. Her point when a leader follows spiritual principles, leading by example building trust, providing positive energy, along the way; if a leader creates an organizational memory that takes into consideration everyone is working in the organization toward a common goal, the leader is building trust—good will for lack of a better expression. Then when a leader makes a mistake, an error in judgment, but has done so in good faith, the leader can draw back some of that positive energy to sustain him or her. This gives the leader the time to learn and to steer a new course. It's perhaps a modern image for the age-old concept that "you reap what you sow". As the ground stores and protects the seedling until it grows and is ready to be harvested, that karmic ATM my friend invented holds the positive organizational energy and returns it to the leader during difficult times. Whether you like farming, banking, or biblical analogies, David, the principle teaches that a good leader can make mistakes but those mistakes aren't fatal.

WRIGHT

You mentioned earlier that Deepak Chopra influenced your thinking on spiritual leadership. Would you tell us how?

HOWELL

Yes, and first I'd like to say, David, that because of this project—the *Stepping Stones* project—I became much more aware of and familiar with his work, so it's became an important turning stone in my development of spiritual leadership concept. In applying his principles I have created the "Seven Laws of Spiritual Leadership." I give Deepak Chopra all the credit for having developed the concepts in general. I'd like to apply those principles to leadership. I also thank you for bringing us together.

The first law, as you know, is the *Law of Pure Potentiality* and in an organization, that is the collective consciousness of the individuals who make up the organization. Therefore, the collective wisdom of the individual employees is the organization's potentiality. In the process of vision-setting, the leader should facilitate the discovery of the organization's essential nature, just as Chopra talks about the individual's essential nature. The leader should help to create an atmosphere that encourages the essential nature to be inseparable from its written mission, its strategic vision, or the individuals' goals that form it. That is the energy of pure potentiality.

We would then encourage each individual to be self-empowered as he or she follows that law on his or her own, and as he or she contributes to the process of working toward a common goal.

Now, on the other side of the coin, the more traditional way of thinking is a fear-based organization. It is one without a common vision where the operating principles are control, separation, obligation, and tit-for-tat. A fear-based organization survives by buying and selling approval. On the other hand, in a spiritual organization, the individuals are unafraid of their leadership, so they're unafraid of any challenge. It is both a humble organization on the one hand and proud. This is the concept Chopra talks about when he refers to individuals being humble and yet proud. The leader as servant must surely find a home in such an organization.

Again, from my own path, I remember my new Vice President always expressing concern when someone from the staff came to see me directly or as they said, "outside of the chain of command." I remember thinking, believing, and then saying, "I am their CEO just as much as I am yours." I believed it was important to be viewed as everyone's CEO. This empowered me to be out and about in the organization. I know my attitude and my example also drew like-minded people to the positions of vice president and to staff positions all the way along.

I believe that if you foster such an attitude, people become bonded to you and you to them in a way no outside force could dictate or mandate. The spiritual leader, by example, demonstrates the attention to purpose, caring, and appreciation for those in the organization and a true love for the mission. The end result is an organization in a state of grace. The harnessing together of like-minded people operating in that way could change the very nature of organizations.

The second law is the *Law of Giving*. Chopra talks about the giving and receiving of energy, and likewise, organizations are in the business of giving and receiving energy in the form of the organizational mission or purpose. The leader's job is to keep the energy from being blocked; to encourage principles of giving through the free exchange of information, ideas, suggestions, and allowing change. I talked earlier about not hoarding information inside the C suite, and that's an example of the kind of energetic blocking that would keep the organization from reaching its full potentiality.

Now, I want to mention financial incentives in an organization. Organizations are created to allow individuals to exchange the energy of their talents, gifts, expertise, needs, and desires. Money may certainly be the symbol of those exchanges, but I don't believe we should confuse money with intention. I think the organizational intention should not be—and cannot be—only to generate the symbol that we call money. The organization's intention should also be to create and increase well-being for those it serves; that will be the organizational equivalent of happiness. If you can imagine an organization as being happy, I'd like to think we could then we have an organization truly in the state of giving. I've witnessed happy people in organizations so I know they exist. People are paid fairly for their efforts and customers get a fair product for their dollars—that's not the purpose, just a symbol of the exchange.

Chopra talks about bringing a gift to everyone you meet as a practice—as a way of practicing the Law of Giving. In an organization, I think a leader can do likewise. As CEO, I made rounds throughout the organization—all shifts, all locations—and the gift was simple. It was conversation, recognition, remembering names, maybe children's ages—the small things that didn't cost me anything, but the change of human energy was palpable, and I do think it changed the nature of the organization. We kept monetary energy moving also. We put most of the pay increases into general cost of living increases. Bonuses were reserved not just for management, but for each member of the staff based on individual and overall performance.

Next is Chopra's third law, the *Law of Karma,* or *Cause and Effect.* David, you and I both know that people don't often talk about karma in an organization but I'd like to encourage that discussion. I strongly believe that organizational karma exists both internally as it relates to those inside the organization—to itself—and in relationship with the outside world. Not only do I believe organizational karma exists, I believe it may be purposefully and consciously cultivated, not just left to chance.

One way to encourage positive organizational karma is for the leader to consistently process each decision, not in a vacuum, but in relationship to the karmic atmosphere he or she wants to foster. Every spiritual leader should develop a filter through which all decisions pass before they are made. In those contemplative moments you and I have talked about, the spiritual leader asks, "What are the consequences of this choice? What are the intended and the unintended consequences? What are the announced or the hidden consequences?

Will this choice—this decision—be to their betterment?" If I perceive that it will be good for some but not for others, then the choice needs more contemplation. If it is good for only a select few, then it should be set aside altogether. But if it brings benefit to all, or at least harm to none, and benefit to many, then I believe that decision is what my gut feels is good karma.

That decision will feel right, and it will feel right with a certain amount of clarity. Without being able to predict the future, the leader will know it's the right decision. To me, that "knowing" is the karmic part of it—the holistic feel for decision-making—not just looking at the nuts and bolts, the numbers, the strategic plan, but making the focus an intuitive decision-making process that takes all of those as well as spiritual principles into consideration.

I'm certainly not suggesting that a spiritual leader will never make a mistake—we are human and we are flawed. But if our heart is in the right place then we learn from the experience and we adjust to foster the best possible outcome regardless. We'll set the organization right; we'll accept the blame and responsibility and move on with a renewed supply of karmic energy.

This concept refers back to that ATM principle I was talking about. I think the ATM is a lovely way to put the law into a context. It is fun, but it is also very modern and easily understood. If we withdraw from an account we've been consistently contributing to, all is good. However, if we're not putting back into it what we're taking out, well, we all know what happens then in finance and in leadership.

This brings us to the *Law of Least Effort*. I love this one because it's certainly not an organizational intuitive. We were all raised to believe that nothing worth having comes easily and success only comes through hard work and effort. So where does the Law of Least Effort fit in? It helps to remember that this law is also known as the Law of No Resistance. Further, let's think of it organizationally as the law of harmony and acceptance. It's in that context we may begin to understand what it can mean for an organization. I believe the spiritual leader honestly accepts the people with whom he or she works exactly as they are.

Yes, David you could sigh at me though you didn't and ask, "Gee, Bonnie, do you mean every one of them?" Yes, as impossible as that sounds, I mean everyone.

Follow my chain of thinking here and see if you don't come to the same conclusion. It helps to go back to what we talked about earlier. *Remember, no one ever does anything wrong.* You will recall that concept from earlier in the interview. In short, by the time any individual does even the most awful thing by anyone else's standards, the perpetrator has already convinced himself or herself it's the right thing to do or that he or she didn't have any choice. If, then, I believe no one ever knowingly "does anything wrong,", then I can accept each individual employee as he or she is and be confident that these individuals believe they are doing the right thing. That's not to say I condone every behavior. I will still need to offer guidance, correct misconceptions about organizational realities, and, as a last resort, provide consequences for wrong actions. However, I will know that the individual believed he or she was doing the right thing, just as I believe I am doing the right thing. It's a different perspective than believing there are "bad" people who knowingly do "bad" things.

Next, from that vantage point, I accept that the entire organization is as it should be. Then I acknowledge that the organization not only has a place for each one of those individual employees, but has a need for them and their energetic contribution.

Now, stay with me. From there we will find it possible to accept that everything is as it should be, every moment is complete—in and of itself—and will inevitably lead to the right place for the organization. This may be a hard concept to accept when you're in the swamp day- in and day - out, when things aren't going as *you* think they should go, and you've bought the traditional idea that it's your job to singlehandedly do something about it. However, wouldn't this law of least effort give us a lot more peace, a lot more happiness within the organizational structure? This is something to strive for, not only as leaders but for all the individuals who are making contribution to the organization every single day.

This is only a short step, then, to embracing the Law of Acceptance and Harmony, right, David? Good, I'm glad you agree because it's a law important to come to grips with and is a critical step in developing spiritual leadership.

From there let me convince you to adopt a no-blame principle for the spiritual leader as well. We need to add this caveat in order to truly accept that least effort, not command and control, will lead to organizational success. If the leader accepts that everything is as it's supposed to be, no matter how it seems to be at the moment, then we must believe that the organization is always where it needs to be for some reason, even if it seems wrong by someone else's judgment. If it seems wrong by the leader's own judgment, then he or she needs to stop and look for the lesson instead of looking for the culprit. The rule is: don't assign blame, including blame aimed at oneself.

To understand what is being said here, I like to use a traffic analogy. There was a time that I used to get absolutely frantic in a traffic jam. I would inevitably move through a litany of blame, including and especially blaming myself for having gone down this road to begin with. Then one day, in a moment of enlightenment, I realized that "I don't know what I missed." By that I mean that perhaps, if I had gone down another road, the traffic would have been worse. Perhaps I would have gotten in an accident. I think you get the gist of that analogy. Now, I remind myself not to assign blame by saying, "Yes, it seems bad, but I don't know what I missed." I find this as strangely comforting in the middle of board meetings as I do in the middle of a traffic jam.

That message becomes part of the leader's foundation and it naturally leads to another component of the Law of Least Effort, which is defenselessness.

Chopra develops this concept for the individual and it may be a little stretch for the organization, but I explain it this way: Blame has an equally evil sister. Her name is self righteous justification, and it's as destructive in its own right as is blame, though it comes from a different place. If leaders are not inclined to blame themselves and find no other likely candidate then they might naturally turn to justifying why the discredited decision was right in the first place. That is very different than acceptance of an outcome. If I accept the outcome, then I take responsibility. I learn and move on and I am then engaging in spiritual leadership.

If, on the other hand, I try (usually using my power and control) to justify the decision, jam it down everyone's throat, and continue on the same course, then I am exercising power and control, not spiritual leadership. Further, if I even convince myself it wasn't a wrong decision in the first place then, of course, I'm just going to keep traveling the same path. I learn nothing and ignore the consequences. In the old Shakespearean tradition, that could be characterized as a fatal flaw or, in our terms, defensive justification. As in the Shakespearean plays, a fatal flaw will bring down a king or a kingdom and that's no less true in organizations.

Often, especially early in my career, I engaged in defensive justification. The fact that it wasn't fatal to me or the organization is more about luck than anything else. Chopra talks about defenselessness, meaning that you don't have to jump to your own defense all the time. However, I didn't always understand that part. For the purpose of illustrating the point, I'm going to tell you a story that demonstrates the principles of acceptance, responsibility, and defenselessness, as well as defensive justification.

One of my department heads, who was in charge of purchasing, was very well thought of in the organization and in the community. Unfortunately, well into his career, he was accused and found guilty of accepting kick-backs from certain food vendors.

Now, this department head was excellent at what he did, saving the organization millions of dollars while achieving the highest level of quality for needed goods and services. As a side note, I trusted him completely. He was responsible for all purchases from medical equipment and supplies to cleaning supplies and, yes, food items.

We had an anonymous hot line for employees to report abuses of power and authority and he was reported. When confronted, the department head noted that in other industries, people in his position received a portion of the savings they achieved as a bonus, so he felt justified in taking a vendor kick-back. He noted that it was only on food items, not on medical supplies. This was his defensive justification. The illegal activity had been going on for two years prior to the anonymous report. He had to be fired.

The Board of Directors rightfully asked why he had not been caught earlier by our checks and balances rather than by an anonymous tip. At that point, I did not argue with the Board, I went about setting up better checks and balances. I also argued for not pursuing a legal case against our department head because we were partially at fault for not having an appropriate system in place.

I would like to think that in this story, all the principles of acceptance and defenselessness came into play though I didn't recognize it at the time.

The next law is the *Law of Intention and Desire.* To recap what Chopra teaches: all living things are made up of energy and information. Likewise, I argue that an organization is a living, breathing cosmos of that same energy and information, however, in a collective form. In fact, unlike some of the earlier renditions of Chopra's Laws of Success, this one may in fact be a little easier to understand in an organizational context than in an individual human one. However, David, it could be that it only seems this way to me because I study organizations.

Let's spend a moment differentiating between attention and intention, starting with attention. Chopra talks about the Laws of Attention and Intention and books about raising children address the same principle—whatever we focus our attention on will prosper, and that which we ignore will wither and die. Authors of books on child rearing write about various forms of child abuse; many argue that the worst form of abuse is to ignore a child. A child who is truly ignored will die as surely as if that child were malnourished or even beaten.

That is scientifically true, and I would submit that it is true for organizations as well. Children and organizations, partners, and positions, will sooner die from lack of attention than anything else. And a closely related corollary is this: what we pay attention to will flourish.

As parents or leaders, we often find that have we inadvertently encouraged a behavior we were trying to do away with by focusing on that behavior. We failed to realize that negative attention is better than no attention at all. Whether by accident or design whatever we pay attention to will flourish; it is without equal in organizational or parental motivators.

Then how does the Law of Intention feed into organizational behavior? Let's discuss the relationship of attention and intention. Very simply, intention is the process of actively choosing those things upon which to focus our attention. This isn't as simple or as straight-forward as it sounds. So, much of the time what we pay attention to is accidental—we didn't intentionally pay attention to it, it just happened and therefore, the end result can be unintended consequences. It is sad to note that most executives give not one iota of thought to the Law of Unintended Consequences, which is inadvertently putting into motion a series of events by placing their attention on anything by accident. Intention adds purpose and meaning to attention.

213

Now, added to that formula, I give you one more important concept: if I want to give my attention to only those things that I truly want to encourage, if I want to focus my attention with intention, I must practice these laws while avoiding their negative side, which is becoming attached to a particular outcome. Chopra very eloquently convinces us that we should not be attached to a particular outcome, even as we are practicing attention, intention, and noting the law of unintended consequences. So does that mean that if I do favor a particular outcome, I've already forgotten the other laws of spiritual leadership? If I am now focused on a specific future as the only possible "right" outcome, have I missed the mark? I have missed the mark only if I have assumed that by a proper execution of attention and intention that it is possible to predict, and thus control, the outcome. If I believe I control and command, then I've lost sight of my role as spiritual leader.

Learning to let go of future ideas of organizational "good outcomes" is a necessary component and a key issue in organizational behavior and spiritual leadership. So many leaders try to control not only what happens during their own tenure but beyond it to include the "life of the organization." Such leaders attempt to cast the future of their organization in concrete, usually in a thinly veiled attempt to preserve one's own legacy. This is not possible to do and not desirable from the organization's or even the leader's point of view. Further, pragmatically speaking, attachment to a particular outcome will unnecessarily expand the definition of or the perception of failure. It will also damage one's current credibility as leader.

Why would we want to expand the definition or the perception of failure by attaching ourselves to a particular outcome when so many other possibilities may be equally as positive for the institution we are leading at a particular time? The perception of failure, because we allowed only one definition of success, will potentially start a vicious downward organizational spiral. The culture may revert back to blame, defensiveness, punishment, and separateness that will take a long period of rebuilding time.

Enough of these faulty attachments and you may very well overdraw your karmic ATM account. (I'll expand on this concept in a minute when we discuss the sixth Law of Spiritual Leadership.) So once again, if we find ourselves attached to only one possible future, we'll use our contemplative space to reassess motivation and perhaps to back up, try again, and use those other laws of spiritual leadership. Like everything else, it takes practice, practice, practice.

Before going on, let me add one more corollary to this fifth spiritual law of organizational behavior. Right now, in what might seem a total contradiction of what I just said, I want to suggest that by using our experience, attention, and intention, we can predict and avoid obstacles *in our own behavior* that would detract from achieving the organizational good. More importantly, I'm not saying a spiritual leader doesn't try to figure out what might happen if a certain decision is made. Studying the possible unintended consequences of our decisions is a good thing. However, I am suggesting that we shouldn't assume that, as leaders, we have to know, or will know, or can know exactly what form that organizational good will take in the future.

This doesn't mean giving up on specific organizational goals. Of course not; just hold them gently, focus on their intent, and watch for obstacles that might suggest you should re-think your course. In short, give everything you have to fulfilling the spirit of the goal, but don't hold fast to the detail. Think of it as a child's coloring book. Since we're using child-rearing today as our vantage point, the outline of a picture is there but the exact color combination, well, maybe that's best left to the universe, or at least to the imagination.

WRIGHT

Now, let's see, that brings us to the Sixth Law of Spiritual Leadership. Would you talk about that one in a little more detail as promised?

HOWELL

Yes, David, the sixth law of spiritual leadership is the *Law of Detachment*. As applied to spiritual leaders and the organizations they lead, the law of detachment frees us to creatively meet each new challenge and each new situation without needing to seek the security of what is already known. The spiritual leader never has to say, "We tried it that way and it didn't work" or worse still "We've always done it this way." Spiritual Leadership's security is self-generated. It does not need to lash itself to the deck in any storm, hanging on to what seems to be safe. The spiritual leader understands that no organization can continue to do what it has always done and expect to be successful.

On-going success is doing the right thing at the right time for the right reason and this cannot be a static environment. Being open to ever-changing, endless possibilities enables an organization to be there for the long haul. Likewise, that organization attracts adventuresome, forward-thinking people who are game for the excitement of changing times. They thrive on the uncertainty, the adventure, even the joy of an ever-dynamic organization.

I remember my administrative meetings, my department head meetings, and my staff meetings as being fun. They were full of challenge, sometimes even impending disaster, but we were always laughing because every danger averted or experienced opened up a new world of extraordinary opportunity. We were detached from a particular outcome because we had embraced the law of detachment. We used to laugh at the old adage "if the only tool you have is a hammer, everything looks like a nail."

The law of detachment teaches that the spiritual leadership challenge is not to find a way to turn everything into a nail but to learn from new experiences and add new tools to your toolbox. We kept adding to the toolbox and found it to be a much more positive and rewarding experience than remaining attached to our lone hammer.

WRIGHT

You have some interesting theories on why all organizations should be spiritual, not just the ones that we label as religious organizations. Would you talk to us about that?

HOWELL

Absolutely, and the question brings us to the final Spiritual Law, the *Law of Dharma* or one's purpose in life. It's a very good way to answer your question and finish the Seven Laws of Spiritual Leadership. These laws could also be called the Seven Laws of Organizational Success.

Chopra talks about the unique talents of an individual. He argues that no one else is able to do exactly what he or she does better than he or she can. People's talents and their places in the world are distinctive. Likewise, I believe that each organization has a unique purpose or mission, one that it is able to accomplish better than any other, even similar institutions.

To expand that principle, think of it this way. Individuals who are attracted to (or called to) an organization at a specific point in time bring a set of talents that have never been or ever will be exactly duplicated in their collective. How then could they not create an organization as exceptional as they are? I think that is the beginning of the definition of a spiritual organization—a group of specific individuals attracted to an organization at a specific point in time. The group brings a set of talents that has never been or will ever again be exactly replicated. If they are given the tools and the encouragement to work with singularity of purpose toward a common goal—a goal of providing a distinctive service or set of services to their community—how could they be other than successful? The organizational spirit will bring abundance to the lives of those who serve and are served according to the organizational Law of Dharma.

To re-cap for emphasis, and to end our discussion today, let me summarize. If each individual is given the encouragement to use his or her special aptitudes, if they are given the opportunity to work with singularity of purpose toward a common goal, if they are allowed to provide a distinctive service (or set of services) to their community, and to their colleagues, how could they be other than a flourishing spiritual entity? Together, their organizational spirit will bring abundance to the lives of those who serve and are served.

To me, there is no better characterization of a spiritual organization than the one we have posed here. I think you'll agree, David, that there is also nothing in that definition at all limited to religious institutions. It can and should be the description of every organization, as well as to society at large.

I don't pretend to believe it will be an easy task to turn every organization into a spiritual one. Our organizations, for the most part, were designed to isolate and protect us from perceived threats (competition) and to maximize the benefits to the special and deserving individuals inside the organization.

Just to expand a little and for the purposes of argument, I think you'll agree that we have fostered the idea of separateness in our organizational life as a natural outgrowth of the human separation and even isolation we hold for ourselves. We believe that we are separate beings and from that position, we are naturally suspicious, even afraid, of other equally separate beings. Therefore, we create tribes, religions, countries, and, of course, organizations to protect and defend our isolation. If I wish to say this in a slightly more tongue-in-cheek way, we protect and defend our acknowledged "specialness."

Further, we only want to associate with those whose specialness is similar to our own. Another way of describing this concept is that we engage in enforced isolation in order to preserve our own superiority over other lesser beings. Within our tribe, religion, country, or organization, we decide how to maintain our specialness/separateness by paying attention to only certain ideas, focusing on certain behaviors, upholding certain laws and rituals.

These widely held beliefs about why associations exist have no place in a spiritual organization. In a spiritual organization, we are not special because we are better than or separate from anyone else. We are special because each individual making up the organization reaches his or her full potential, with other individuals, to offer something important to the world.

That's probably a good place to end, David. Thank you for your very astute questions and for the opportunity to participate in *Stepping Stones to Success*.

WRIGHT

I have learned a lot. This idea of spiritual leadership makes a lot of sense. I've made leadership mistakes in the past, and now I know how to do some things differently. I think you've been very helpful here for those who are even thinking about leadership. I really appreciate all the time you've taken to answer these questions.

HOWELL

Well, you have been very kind and made it easy for me to move through this process. I feel strongly about the concepts I've shared. I don't often get a chance to express them and acknowledge their importance in my life, so I thank you.

You have precipitated some important discussions in your series of research topics. You've brought people together who I'm sure will dialog in the future about these and other important topics of the day. Yes, spiritual leadership is common sense executed consistently, in humility, and with the spirit of loving kindness. To quote Native American, Chief Red Mountain, "Lost warriors have only to open their eyes to find the right and good path."

WRIGHT

Today we've been speaking with Dr. Bonnie Howell who has been working in the healthcare field for over twenty years. Dr. Howell served as the president and CEO of a major regional medical center and as chair of the Healthcare Association of New York State. She served as chair of a regional banking system and worked in community planning. Today she is a national speaker and consultant, specializing in one-on-one leadership and team coaching for administrative and physician executives from healthcare organizations across the country.

Dr. Howell, thank you so much for participating in this important *Stepping Stones to Success* project.

HOWELL

Thank you. It's been my very great pleasure and privilege to work with you.

ABOUT THE AUTHOR

Dr. Bonnie Howell has twenty years' experience in the healthcare field. She was CEO of a major regional medical center, Chair of the Healthcare Association of New York State, and is a fellow in the American College of Healthcare Executives. She has a BS in Organizational Behavior, an MPA from Cornell University's School of Business, and a doctorate in Healthcare Administration from the Medical University of South Carolina. She is certified as a spiritual counselor and has a degree in Divinity from the University of Metaphysical Sciences. Dr. Howell has taught leadership at both Cornell University, and New York University. She served as a director of a community bank in Ithaca, New York, for over twenty years and has lectured for healthcare, financial, and corporate clients across the Northeast. Dr. Howell specializes in one-on-one leadership and team coaching with administrative and physician executives for healthcare organizations across the nation. She has three daughters and resides in Jersey City, New Jersey.

Bonnie Howell

4 Beacon Way
Jersey City, NJ 07304
201-524-9753
bhhcmc@yahoo.com
www.DrBonnieSpiritualCoach.com

CHAPTER THIRTEEN

When Failure Turns into Success

An Interview with . . . **Susan Rae Baker**

DAVID WRIGHT (WRIGHT)

Susan Rae Baker is an acclaimed Life and Business Coach, Motivational Speaker, Award Winning Author and a quoted National Expert on www.TheStreet.com and SmallBizAmerica.com.

Susan holds her certification through the Certified Coaches Alliance (CCA). She has made guest appearances on local NBC, CBS, Comcast stations, guest speaker on Fox News NY and Better TV as well as with nationally known radio talk shows speaking about topics such as How to Attract and Retain Great Employees, Retaining Employees Without Spending Money, Burning Down Silos and Tearing Up Turf Wars and The Top Ten Signs You Are in The Wrong Job.

She has become a most respected and engaging speaker, teacher and leader in the field of Life and Business Coaching. She has taken the art of speaking to a whole new level that leaves one feeling as though they have not just learned something new, but also leaves people filled with joy and inspiration. Susan is bringing forth positive change in people who would otherwise remain stuck in a rut of indecision.

Susan's inspirational workshops have brought an awareness of life and business coaching to the eastern shores of Delaware and Maryland Susan's aspiration in life is to help people become what they were designed to be, so that they can live a happy, fulfilling and successful life. Susan's other passion is to make a strong positive impact on the way Corporate America views their employees as she unravels the internal destructive competitiveness within.

Susan is the author of the *Mom's Choice Awards Silver Honoree for Women's Issues* Book, "*The Last Box- A Women's Guide to Surviving Corporate America.*" In this book, she has taken over 30 years of life experience and packed it into a very engaging, thought provoking book that is sure to not only entertain, but to bring an awareness to women in the working world or about to enter it, of the personalities that they would like to aspire to or run from.

The last Box has also been named as a finalist in the Foreword Magazine Book of the Year Award for 2009.

Susan is also completing her second Book, *Defining Moments, a Gathering of Women's Journey's*, targeted for a summer of 2010 publishing date.

Susan welcome to *Stepping Stones to Success*.

SUSAN RAE BAKER (BAKER)

Thank you David, I'm glad to be here.

WRIGHT

So right up front, how do you define success?

BAKER

How do I define success? Well, first I want to start by saying that prior to the *Stepping Stones to Success* project I wrote my definition of success and it goes like this: "Today's failures are just steppingstones to tomorrow's successes." That was a quote I wrote a while back and here we are with *Stepping Stones to Success*, so it's a rather serendipitous moment. The way I see success, it can be defined in so many ways. First of all, it's how you see yourself—how you view yourself—no matter what career you're in and whether you're a mother, wife, or husband.

Look back just long enough to see how much you have accomplished and the strides you have made to get there. Every time you climb the next mountain or solve the next problem, it becomes a successful moment. We all are a success in our own right and most of us have had to fail many times to reach this point.

Success should never be determined by how much money you make, the car you drive, or the house you live in, but by what you have contributed to life in general. Have you been kind, loving, and generous? Have you done some community service to help those less fortunate? Have you lived your life with honesty and integrity? Have you made a difference in someone's life? These are all the qualities of a successful person.

For me, the successes in my life were due to hard work and perseverance, but also because I love to reach out and help people. Every time I do that, I walk away feeling that I succeeded. By that definition you're a success, you did something that made a difference in someone else's life. So it's not who you are, it's what you do, and whether or not you're doing something right and you're doing it well. It's taken me quite a few years to figure out who I am, and what I was meant to be as I worked in many, many fields. It was because of that long journey that I realized I was on a path of discovery to find out what God's intention really was for my life. Because of that journey I realized my true calling was to be a life and business coach. Since that revelation, my work has been extremely fulfilling and because of where I've come in such short time—since that leap of faith—I have already become a success in my field.

WRIGHT

So what's the one most important element to finding success?

BAKER

You've got to start by searching your soul, you've got to find out who you are and what you're passions are. Most people are just going to work and doing a job for a paycheck, then coming home at the end of the day. Just going through the motions every day is never going to bring you to the point of success where you're going to be happy with yourself. You can be successful at any job you're good at, but when you find what your passion is in life and follow that path, that's where you find that true feeling of success because now you look forward to doing that function every day. [Ed. Note: Try to reduce the number of the word "that" used in a sentence. Be sure you use that and which correctly. "Which" should be used restrictively only when it is preceded by a preposition (e.g., the situation in which we find ourselves). Otherwise it is almost always preceded by a comma, a parenthesis, or a dash.]

So whether it's being a doctor or an astrophysicist, maybe you could be a landscaper, a writer or an artist. Whatever you choose to do that comes from a passion becomes a success naturally because you look forward to doing it. You are going to put your best foot forward because you enjoy doing it.

One of the comments I made in my book, *The Last Box: A Women's Guide to Surviving Corporate America,* is that one of the top ten signs you're in the wrong job is you're not looking forward to Mondays. I take a little bit of criticism about that because everybody has his or her own thoughts around it. However, I truly meant it because once I found what my true passion was and started feeling like a success, I looked forward to Mondays—I couldn't wait for Mondays. I actually wanted to get through the weekend faster, so that I could get to Monday.

What I've done is turn it around. Because I work for myself, I can decide what part of each day I devote to working. If a mistake is made, I can only blame myself. The highest power I have to answer to in my office, other than God, is me. Every day I make strides or I work hard to get to the next level because I do feel there are also levels of success.

WRIGHT

So how many times do you think you had to fail before you succeeded?

BAKER

Many times! I failed many times before I realized that the definition of insanity is to do the same things over and over expecting different results. This is definitely the definition of insanity. Looking back, I can see it—I was rather "insane" for a long time. I mean in that in a kind way. I think we all go through periods of insanity because we don't know who we are, we don't know what we really want out of life, we have a feeling deep down inside, when you think back on your childhood and try to remember what you loved—what you wanted to be when you grew up. I think most people already knew.

Here's a great example for you. There were two brothers my sister and I went to high school with. They were always the president of the class, they were always at the head of the class, they were way ahead of the rest of the students in the school and we both saw these same two boys as becoming either president of the United States or as lawyers. Sure enough, the one my sister knew is Andrew Napolitano, the judge we know see on FOX News. His brother, who was in my class, went on to be a lawyer.

So your life is pretty much cut out for you when you're born, it's how your parents help shape you and it's what you do to carry that sword. Of course they don't have to shape you in their own image, they should never do that. Parents know what their children's talents are when they're growing up and they should inspire them to keep moving forward, encouraging their children to do what they love to do. These young men my sister and I knew in high school knew exactly what they wanted to be and made it happen.

Another great example is my nephew's stepdaughter, who is nine years old going on thirty. I saw her recently at a wedding. During the reception, when the music cranked up she was out there, pretending to have a microphone and singing. She was incredible. You could see and feel her passion. She was asked to give a reading at the wedding. She proudly marched up to the front of the room and was the most amazing orator for someone her age that I have ever seen. She was comfortable, she had presence, she had a personality about her when she spoke that was incredible. Needless to say, we were all just sitting there in awe. She wants to be a singer on Broadway, and this is one kid who has a dream and a passion—something you don't stifle.

When a child shows that much innate ability to be something and lives it out every day, you do everything you can to put that child in the right places, in front of the right people. You will encourage that child and give him or her voice lessons and acting lessons to hone and develop innate skills already present.

I am sure I'm going to see my nephew's stepdaughter on Broadway someday. When a parent sees a child's natural ability, talent, and passion and encourages them, that's success.

I think even as adults we are guilty of stifling our own talent and our own abilities because we allow other things to get in the way. Sometimes these things are unavoidable such as you just got married and now you're having children. Life changes, you've got other responsibilities, and you have to put your passions on the back burner because you definitely have to bring home a paycheck. When you get to that point of your life I encourage you to never let your original passion die. Try to find some time for it every week and continue to build on it somehow. Don't let the flame burn out because someday may have to look back when you're eighty and say, "Gee, I always wanted to be that and never did it."

WRIGHT

So what was the driving force that brought you to where you are today?

BAKER

Well, I think it was the fact that I knew every job I took involved something I knew I could do and do well, but knew in my heart that it just wasn't what I was meant to be. I spent a good twenty-five to thirty years in the healthcare field. I loved what I did, but it was about the people I met. I wrote about them in my book; it was a part of my journey and part of what I needed to learn and share with others.

There are different personality types that can trip you up. They can either move you forward or they can help you fail. I got sick and tired of the failures that were literally caused by other people who didn't want me there because they saw me as a threat. The bottom line was that I had to look inward and say, "Okay Susan, how many more times do you want to do this? How many more times do you want to work in that field?" The last one was the financial services industry. I asked myself, "How many times do you want to do this and fail (according to their definition), walk away disappointed, and have to pick yourself up and continue on?"

After having met a life coach who was giving a keynote presentation, I finally realized while sitting there how great it would be to have a career like hers. I would like to be like to her—I would really love to do what she is doing. I started talking to myself, and saying things like, "I'm able to get up there. I have stage presence. I've done a lot of singing, and I've always liked being on stage and I have no fear of being down front." My abilities to speak came to me from my father, who was a great orator and did a lot of public speaking. I really started to search my soul and say, "Okay, I'm not getting any younger, it's time." I was in a position where I could stop what I was doing on that last job, walk away from it, take my certification course, and start my own business.

I immediately started my practice. I was picking up clients despite the obstacles that were ahead of me. I had just moved my entire life in New Jersey to Delaware and it was a culture change for me. I didn't realize that I was going to walk into an area where people had no idea what coaching was about. The affordability of coaching for the people who lived there was slim to none and I had to keep bending with the wind, so to speak, to get around these pitfalls.

Instead of coaching many individuals I was doing workshops, which went well. My biggest clients happened to be men who were business owners. I had started out with women as my niche and ended up working with men in business. It went on from there, constantly evolving and changing as I added motivational speaker, award-winning author, and editor in chief to my designations.

WRIGHT

So what is the one best tip you can give to those who have not found their way?

BAKER

I would say, find a coach; it does help. I mean, if you can sit down and even write down what you love to do, what you are passionate for, and what you have always wanted to be, that is a great place to start. It is also helpful to ask close friends and family members this question, "If I had a choice of careers, where do you see me?" You will get a pretty good idea of what talents others see in you.

I asked one of my bosses that question once, "Where do you see me in this field?" It's a hard question to ask and you have to be ready for an honest answer. The honest answer may hurt or it may actually bring some sense of relief. You might find yourself responding, "I was wondering about that. I always had that in the back of my mind; thank you for validating it." But start asking the people around you who care about you—people you know you can get an honest answer from.

You can take some online tests. I have heard that Careerdirect.com is excellent. That's a great source to see what you're all about and it's another source of validation of your own thoughts and feelings.

Just start exploring now, don't wait so long that you go through all of these years as I did, wondering and struggling and trying to do the right thing and learning later that you didn't have to suffer that long—you could have had a great time doing what you love and helping other people become a success at what they're doing.

WRIGHT

So what can you offer those who feel like failures and can't seem to lift themselves out of that pit of despair?

BAKER

Well, if they can't lift themselves out I would love to say to them, do not despair, but do get help. Either find a counselor to find out what is holding you down, what has you stuck in a rut of indecision, what is making you feel the way you feel about yourself. It's difficult to do, but get some help. Get somebody to help motivate you and get you up on your feet again. Then start exploring and, once you figure it out, just go for it. If you don't, you're going to spend the rest of your life in that same rut.

You can't do it alone, it's like trying to stop drinking or quit smoking. Most people need help stopping those kinds of habits, right? Whether you need medication or join a group (some people actually have hypnotherapy to get them through it), you can't always do it alone; it's a tough road to travel by yourself.

I think the reason why I was able to do it for myself was because of who I am and what my abilities are. I was actually able to see the light. When I left that last job I was able to sit down and literally write a book about it so that I could help others. This was when I realized why I went through that journey. Everybody needs some support system. This system can help people realize the direction that they need to go in.

Sometimes we go through difficult times for a reason. You don't want to interfere with that because there is a purpose behind everything we do and everything that happens to us.

For example, if you've always wanted to be a performer on Broadway, first you've got to get real with yourself and go find a voice coach and ask, "I want you to tell me honestly, can I sing?" You don't want to follow a passion or a dream that that is beyond your capability. You can sing if you can't read music, but it's a little more difficult. If an expert tells you, "I think you should find a different road to go down, you just can't seem to follow a tune, you can't hold a note," then you'll know. But try—you've got to try and you've got to find out what the right direction is for you.

I spoke to a client recently who was going through a career transition, or desiring to. He was still was working at the time. I talked with him about his passions and he said, "Well, if I had it my way I'd want to be a baseball player." He's now in his forties and he has some kids and responsibilities. He realized that being a baseball player was no longer within his reach. Now, it's possible that he could have been great as a baseball player, but he did not have the opportunity—he didn't focus on it when he was young enough and now that opportunity has passed by.

So you have to be real, you need to get help from experts to help you work through your thoughts and your passions to figure out which ones are viable and which ones just aren't.

WRIGHT

So if you could change one thing about your life that would have shortened the learning curve, what would that be?

BAKER

Wow, I would have started coaching years ago. Unfortunately, it was not an option financially because I was raising four children on my own after a divorce. I had to pay the bills to keep the roof over our heads. But had I been able to choose freely at the time, I probably would have just gone straight into coaching. I think my heart was always there, but I never knew about it. If someone had told me about coaching twenty or thirty years ago, that's probably the direction I would have gone.

How could I have shortened my learning curve? I could have sought advice from people of wisdom. I could have trusted God more. I could have followed my gut and held on to faith!

It just occurred to me that this is like professional sports for women. I graduated high school in 1970. Women's sports consisted of not much more than what we did at school in gym class and a few extracurricular sports activities before school which amounted to playing speedball on the blacktop. We were playing that rigorous sport of speedball, not soccer. In my time, we didn't have the opportunity young sports-minded women have now. Today I play golf; I play it well, and I know if I had started thirty years ago, I just might have made it to the LPG Tour. Do you see where I'm going with this?

It's about what's out there, what's possible, and now the world is open for men and women to everything—everything. What was just men's sports are now women's, too. Women have the opportunity to get through college on sports scholarships that were only offered to guys in the past. So there is a world of opportunity for many women.

You need to start as young as possible to truly develop what your passion is for, and if I had done that, I'm sure I would have gone into the field of sports and maybe evolved to coaching when I retired from my career in sports. You do have to have a plan B if you're going to go into some kind of career that can end at a certain age because of its physical demands (we all have this nasty habit of aging).

WRIGHT

So was there anyone in particular who helped you launch into a clearer understanding of who you are and what you were designed to be?

BAKER

There are three people I will name. The first is Laura Berman Fortgang who is a very well-known life and business coach. Laura is from New Jersey (I grew up in

Bloomfield, New Jersey). She and I connected when I went to a conference. When I heard her presentation, I thought, "You know, she just gave me some great advice about someone I was working for." At the end of her talk, I had the opportunity to talk with her and realized this would be a great career for me. I would say that she was the one who inspired me to be a coach. I'm not sure she realizes that. I believe I did write her and I actually sent her one of my books.

Other people include those who actually let me go from some of my jobs, believe it or not. It's a painful thing to have happen but they actually helped launch me into what I'm doing now. They literally moved me out of the way from something I really didn't love. I was doing it, and I was doing it well, but I didn't love it. I also realized that, again, I don't want to work around particular personality types such as the hidden agenda queen, or the HR diva (I mention them in my books). They can really either make you or break you. They were breaking me every time because it can be a bad experience to be a woman out in corporate America where there is a lot of cattiness. Many women fear that you're going to get in their way, especially when they see how well you can perform. They'll help you get out of the way—right out the door! But the few I can think of have really done me a favor by moving me out because I walked right into the next best thing.

The last job I left, I brought my box of personal belongings home, put it in the garage, and wouldn't look at it because I wasn't feeling like a success right then. I was feeling more like a big failure. The next day I walked back into the garage and I looked at the box. I pointed my finger at the box and said, "That's the last box—that's the last time I'm going to carry my belongings home from the workplace and walk 'the walk of humiliation.'" I ended up sitting down during my husband's recovery from triple bypass surgery and started writing my first book called *The Last Box: A Women's Guide to Surviving Corporate America.* The first night I decided, "Okay, I'm going to take the advice of other authors and I'm going to try to finish a page a day."

Well, I did three chapters that night; they just flowed. If I had my way, I would reach out to those people who let me go and send them my book with a thank you note—"Thank you for letting me go!"

WRIGHT

What is the most common denominator you've observed among your coaching clients?

BAKER

Indecision and fear. Fear is usually the number one problem that most people face. Whether it's in their business or in their personal lives, fear and anxiety set in from the start. They all have a fear about something and it's usually about growth—some are afraid to grow. Their inability to make a decision keeps them from moving forward in life.

WRIGHT

What do you think is the most powerful thing you have learned and can share with others about forgiveness?

BAKER

Forgive as quickly as you can—don't hold grudges. Your life is too short to not forgive people. I think people hold on to grudges and decide they're going to hate someone because he or she "did them wrong." This behavior is only zapping your own energy. You are wasting your time and you need to release people from whatever it was they did and just get on with your life. It's also important, if you can find a way to do it, is to talk with them personally. This is the biggest release you can have. Say, "I know we've had our differences, but I want to let you know that I've forgiven you." Hopefully, this won't spark another whole round of rehashing the problem. If it does, you can just say, "I'm sorry you feel this way. I wanted you to know I've forgiven you and want to put it to rest."

My own husband has allowed other people in his life to make him feel like less of a person, but he also allows himself to hang onto to past hurts and grievances. He often displays the inability to forgive. There are certain things that have happened to him in his past, and some in his present, that he has allowed to cause him much internal stress. These events are literally making him sick.

Why would you allow what somebody else did to you affect you enough to make you sick? Sometimes these people have already passed on but the memory of what

232

happened still hurts you internally and is still slowing you down. That person might have been a father or a mother when you were little who always told you that you're nothing but a failure, you're stupid, you're dumb, you're this, you're that. The worst thing we can do to children is to call them names and make them feel inferior. We don't realize that these words can stick with someone for the rest of his or her life. People who are in this situation wonder why they've never become what they wanted to be. They don't realize it's because they have a voice in the back of their head—a memory of someone telling them that they are stupid, they're dumb, and they're a failure.

I saw this happen in my own family, with my own brother. For the last thirty-seven years he has held onto a grudge about my sister and me getting married at the same time and leaving him alone. He wasn't alone—he was young and lived at home with both our parents. He was feeling abandoned. The point here is that even as an adult, he has never let go of that feeling. It has eaten up so much of his precious energy and time.

I also see this problem in my husband's life and it hasn't helped him one bit. There are certain things that seem to haunt him, such as feeling that he didn't spend enough time with his father when he was dying. I said, "First of all, I don't think your father would want you to feel this way, I really don't. I'm sure that if he even felt any negative feelings toward you because of that, he's already forgiven you. He doesn't love you any less. You've got to let it go or you've got to go get counseling and help find a way to let it go. It will definitely eat you up inside for the rest of your life if you allow it to." I've seen too many examples of the inability to forgive in people I have met. They allow their past to ruin their future.

WRIGHT

So in today's economy, what would you say is the best advice you can give someone who wants to start their own business?

BAKER

Starting your own business in this economy it is a really touchy subject. If you have a decent job that provides a good paycheck and you can pay your bills and you're not struggling, hang in there for now but start doing your research. Start doing your soul search. Maybe you can do it a little bit during the week in the evening when you're home and just take an hour out each night or a half an hour to do some online assessment programs to find out where your true strengths are. Start talking to people you can trust. Once the economy starts to lighten up a bit and things start to change, there will be more opportunities to move forward with your plans.

I think it's a very difficult time right now. If you are going to start a business, you'd better think really hard and do a lot of research. Find out what type of services do people need, versus what they want? People aren't spending a lot of money right now unless it's something they absolutely have to have. However, lot of people are still going out to eat, they're still treating themselves to ice cream, and they're still doing some fun things. Try to look at the whole picture and say, "If I'm going to start a business, what do people need regardless of the economy?"

WRIGHT

So what's the best advice you can offer to someone who wants change careers at this challenging time?

BAKER

Oh, same thing. If they're going to change careers, if they're still going to work for somebody else, there are not a lot of jobs available. There are a lot of people out of work—the highest number ever. I think it's over nine million people, the last I checked. The market right now is flooded with people looking for a job, not even a career—a job, a paycheck—because eventually their unemployment is going to run out and they're really going to be stuck. So if you have a decent job that is paying well, you're not dreading it every day, and it's not making you sick, hang in there for now, but start your search. Don't waste time. When the time is right you can move on it and make a proper change. Hopefully it will be one that you're going to enjoy and one in which you will find success.

WRIGHT

Well, what a great conversation. This is some really good commonsense information that will be good for our readers, especially in this economy. I think you've really helped a lot. I really appreciate the time you have spent with me here today answering all these questions. I know this chapter is going to be a good addition to our book.

BAKER

Here is more advice: always set goals for yourself. My goal this year was, and is, to be on national television. The day arrived twice when my agent called to tell me that she was pitching me to CNN and then to Glenn Beck to go live. I stayed on call, but the subject passed by pretty quickly so they didn't need me after all, but any day now, the next call will land me a spot on national television.

I pray a lot. That would be my last piece of advice—pray a lot about what you're considering doing and just really look to the Lord for wisdom and grace.

WRIGHT

Today we've been talking with Susan Rae Baker who is a business coach, a motivational speaker, and author. Susan has become a most respected and engaging speaker, teacher, and leader in the field of coaching. According to her, she is making some really serious moves, all under the umbrella of what she really loves to do.

Susan, thank you so much for being with us today on *Stepping Stones to Success*.

BAKER

Thank you for spending this time with me.

ABOUT THE AUTHOR

SUSAN RAE BAKER is a Life and Business Coach, Motivational Speaker, Award Winning Author and nationally known Expert for TheStreet.com and SmallBizAmerica.com. She has appeared as a regular guest on local NBC, ABC and Comcast stations along with nationally known radio talk shows speaking about many topics such as: How to Attract and Retain Great Employees, How to Resource Your Humans, Burning Down Silos and Tearing up Turf Wars, Rebranding yourself for the next Best Job and The Top Ten Signs You Are in The Wrong Job.

Susan's first book, *The Last Box: A Women's Guide to Surviving Corporate America* has won the Silver Honoree Award from the prestigious Mom's Choice Awards 2009 for Women's Issues, and is a finalist for the Foreword Magazine Book of The Year Award.

Her aspiration in life is to help people become what they were designed to be, so that they can live a happy, fulfilling and successful life. Susan's other passion is to make a strong positive impact on the way corporate America views their employees as she unravels the internal destructive competitiveness within.

SUSAN RAE BAKER

20 Gadwall Circle
Bridgeville, DE 19933
443-944-2717
www.future-endeavors.net

CHAPTER FOURTEEN

Wisdom at Work

An Interview with . . . **Dr. Joni Carley**

DAVID WRIGHT (WRIGHT)

Today we are talking with Dr. Joni Carley. Her international consulting practice serves successful leaders, professionals, and entrepreneurs. Much like Olympic coaches working with athletes who are already strong, Dr. Joni helps her clients strive for the gold and get there. In her work at the United Nations and in the private sector, her expertise in values-driven leadership helps her clients create an abundant triple bottom line in terms of people, profits, and the planet. Joni holds a doctorate in the Reinvention of Work and she's been coaching, speaking, and teaching for more than twenty-five years. Dr. Joni's blog, "Wisdom at Work↔Wisdom in the World," her products, services, talks, and her workshops don't just inform, they transform.

Her Wisdom at Work coaching methodology has proven effective in addressing core issues to produce sustainable results. Audiences say "she changed my life," "inspired me," and that they'll "use her material for the rest of my life." That's probably because Dr. Joni's content draws from a unique depth and breadth of experience, ranging from the jungle to the boardroom, from the UN to college campuses, from coaching corporate, governmental, and nonprofit/NGO leaders to solopreneurs.

Dr. Joni Carley, welcome to *Stepping Stones to Success*.

DR. JONI CARLEY (CARLEY)

Thank you, it's great to be here!

WRIGHT

You believe that success is all about choices, don't you?

CARLEY

I believe it's all about making wise choices. Choosing wisely can make or break your career. I've had the privilege of working with some wonderful leaders who have taught me that people who reach the top do so because they make the wisest choices. Wise choices create the types of careers that leave great legacies and wise choices create successful organizations.

Since the only constant in life is change, success is dependent on the choices we make while we're negotiating change. So the trajectory toward success is just one choice after another. In that sense, our steppingstones are our choices. Daily choices form the building blocks of our potential. First and foremost, leadership is having decision-making authority.

My work is aimed at helping clients close the gap between where they are and where they want to be by helping them recognize and then act on their wisest choices. Wise choices are more than simply smart choices. They're a meeting of heart and mind, of gut-generated information combined with hard data. Wisdom means capitalizing on that funny feeling that says "wait" even when all the facts say "go." Wisdom balances the internal with the external, the hard evidence with soft evidence, and the people values with the profit values.

Our "Wall Street Wonders" are great examples of leaders who made many smart decisions that were even confirmed by standard indicators right up until the market crashed. That's because for millennia we've squelched the voice of wisdom and that has compromised our ability to balance being "head smart" with being "heart smart." I call this balance the "Yin and Yang of Success" in my talks and in an article on my Web site: http://jonicarley.com/complimentary-downloads/articles/yinyang.

The 2008–2009 stock market collapse demonstrated that "smart" choices made without heart can lead to major problems. On the other hand, choices made only from the heart can lack substance. Beneath the financial crisis was a moral one. When leaders take the time to apply the lens of wisdom, not only are their actions more ethical, they generate a special kind of spark, as if they're bringing together a positive and negative electrical charge. It is almost metaphysical when you craft your intuitive instincts together with your knowledge base.

Wise choices lead to less drama, in spite of the fact that wise people tend to attract more opportunities. They also take more risks than their intellectually oriented colleagues and high caliber leadership demands meaningful risk-taking. The path of wisdom leads to a more abundant and more sustainable triple bottom line in terms of people, profits, and the planet (the 3Ps). And, wise people tend to sleep well!

WRIGHT

If smart choices aren't always wise, are wise choices always smart?

CARLEY

Yes. Look at Gandhi. He opted for wise choices instead of the "smarter" choices advocated by the powerful people around him. He was a lawyer and today most lawyers are trained to manipulate the law to win at any cost. But Gandhi never allowed legalities to trump justice or winning to trump compassion. Legality requires smarts but true justice relies on wisdom. I see the smart/wise conflict in play at the United Nations and in the private sector because values-driven leaders who refuse to compromise their wisdom—no matter what the affect is on their short-term career goals—tend to leave great legacies.

In terms of the number of cases he won or the fees he collected, Gandhi's career appeared mediocre. All the time he spent in jail would seem to spell failure.

But, because he understood the distinction between wise and smart choices, his career (and life) has become a model—in fact, a gold standard for success. Gandhi's actions were well ahead of his time but there is now a critical mass of leaders across all sectors who are creating a new values-driven paradigm. These are the people I work with at the United Nations and in my private practice (Complimentary MP3—"Mastering Leadership" at www.drjoni.com).

People who choose to work at the United Nations are usually driven by their values; they're dedicated to making a difference. And, the UN's Charter, the Millennium Development Goals, and the UN Global Compact principles perfectly reflect great and wise vision. Unfortunately, just like in many less values-oriented organizations, what shows up in day-to-day work lives can feel very, very disconnected from the vision that people signed on to in the first place. The result is a stagnation of organizational mission and lackluster career trajectories.

To combat this problem at the UN, we're using a coaching methodology designed to help create more fertile ground between the values that attracted people to their positions and the extreme protocol and hierarchy that can fill their days. Using a coaching approach means that leaders and their teams create specific concrete actions to reconnect their vision and values with their duties.

Our work at the UN, through Global Vision Institute, is dedicated to creating a values-driven international community. We help people unleash the deep drive that's at the heart of their work. Their evaluation forms tell us that reconnecting with their vision and values not only helps them feel recharged but leads to taking positive action. I see the same thing with my business and non-profit clients—*the ones who keep the values conversation alive are the people and organizations that thrive.*

Leadership studies have shown that executives can make wrong decisions 50 percent of the time and still be considered good leaders! That's because they're keeping things moving while staying accountable—which makes good leadership but it doesn't make great leadership. Great leaders make sure their decisions pass the test of wisdom. Each choice they make is one that feels good in the gut and satisfies the mind. Wise decision-making is based on solid information as well as core values.

We tend to think that choices are about right and wrong, but everybody knows that you can make a choice that looks completely right and then you end up thinking, "Boy, I wish I hadn't made that decision." And, how often have you thought a decision was a huge mistake only to have it turn out to be the best thing that could have happened? That's why it's really not about right and wrong; it's really about discernment. Discernment comes from being mindful as well as "heartful," which turns out to be a winning combination.

An important reason that successes increase so dramatically with coaching is that coaching is all about discernment, which, neurologically, is a higher-level decision-making process. Olympians can't get to their best without their coaches. Likewise, leaders who exercise their discernment with a coach are more likely to realize their visions. I specialize in moving you from bronze to gold.

WRIGHT

You have a unique perspective on success. You consult with a wide range of professionals, you have a doctorate in the Reinvention of Work, and you've also traveled around the world discovering ancient and modern keys to realizing human potential. So, what are the steppingstones to success and how do you know when you get there—wherever the "there" of success is?

CARLEY

That's a great question because there really is no "there" of success. Success is a moving target and so are the steppingstones toward it. There is no evidence that there is one ideal way to success and if we just get it right, we'll be successful and if we don't, we won't. Having a fixed notion of success is really a trap, unless it's a huge dream like Gandhi had for liberating India. If he had just kept on practicing law, and doing a little community work on the side, he would have better met day-to-day definitions of success. But, instead of gauging his success by cultural norms, he followed his vision and inner wisdom.

We often mistake success as a stagnant endgame, but it's much more dynamic than that. It reminds me of the Zen saying, "If you meet the Buddha on the road, shoot him." Zen followers believe enlightenment is a forever unfolding experience and that anyone claiming to have arrived at enlightenment as an endpoint shouldn't be trusted. That's because enlightenment, like success, isn't about arriving and then being done.

Most of my clients define success by how much joy and satisfaction they have, as well as by the ease with which they can live to their hearts' desires. They also define it as being able to make a difference in other people's lives. I'm often struck by how many end up enjoying financial abundance even when that wasn't their primary coaching goal. At the same time, it's fascinating how many say they want to make more money, but what they want more than that is satisfaction.

So if success isn't a fixed destination, it stands to reason that the steppingstones aren't fixed either. If you mapped out every single steppingstone during a river walk, you would miss exploring all the nooks and crannies that nature is always creating. But without some plan for crossing the river, you could drown. Still, if you never venture off your pre-determined path, you lose the possibility of finding even better opportunities. Take my own field of leadership coaching, for example. Formulaic models are popular but they can end up being less effective than more adaptive methodologies because no fixed system can adequately account for changes in the stream or changes in a dream.

You couldn't ever perfectly map your path across a river anyway because rivers, like the path of leadership, are always changing. Leadership studies indicate that adaptability creates greater success than rigidity. Keeping your focus in the moment might mean that you don't step on the stone that you thought you would. But altering your path doesn't mean that you're any less focused or that you've somehow failed. Steppingstones to success are no more permanent than steppingstones in the river, but people are often resistant to changing their own professional paths and to you changing yours.

My most successful clients are always wrestling with questions of change. I'm often hired at a transition time but many people continue working with me for years because, once the dramatic stuff has settled down, they realize that coaching helps maintain a kind of vitality that best accommodates change. Good leadership coaching helps you maintain the integrity of your long-term vision while keeping you agile in the moment.

I firmly believe that quality coaching must include values work because the data shows that values-driven leadership generates a high return on investment that is sustainable over time.

WRIGHT

What is values-driven leadership?

CARLEY

The phrase is fairly self-explanatory. It is leadership that emerges from a foundation of clear core values rather than from the drive for profit at any cost.

Values-driven leadership is an emerging paradigm that's based on trust, virtues, relationship, transparency, philanthropy, ecology, co-creativity, abundance consciousness, and partnership. It creates dignity in the workplace and develops organizations that are vital community members that honor all stakeholders. Best practices include creating the time and space to develop vision and to strengthen individuals and their relationships. Values-driven organizations act with enlightened self-interest.

The emerging values-driven leadership paradigm requires that we walk our talk. If we really want liberty and justice for all, then we have to do business with companies that don't exploit employees or pollute their neighborhoods. Therefore, the task for leaders is to devise new sets of rules and new ways to measure success. Values-driven leaders see values as steppingstones, but that doesn't mean they compromise their dedication to solid research, strong profits, and robust productivity. They recognize that success needs to be measured by how they do what they do as well as by what they actually do.

The definition of success is morphing. Values-driven leadership used to be seen as a weakness—it was too soft, unquantifiable and even considered flaky. That's partly because the concept emerged along with what's sometimes called the LOHAS sector, meaning Lifestyles Of the Healthy And Sustainable.

LOHAS leaders are everywhere now. Though it's sometimes still linked to the Birkenstock and granola industries that spawned it, the LOHAS sector is now a $355 billion chunk of the economy and it's growing at 10 percent a year. Not all values-driven leaders are LOHAS sector members but I submit that all have benefited from LOHAS distinctions, which have also informed the Socially Responsible Investments (SRI) sector.

We have tangible proof that this new approach works. During the recent crash, the SRI stocks and mutual funds didn't experience the volatility of the rest of the market. Both the stock market and the research are starting to prove that ethical action and values-driven decision-making are steppingstones to sustainable success. That's why more and more companies are dedicating resources to corporate social responsibility (CSR).

WRIGHT

It's a new approach to many people and corporations. But you have twenty-five years of experience and a doctorate in it! What do you think about the more recent developments in this field?

CARLEY

It's really an ancient way of thinking but it's new to most of us. The profit-at-any-cost mentality about success is shifting toward a different mindset because that old paradigm is setting new benchmarks on the scale of failure. We've all been told that sometimes you have to use people as a means to your own ends, that you really can't do well and do good at the same time, and that you should get the next guy before he gets you. We even made "do-gooder" into a bad word! Yet, something in us knows that the Golden Rule rules.

On an individual basis, values-driven businesses aren't as likely to have stellar returns in the short run, but they sustain and they demonstrate extraordinary vitality. The 3P's (people, profits, and the planet) are in the organizational DNA of values-driven businesses. Triple bottom line awareness is beginning to penetrate old paradigm organizations because these companies have to shift. The writing's on the wall: we're at a stage in our evolution where we have to make profound systemic changes so that we place more appropriate value on what really matters.

I wrote a post called "10 Reasons why Greedy Jerks Make the Worst Leaders" (http://jonicarley.com/complimentary-downloads/articles/10-reasons-greedy-jerks-make-the-worst-leaders) as a simple way to examine what weakens foundational pillars. The recent financial meltdown brought us face-to-face with the reality that a lot of what we see on television about success is just not working out for millions of people. Truly great leaders never bought into the dog-eat-dog myth of success. Instead, they developed their passion for compassion and became great by being good.

244

We're evolving from models of radical antagonism toward partnership models. After all, we are all interdependent on the expression of core values. I think coaching is so beneficial because its respect for values helps naturally develop partnership, which is definitely a steppingstone to success.

WRIGHT

The word "steppingstones" is an interesting metaphor, isn't it?

CARLEY

It sure is! I've seen stones used in fascinating ways in many different cultures around the world. In the West, we think of a stone as rigid and fixed and strong. But Native Americans called stones "the stone people," sculptors see a figure to be freed, the Bible talks about a stone in your shoe, and Buddhists stack stones while praying.

The most fascinating stone tradition that I ever experienced was in Ecuador where I spent several weeks traveling from high in the Andes to deep in the jungle to learn from tribal elders. I met a woman shaman who had trained through a very ancient lineage. Her name was Maria Juana. (I kid you not, and no, she didn't partake!) Before we got there, our guide had been trying and trying to reach her but he couldn't get through to her or anyone else in the village. He warned us that we might not find Maria once we reached her village and, if we didn't see her, we would go to the local market and just move on.

But when we pulled up to her little wooden house, Maria was completely prepared for us. She had set out the right number of glasses and snacks and had already been making spiritual preparations for our particular group. When our translator asked her how she knew we'd be there, she said her "huacas" told her that we were coming and she pointed to a tray of about fifteen different sizes and types of rocks. It sounds unbelievable, but I'll tell you, her diagnoses and insights were amazingly accurate for all five people in the group.

Maria Juana helped me understand *heuristics*—the act of arriving at a decision not by following set rules but by being completely present to your sense in the moment. She taught me how fine-tuning to your immediate presence provides valid, actionable data. In this culture, we often dismiss, even ridicule, the world of precognition. But imagine if we could train our leaders to have her kind of presence! I find that the more clients develop a kind of heightened sensibility, the greater their competitive advantage.

The old saying, "plan your work and work your plan" still holds; it's advisable to have a plan and to follow it. But we're also finding that to reach higher levels of success, a plan-and-goal orientation has to be balanced with the heuristic ability to discern in the moment whether or not a particular steppingstone is the ultimate best choice.

Leadership coaching is all about negotiating that cutting edge of discernment. Strong leadership, by definition, is frontier territory that can be very lonely, unclear, and challenging. Just like a frontier on land, living at the professional forefront creates tension, confusion, and even chaos. It's easier to conform to the norm than to transform.

Because my clients tend to be at professional frontiers where challenges are always evolving, they have to develop their inner compasses to maintain a winning edge. Since they often find themselves with no road maps, fine-tuning their inner guidance systems ends up being a highly effective use of their time, although hard to reconcile within standard time management practices. I've seen people do well by staying the course on pre-determined paths. But, the opportunity to reach greatness only comes when leaders have the discernment and flexibility to hop on unexpected steppingstones because they can lead to unplanned-for successes.

Oprah stays true to her heart and mind to the point that it's actually her brand identity. In fact, Oprah has said that she never set a goal. She just knew intuitively that a more heuristic, or non-formulaic, more experiential, way was just as valid as the path that her television news colleagues were pursuing in their very goal-oriented, highly competitive field.

Oprah's a great demonstration of the heartedness that's part of greatness. But having her kind of heart is not for the faint-of-heart because, though simple, it is not usually an easy path. It's a lot easier to follow a goal-driven, predetermined path because it's much more predictable and less psychologically and/or emotionally challenging.

The nature of the heuristic path is more chaotic, but ultimately, it's more geared toward people building the lives they want, the work they love, and the world we all want to live in. If we could help leaders better incorporate the heuristics that Oprah and Maria Juana instinctively mastered, we would set new benchmarks for success. Unfortunately, on the ground, incorporating heuristics can be messy and take much more time than it seems like it should. But more recent indicators show that developing a better balance between heuristics and goal-driven approaches yields excellent returns on investment of time, talent, and treasure.

WRIGHT

Speaking of return on investment, judging from the studies on your Web site, the latest numbers on coaching are extraordinary, aren't they?

CARLEY

You know, they really are. And the interesting thing is that the numbers only represent the measureables. I don't believe we have adequate tools to fully assess coaching results yet, but studies show that the return on investment (ROI) in coaching ranges from 150 percent to 689 percent.

One surprising thing in those studies is that what I call coaching at the "leaderful" edge yields a far higher ROI than coaching strictly for problem-solving. Simply working with a coach or mentor to resolve an issue certainly pays off; however, the big payoffs happen when clients aren't in crisis but are coaching the way Olympic athletes do. Olympians don't go to coaches just to fix broken ankles or transition to new teams; they hire coaches to keep moving beyond the status quo. By using coaching to do the "soft" work of values alignment and vision development along with problem-solving and task execution, you can unleash formidable forces of passion, commitment, creativity, partnership, and action.

Before turning to full-time consulting, coaching, and speaking, I was a director of a philanthropic foundation and helped start up a community foundation. I have also sat on many boards of directors of non-governmental organizations. Over the years, I've coached and consulted with hundreds of successful professionals throughout a wide range of sectors. My experience tells me that success really can't be pinned down to a dollar figure. Is money important? Absolutely! But you get the best return on a coaching investment that helps you balance your dollar data with the data from your inner GPS.

WRIGHT

What do you mean by "inner GPS?"

CARLEY

Your inner GPS is a lot like a real GPS—the Global Positioning System receiver in a car that lets you type in where you want to go and automatically tells you how to get there. Both your inner GPS and a mechanical GPS are highly accurate guidance systems, but the inner one is hard-wired for reaching your full potential and it always leads toward your greatest good.

From searching for answers all over the world and from working with extraordinary clients, I've learned that reaching full potential is a constant unfolding of personal vision and the capacity to realize it. Whereas a real GPS receiver takes you to a particular destination, the journey with your inner GPS is a lifelong, ever-unfolding path. You don't just fully "potentiate" one day and then you're done.

One big difference between the two is that our internal GPS can be much trickier to access because unlike the mechanical one, it gets a lot of static from the world around us and from our own internal racket. Both GPS systems point the way toward our desired destinations but our personal one is more challenging to follow. Much of coaching is about helping clients clear the static so they can better access their own GPS's for a smoother, more efficient journey to success.

It's difficult to quantify what tapping into that internal GPS looks and feels like. Some people describe it as a flow, or a zone, or a vibe. Different people have distinctive sensations; some feel it in their stomachs, some on the backs of their necks, some "hear" it in their minds, and others just feel a general sense of things. Regardless of the manifestation, the more people follow it, the clearer it gets.

Unfortunately, current productivity models are based on old paradigm systems that totally disregard the intuitive and other "softer" indicators. It's clear now that leadership development methods that don't account for the inner GPS factor are under-developed, yet they're still over-relied on. We are beginning to create the instruments to quantify so-called "softer" indicators, but it will take generations before we can fully integrate "flow/zone/vibe/knowing" kinds of measurements into organizational assessment tools. The more we do, the more we will capture the moral spark that fuels the best of best practices.

I've done transition coaching with people who thought that they were going to be entrepreneurs but ended up going the corporate route, and vice versa. Just like a mechanical GPS receiver, their inner GPS's allowed for recalculation. I've never seen it fail—the inner GPS is incredibly accurate. Nonetheless, when it steers you off the path you thought you were on, it can be disorienting and can lead to personal and interpersonal misinterpretations, some of them quite damaging.

The mechanical GPS has a very non-judgmental way of simply saying "recalculating" when you make a mistake or change your mind or choose to go a different way because you knew more about the road you were on than the GPS did. Attuning to the internal GPS isn't nearly so accommodating because we have to interpret it through the personal and cultural cacophony around us.

For example, imagine if your spouse or boss was navigating and you missed a turn; it's unlikely that their words would be as neutral as your car GPS's simple "recalculating." In fact, as great a coach as a spouse or colleague can truly be, the lack of attachment to outcomes is part of what makes professional coaching so effective. Because, in the coaching relationship, when it's time for a shift, there is no judgment, no fuss, and no grounds for divorce—just a conscious recalculation.

It won't always take you on the route you've envisioned, but your inner GPS will take you exactly where you want to go. We all know the best choices for ourselves. Sometimes, though, the voice of wisdom is impeded by the static of old-paradigm success indicators, of other people's needs, of defining "right" according to arcane standards, and of old stories about who we are and what we do.

For example, I have a client I'll call Lou who lives in Los Angeles. Lou hired me after he started a radical sabbatical. He'd risen high in the ranks of the advertising industry at a very young age and had totally burned out, but he'd saved enough money to take a year off. We spent months exploring possibilities from his moving to a small town and opening up a little ad agency or getting a job in somebody else's, to opening up his own wine store or a travel agency. You name it, it came up over the "research and development" phase of Lou's transition.

He started exploring values-driven leadership and the more he learned about it, the more it resonated. He thought it could never happen, but he ended up going back into the ad business, earning a healthy three-figure income as a partner in one of the world's top three firms. While it's almost the antithesis of a values-driven industry, he's in a position to introduce values-driven distinctions into the culture every day. He got the position three years ago but we've continued our coaching sessions to ensure he is doing his job in the most joyful, leaderful, life-enriching way possible.

Another client, Linda, recently turned down a position that would have paid more than $500,000 a year. My mother asked me why somebody wouldn't fire me for missing out on that kind of opportunity! But Linda's internal GPS was clear that at this stage in her career, she's feeling led to make a difference. That particular job wouldn't have changed the world enough to satisfy her.

WRIGHT

Is the inner GPS spiritual?

CARLEY

It can be, but not everybody experiences it that way. We can all be successful, wise, and good, regardless of our spiritual orientations. Our inner guidance system is certainly mysterious—the more we understand it, the more questions we have. It has a lot to do with values because they function like internal GPS coordinates. Nothing derails the journey to ultimate success faster than compromising your values. When we stay true to our unique value systems, we move toward full potential with every choice we make. A strong GPS signal requires ethics, compassion, and the understanding that personal development is critical for professional growth.

Taking time to deliberate and to wrestle with your core values helps you make wiser choices. Developing a reliable inner GPS requires dedicated time, space, and focus. People use many ways to tap into the GPS "zone"—organized religion, walking in nature, playing an instrument, meditating, running, and so on. Even though they seem unrelated to work life, those kinds of activities can catapult careers.

Personally, I'm on a spiritual path of many paths. But whether or not clients have any kind of spiritual leanings, they develop reliable GPS's when they choose to live life without any blinders—when they refuse to ignore what's going on in the world around them and they demand authenticity, dignity, truthfulness, civility, and compassion.

WRIGHT

Can you help your clients learn to rely on their own GPS's?

CARLEY

Yes, I can. I know from experience that if you master the courage and discernment to follow your inner guidance you'll rise far beyond standard measures of success. It's only logical because, ultimately, only you know what's best for you. You're the expert on when it's time to build your soil or time to fruit, when it's time to step up or stand still or to say yes or say no. Leadership coaching helps you discern when it's time to load a new destination into your GPS, or to follow its direction, or to trust your instincts to take a detour.

This might seem like bad business on my part, but my objective is to make myself obsolete. My goal is for clients to become their own best coaches by relying on their inner GPS's, which is not as easy as it seems because it not only requires staying on top of your professional game but also keeping up with personal homework.

WRIGHT

When you say "personal homework," I imagine you mean taking care of your "baggage" or doing self-reflection. Is your work similar to a therapist's job?

CARLEY

No—leadership coaching is very different from therapy or even life coaching. I have a holistic approach to professional development, so personal issues do come up. But, I'm definitely not a therapist. Although I do believe that the more you work out your "stuff" the more available you are when opportunities arise, my work is not therapy.

The difference between therapy and coaching is like the difference between an Olympic coach and a physical therapist. Therapists work on healing what's hurting, digging into the causes, and naming the pathology. Coaching is about real-world, inspired action. Therapy is important work; I don't hesitate to refer people to it. I don't do therapy but I do support clarifying unresolved issues because they can become roadblocks on the path to success.

Everybody's got personal issues—even if you had perfect parents and nobody ever teased you—they're just part of the human condition. The coaching context uses issues as steppingstones to change. People who have experienced the kind of personal exploration and development that therapy offers can sometimes move forward faster in coaching; but if they've spent too much time contemplating themselves, it can perpetuate a personal narrative that's stuck in a cycle of limitation. Good leaders take time to self-reflect but, instead of getting into ruts, they turn their insights into gold and sometimes my job is to support that process.

It takes a lot of tenacity to break through old ideas of what success is, and sometimes the process creates psychological discomfort. In the therapy model, you would dissect that discomfort and connect it with past experiences, whereas coaching turns the scars into stars to create a stronger personal foundation for supporting professional excellence. Many people are unconscious of how much their personal issues show up at work. When they raise their awareness of themselves, they become clearer leaders who are much easier to work with.

One problem with the coaching field is that many coaches believe you have to be positive 100 percent of the time and never embrace the negative stuff. But, just like a seed has to fall apart in dark soil in order to grow, sometimes we have to fall apart into our challenges in order to get to the win. For some, the falling apart requires a therapist; for others it's an opportunity to coach toward restacking the deck exactly the way you want it. To do that in a more personal way, hire a life coach; in a more professional way, hire a leadership coach.

WRIGHT

You seem to bring a unique depth and breadth to your work. Your clients must appreciate your perspective.

CARLEY

Thanks—I hope so! I certainly have a passion for my work. I've learned so much from scientists, cutting-edge personal and professional development experts, scholars, and other thought leaders. I've explored human potential in a monastery in Thailand, in a seminary in New York, with shamans in the Amazon jungle, tribal leaders in the African bush, and in boardrooms, as well as countless classrooms. I've participated firsthand as many board members and business and organizational leaders debated their next steps. I've come to the conclusion that we are now making an evolutionary quantum leap in our definitions of leadership and professionalism.

"Quantum" is an interesting word because when you put it with the word "leap," it means a big, dramatic movement. But "quantum" as a noun means the smallest of the small, like a photon, which is so tiny that scientists don't even know whether it's a particle or a wave. Some of the biggest leaps in my own life have been almost invisible to the naked eye. I have the privilege of partnering with clients through the big leaps as well as the little moves that create profound differences in career paths.

What sets my methodology apart is that it isn't just about linear movement. Too much leadership coaching is still based on old paradigm distinctions and on one-size-fits-all methodologies. I find, though, that when the voice of wisdom is amplified, it naturally strengthens leadership. It seems like a paradox—if you pay attention to the "softer" things by going for breadth and depth instead of just focusing on a series of goals, it will make you weaker. But history and leadership studies, as well as my professional experience, have shown the opposite.

WRIGHT

So how exactly do you work?

CARLEY

Much like an Olympic coach partners with an athlete on the road to success, I help clients and organizations negotiate their paths. I work mostly by phone, either with individuals or in MasterMind groups, and I also do on-site consulting. I have a number of different one-on-one coaching plans that are explained on my

Web site. People usually register online and/or they e-mail me at manager@drjoni.com to schedule the first session or to talk about custom on-site solutions or keynote talks and workshops or seminars.

Not that long ago, I realized that such high caliber clients could, in fact, contribute to each other's successes so I started Wisdom at Work MasterMind Coaching groups. These groups are usually limited to five members who meet over two months by phone, and the package includes deeply discounted individual sessions. By putting their businesses "on the table" to work intensively *on* them, group members unleash possibilities that they just can't get to while working day-to-day *in* their businesses. MasterMind Coaching groups are a good bargain because members tend to share resources and insights generously; so in addition to getting more economical coaching with me, participants fuel one another's sparks.

I also offer a Wisdom at Work self-coaching program on my Web site.

WRIGHT

What an interesting conversation, I've learned a lot here today; you've given me a lot of new information. I really appreciate the time you've taken this afternoon to answer my questions.

CARLEY

Well, thank you for asking them! It's been my pleasure.

WRIGHT

We've been talking with Dr. Joni Carley, a knowledgeable and entertaining speaker whose international consulting practice serves successful leaders, professionals, and entrepreneurs.

Dr. Carley, thank you so much for being with us today on *Stepping Stones to Success*.

CARLEY

You're welcome and thank you!

ABOUT THE AUTHOR

DR. JONI CARLEY'S international consulting company serves successful leaders, professionals, and entrepreneurs. Just like Olympic coaches work with athletes who are already strong, Dr. Joni coaches individual clients, organizations, and MasterMind groups to go from bronze to gold. She's also a dynamic keynote speaker and workshop leader for companies and organizations of all sizes.

She has incomparable expertise in facilitating transformation from the inside out, and in helping to close the gaps between where you are and where you want to be. Her clients maintain a sharp, "leaderful" edge so that they produce an abundant triple bottom line in terms of people, profits, and the planet.

Dr. Joni has been coaching, speaking, and teaching for more than twenty-five years. She has traveled the world to learn from and collaborate with leading personal and professional development experts and she holds a doctorate in The Reinvention of Work. Her leadership coaching addresses core issues for sustainable results so that her clients do more than excel—they leave legacies.

Keynote and workshop audiences have said: she "changed my life," "inspired me," and that they'll "use her material for the rest of my life" because Dr. Joni's content draws from a unique depth and breadth of experience ranging from the Amazon jungle to the boardroom, from the United Nations to college campuses, and from working with top-level corporate executives to solopreneurs.

Her blog, *Wisdom at Work↔Wisdom in the World,* is an entertaining and enlightening professional resource (available on her Web site).

DR. JONI CARLEY
910 Twyckenham Rd.
Media, PA 19063
610-566-9927
joni@drjoni.com
www.drjoni.com
(enter "stones" at checkout for a 10 percent discount on products)

CHAPTER FIFTEEN

Developing Sales Team - Organically

An Interview with . . . **Dave Kurlan**

DAVID WRIGHT (WRIGHT)

Today we're talking with Dave Kurlan. Dave is the best-selling author of Baseline Selling: How to Become a Sales Superstar by Using What You Already Know about the Game of Baseball. He hosts Meet the Sales Experts, a weekly business radio show and is a top rated speaker and the leading expert on the subject of sales force development. Dave has published more than five hundred articles on sales and sales management. He is the Founder and CEO of Objective Management Group, the company that continues to pioneer the sales assessment industry. He is also the Founder and CEO of Kurlan and Associates, a national sales development firm.

Dave, welcome to Stepping Stones to Success.

DAVE KURLAN (KURLAN)

Thank you, David. It's nice to be here.

WRIGHT

So how do baseball and sales come together for you?

KURLAN

That's a great question. I've been a lifelong sales guy. I've been selling since I got out of school and I've been in the sales development business for twenty-five years. I've been a lifelong, diehard Red Sox fan which, until 2004, when they won their first World Series in 86 years, was a painful thing to be. Back in 2004 it dawned on me that there ought to be a way to put those two things—sales and baseball—together. I was moved to write a new book at that point. I was frustrated as a sales development expert; I was frustrated with what was happening in the sales training industry. At that time, our company, Objective Management Group, had data on 250,000 salespeople we had assessed and 74 percent of them sucked! At that time there were fourteen million salespeople in the United States, and I just couldn't understand why three quarters of them were so bad.

It caused me to take a critical look at what was going on in our industry and I concluded that it was really the fault of the experts in our industry—authors, experts, trainers, and gurus—and I was part of that mess. We had all complicated selling to such a degree with our seven, ten, and twelve steps along with non-intuitive acronyms and hokey techniques. It had become so difficult for salespeople to not only learn it, but apply it, that most of what was being taught wasn't being used.

So I saw baseball with its simple analogy of first base, second base, third base, and home as a great metaphor to simplify the sales process using some of the things that we know and love about baseball as examples for what really has to happen when we're selling.

WRIGHT

Interesting.

You pioneered the sales assessment industry. How did that come about?

KURLAN

Well, I guess I'm a guy who just gets frustrated a lot. Back in the 1980s when I was training a lot of salespeople for companies, I was frustrated because I could turn some salespeople into superstars, and I could help others become great, but there were always around 30 percent of the salespeople in every company who resisted. They didn't improve, results didn't change, they weren't motivated to change, and it frustrated me. I kept asking myself why I couldn't achieve greater success with a greater number of salespeople.

So I turned to assessments for an answer. I thought that the insights contained in assessments would help me develop a better understanding of this group of salespeople and I did get a better understanding. But they completely failed to help me help these people any more than before, so I was forced to develop my own assessments.

Back in the '80s, the goal of the first assessment I created was nothing more than to smoke out the salespeople who made up the 30 percent I wouldn't be able to change or help so my clients and I wouldn't waste resources on them. But over a short period of time it became much more than that because I had a way of looking at things differently than behavioral scientists.

Behavioral scientists would publish an article and say something like, "We interviewed one thousand salespeople and we determined that the successful salespeople had these nine traits in common. Well, they did have those nine traits in common, but the unsuccessful salespeople had those nine traits in common too! So those nine traits failed to differentiate the top salespeople because they were common among all the people who were in sales.

So I set out to see what was different about the lousy salespeople instead of what was different about the great salespeople. And those differences eventually became the basis for the assessments we created over the next twenty years. Those first assessments created in the early '90s evolved into the assessments we provide today.

When we work with companies and help them grow revenue, we begin with sales force evaluations. We look at the people, strategies, systems, and processes. As a result of the information we obtain and our proprietary analyses, we're able to answer questions like: is the sales force capable of executing the company's strategies? What affect is sales management having on the salespeople? Has the company been hiring the right people and, if not, what must they change in their hiring criteria and selection process? Who can be trained and developed? How much better can they become? What would the return on the investment be?

Many companies are beginning to recognize that many of their salespeople behave more like order takers and account managers. They really need them to make a transition to being more proactive—more like hunters and closers. They also need them to be more consultative so that they're listening more effectively and asking better questions. We wanted to be able to answer questions like, "Which of your salespeople can make that kind of a transition?"

So, circling back to how the assessments came about, it was really born out of frustration. Unlike most assessments that are created in a social context, ours was actually designed and built specifically for sales. The questions are all asked in a sales context and we're able to accurately report sales findings. When I become frustrated, it often leads to industry-changing philosophies, tools, systems, and processes.

WRIGHT

So why should a company evaluate its sales force?

KURLAN

Well, that's another great question and they shouldn't, unless they're frustrated with their results. If they have a sales force and everybody on the sales organization is overachieving, there is certainly not much reason to dig deep and learn what has to change in order to get better results. But let's say the company has a sales force like so many sales organizations today. While 10 percent to 20 percent of its salespeople are overachieving, 20 percent to 25 percent are failing and everyone else is underachieving. It would certainly be beneficial to find out the underlying causes for that and why revenue isn't where it needs to be. If the company has a history of hiring salespeople who don't rise to the cream of the crop, the leaders in the company would be able to learn what they're doing wrong and what they could do differently to become much more effective finding, interviewing, selecting, hiring, and retaining successful salespeople on a consistent basis.

WRIGHT

Once you've shared the results of a sales force evaluation, what happens next?

KURLAN

Most company leaders are somewhat surprised to hear the results. By surprised, I mean, "We had no idea that this is why these salespeople weren't finding new business" or "So that's why we were only closing four out of one hundred proposals" or "We had no idea that was the reason our margins were so low," or "Now we understand why so many closings were delayed." They find it very insightful.

After we've spent three to four hours reviewing the findings and putting an action plan together, the leaders will want to fix the problems we identified. The next step is usually a process of fixing everything that ails them.

WRIGHT

So what are the keys to developing a sales force?

KURLAN

There are a number of keys. First and foremost, a company must work with an expert on the outside who has done this many, many times, in many, many industries, and really knows his or her stuff inside and out. It's not a time to be taking chances with somebody who has done it once or twice or did it in their own business.

Second, you must be working on the right issues. Most firms that work with sales forces are sales training companies, limited to providing training, and it's seldom in the context of the very systems, processes, strategies, and infrastructure that must be modified or created, and it's often not in the context of desired results. So it's really important that it be an integrated approach, through sales force development, as opposed to sales training.

Third, along the lines of integration, all of the issues have to be dealt with. You can't just say, "We will fix the underperforming salespeople" because if you train the salespeople and you haven't first created the necessary sales infrastructure, or developed sales management, the sales training won't have the desired result. If you only fix the sales management team, but you don't develop the reps, the sales managers don't have the ability to develop those salespeople either. And if you work on training sales management and the reps without getting the right infrastructure in place, then it's difficult to track, analyze, troubleshoot, coach, hold salespeople accountable, and predict revenue.

So ideally, you first work on the sales infrastructure—systems, processes, tools, pipeline, and metrics. Then you work to develop the sales management team and make them proficient in sales process, sales coaching, sales motivation, and sales accountability. Then you work on recruiting, making the required changes with regard to selection criteria, and the recruiting process. You cast the net further so you capture more candidates. You assess those candidates in the very first step of the process, filtering out the people who aren't right for the job. Then you conduct phone screening, interviews, hire the right salespeople, and turn them over to sales management for on-boarding.

Finally, when all the right people are in place, the infrastructure is in place, and the sales management team is ready, it's time to develop the salespeople. That should include competency development, skill development, sales process, and the thing that most companies ignore, helping them overcome the weaknesses that prevent them from executing what they learn. If you merely give them skills, they will have a new vocabulary but still won't be able to do anything that they weren't able to do before. But, if you help them overcome their weaknesses, and their discomforts dissipate, then they'll be able to utilize the process, skills, strategies, and tactics that they are shown how to use during sales team development.

WRIGHT

So what are some of the biggest challenges to sales management improvement?

KURLAN

The single biggest challenge affecting salespeople and sales managers is the very thing that got them into sales and sales management in the first place. Most of them are likable, sociable, get along great with people, and the group I just described has a need for people to like them—they have a need for approval. It prevents sales managers from being tough, firm, demanding, holding salespeople accountable, and asking tough questions during coaching and debriefing sessions. It prevents salespeople from asking good, tough, timely questions. Those questions would uncover the compelling reasons to buy, eliminate objections, and get opportunities closed. Need for approval is a huge obstacle to achieving excellence in either sales or sales management.

WRIGHT

Can anyone learn to sell or are people born to sell?

KURLAN

Clearly there are some people who are born to sell and there are some people who are born not to sell. But in between there is a huge population of people that could learn to sell and whether or not they succeed depends first and foremost on how badly they want to. If the desire to be successful is strong enough and the commitment to do what it takes is great enough, then absolutely, that group can learn to be good because they have the incentive to overcome weaknesses, obstacles, and challenges.

Let's take another group of people who seem to have the innate talent and personality, and who are likeable and friendly. If they don't want it badly enough and they're not committed to achieving that level of success, then at best, they're destined for mediocrity, and more likely a miserable journey in the field of sales.

WRIGHT

So what are some of the biggest obstacles that prevent salespeople from being great?

KURLAN

In addition to the need for approval, there are some other weaknesses that get in the way.

One of the weaknesses I identified back in the 1980s was something I call the "Non-Supportive Buy Cycle." Businesspeople are familiar with the term "sales cycle"—the amount of time between when a prospect is identified and when he or she pays for what is bought. The Buy Cycle identifies the way individuals go about the process of making a major purchase. There are several components to the Buy Cycle: whether they comparison shop, price shop, conduct research, think it over at decision-making time, and how much is "a lot of money" to them.

The Buy Cycle becomes non-supportive when their behaviors don't support the ideal outcomes we would want from a sales process. If salespeople comparison shop, they're going to be less effective when their prospects want to speak with them and four or five of their competitors. They'll simply understand that and won't be able to execute the strategies and the tactics that neutralize the buying strategy.

The same applies when a salesperson who is a price shopper meets with a prospect who is looking for the lowest price. The salesperson automatically thinks, "I must have the lowest price" but, in reality, most business does not take place based on price alone. Most business is based on many other criteria, but salespeople with this belief will be vulnerable to prospects who want to buy at the lowest price because they think it's normal.

Salespeople who think it over for any period time are vulnerable to prospects who, at closing time, say, "We need to think about it." Then the salesperson thinks, "That makes sense. When can I follow up?" Salespeople who don't need to think it over think to themselves, "Well, this isn't right," and start asking questions like, "Why?" or "I must have missed something" and "Usually when somebody says he [or she] needs to think it over it's because I did something wrong or the person is not sold on this. Can we back up and talk about it?" Salespeople with a Non-Supportive Buy Cycle aren't able to use the strategies and tactics that help to overcome indecision. They empathize with objections, but empathy is only important when it's to empathize with a problem they can solve.

264

The Non-Supportive Buy Cycle also includes something I call "low money tolerance." When a salesperson thinks $500 is a lot of money and he or she is selling something for $10,000, the salesperson is quite vulnerable to a prospect who says, "Wow, that's an awful lot of money." The salesperson is dead in the water because that's $9,500 over his or her choking point. So once again, even if salespeople have strategies and tactics to overcome this objection, they don't come from conviction because they don't believe it themselves. The Non-Supportive Buy Cycle is deadly for salespeople. It gets in the way and costs companies millions and millions of dollars in lost revenue because it causes salespeople to be so ineffective.

WRIGHT

That really makes sense. This is the first time I've ever heard that.

You talk a lot about over achievement. Will you elaborate for our readers?

KURLAN

Sure. If your company has an accounting department, a CFO, or a bookkeeper, financial accounts are reconciled, and a report is filed with the CEO at the end of the period. Imagine the CFO saying, "We just finished reconciling the books for the second quarter and we were able to account for almost 92 percent of your money." If the CEO heard something that ridiculous, the CFO would be gone. Imagine a quality control director telling the CEO, "Last month, quality control identified that we were at 92 percent." Since it's supposed to be at 99.99999 percent, the quality director would be out. Think about any department where there is a measurable that must be met and when it's not damn near 100 percent, it's unacceptable. But for some reason we've come to accept so much mediocrity from the sales organization, that if the VP of Sales reports that "We were at 95 percent of quota last month," everybody is having a party, doing a dance, back-slapping, and making arrangements for a celebration. But they failed! 95 percent is failure.

So I don't believe it's appropriate to ask or talk about whether we are reaching our goals or not. I think doing so just sets us up for more failure because the "or-not" option is still in place. In order for companies to move beyond failure, they must have higher expectations, along with systems, processes, tools, and programs in place that support those expectations. Companies must think about only overachievement. Overachieve or achieve, but underachieving is no longer accepted in our company. They must hire and fire, and train and develop—all with overachievement in mind.

Here is a shortcut. You know the 80/20 rule, right? It states that 80 percent of our sales force is going to suck or that 80 percent of our business is going to come from 20 percent of our salespeople. Get rid of that rule and replace it with my 100/0 rule, where 100 percent of our salespeople will overachieve. Once that's in place, you will totally change the way you deal with your sales organization from sales management on down to the salespeople. I just have a problem with mediocrity.

WRIGHT

So how can a company dominate its market and consistently beat its competition?

KURLAN

One of the secrets to market domination and consistently beating the competition is to try not to do it so much through marketing but to do it through sales. If it's a transactional product—something we'll all go to the store and buy—then it must be done through marketing. But if it's an expensive product, capital equipment, or a competitive product and if we're the underdog, if we have a story to tell, or it's complex, then it has to be done through the sales organization. The best way to consistently beat the competition is to understand who the enemy is. The enemy is not the competition, not ourself, and not our company. The enemy is resistance, and most salespeople in most sales organizations don't effectively know how to overcome resistance.

The secret to overcoming resistance is to not defend, explain, validate, provide reasons, features, benefits, and bullet points. It's just to acknowledge that the person stating his or her opinion is probably right. That lowers resistance. It's not until resistance is lowered that salespeople can effectively sell anything. So you can achieve market domination by understanding who the enemy is and knowing how to overcome it.

WRIGHT

That is very interesting.

Well, what a great conversation, Dave. I really appreciate all this time you've taken with me this morning to answer these questions. The take-away I have is that the bottom line to selling is an inside job, isn't it?

KURLAN

Yes it is, and when a sales organization is properly tooled, staffed, and managed, that inside job becomes an outside job.

WRIGHT

Very interesting. Thank you so much for being so willing to share all of these thoughts about selling and building companies' sales forces with me. I really learned a lot and I'm sure our readers will also.

KURLAN

It was a pleasure to take part. Thanks for inviting me.

WRIGHT

Today we've been talking with Dave Kurlan. Dave is a best-selling author and business radio talk show host. He is a top rated speaker and leading expert on the subject of sales force development. His company is a pioneer in the sales assessment industry. Listening to him today I believe he knows what he is talking about, at least I'm listening.

Dave, thank you so much for being with us today on Stepping Stones to Success.

KURLAN

You're very welcome.

ABOUT THE AUTHOR

DAVE KURLAN is the best-selling author of *Baseline Selling: How to Become a Sales Superstar by Using What You Already Know about the Game of Baseball*. He hosts *Meet the Sales Experts*, a weekly business radio show and is a top rated speaker and the leading expert on the subject of sales force development. Dave has published more than five hundred articles on sales and sales management. He is the Founder and CEO of Objective Management Group, the company that continues to pioneer the sales assessment industry. He is also the Founder and CEO of Kurlan and Associates, a national sales development firm.

DAVE KURLAN

114 Turnpike Rd., Ste. 102
Westboro, MA 01581
508-389-9350
dkurlan@kurlanassociates.com
www.davekurlan.com

CHAPTER SIXTEEN

Develop a Disciplined Life
An Interview with . . . **Dr. Denis Waitley**

DAVID WRIGHT (WRIGHT)

Today we are talking with Dr. Denis Waitley. Denis is one of America's most respected authors, keynote lecturers, and productivity consultants on high performance human achievement. He has inspired, informed, challenged, and entertained audiences for more than twenty-five years from the boardrooms of multi-national corporations to the control rooms of NASA's space program and from the locker rooms of world-class athletes to the meeting rooms of thousands of conventioneers throughout the world.

With more than ten million audio programs sold in fourteen languages, Denis Waitley is the most listened-to voice on personal and career success. He is the author of twelve non-fiction books, including several international bestsellers. His audio album, "The Psychology of Winning," is the all-time best-selling program on self-mastery. Dr. Waitley is a founding director of the National Council on Self-Esteem and the President's Council on Vocational Education. He recently received

269

the "Youth Flame Award" from the National Council on Youth Leadership for his outstanding contribution to high school youth leadership.

A graduate of the U.S. Naval Academy Annapolis, and former Navy pilot, he holds a doctorate degree in human behavior.

Denis, it is my sincere pleasure to welcome you to *Stepping Stones to Success!* Thank you for being with us today.

DR. DENIS WAITLEY (WAITLEY)

David, it's great to be with you again. It's been too long. I always get excited when I know you're going to call. Maybe we can make some good things happen for those who are really interested in getting ahead and moving forward with their own careers in their lives.

WRIGHT

I know our readers would enjoy hearing you talk about your formative years. Will you tell us a little about your life growing up in the context of what you've achieved and what shaped you into the person you are today? Do you remember one or two pivotal experiences that propelled you on the path you eventually chose?

WAITLEY

I believe many of us are redwood trees in a flowerpot. We've become root-bound by our earlier environment and it's up to each of us to realize that and break out of our flower pot if we're going to grow to our full potential.

I remember my father left our home when I was a little boy. He said goodnight and goodbye and suddenly I became the man of the family at age nine. My little brother was only two, so I had to carry him around as my little shadow for the ensuing years. To this day my kid brother has always looked at me as his dad, even though there is only seven years' difference between us. He'll phone me and ask what he should do and I'll tell him, "I'm your brother, not your father!"

Our dad was a great guy but he drank too much and had some habits that took a firm hold on him. He never abused me and always expected more from me than he did from himself. I had a push-pull—on the one hand, I felt inadequate and guilty when I would go to succeed but on the other hand, Dad kept feeding me the idea that he missed his ship and I'd catch mine. The only thing I could do to get out of that roller coaster impact was to ride my bicycle twenty miles every Saturday over to my grandmother's house. She was my escape. I would mow her lawn and she would give me such great feedback and reinforcement. She told me to plant the seeds of greatness as she and I planted our "victory garden" during World War II. She told me that weeds would come unannounced and uninvited—I didn't need to worry about weeds coming into my life, they didn't even need to be watered.

I said, "Wow! You don't have to water weeds?"

"No," she replied, "they'll show up in your life and what you need to do, my grandson, is model your life after people who've been consistent and real in their contribution as role models and mentors."

She also told me that a library card would eventually be much more valuable than a Master Card. Because of my grandmother reading biographies of people who'd overcome so much more than I was going through, I thought, "Wow! I don't have any problems compared to some of these great people in history who really came from behind to get ahead." I think that was my start in life.

I went to the Naval Academy because the Korean War was in force and you had to serve your country, so the best way was to run and hide in an academy. If you earned enough good grades you were put through without a scholarship or without money from your parents. Since my parents didn't have any money, it was a great way to get a college education.

I became a Navy pilot after that and learned that if you simulate and rehearse properly you'll probably learn to fly that machine. But much of it has to do with the amount of practice you put into ground school and into going through the paces. As I gained experience being a Navy pilot, I eventually decided to go on and get my advanced degree in psychology because I wanted to develop people rather than stay in the military. I pursued a program where I could take my military and more disciplined background and put it into human development. That's basically the story.

I earned my doctorate, I met Jonas Salk, and Dr. Salk introduced me to some pioneers in the behavioral field. Then along came Earl Nightingale who heard just a simple taped evening speech of mine and decided that maybe my voice was good enough, even though I was a "new kid on the block," to maybe do an album on personal development, which I did in 1978. It surprised me the most, and everyone else also, that it became one of the bestsellers of all time.

WRIGHT

Being a graduate of Annapolis and having been a Navy pilot, to what degree did your experience in the Navy shape your life and your ideas about productivity and performance?

WAITLEY

David, I think those experiences shaped my life and ideas a great deal. I was an original surfer boy from California and when I entered the Naval Academy I found that surfer boys had their heads shaved and were told to go stand in line—everyone's successful so you're nothing special. I found myself on a team that was very competitive but at the same time had good camaraderie.

I realized that I didn't have the kind of discipline structure in my life that I needed. I also discovered that all these other guys were as talented, or more talented, than I was. What that shaped for me was realizing that the effort required to become successful is habit-forming. I think I learned healthy habits at the Academy and as a Navy pilot just to stay alive. To perform these kinds of functions I really had to have a more disciplined life. That set me on my stage for working more on a daily basis at habit formation than just being a positive thinker only.

WRIGHT

In our book, *Stepping Stones to Success,* we're exploring a variety of issues related to human nature and the quest to succeed. In your best-selling program, *The Psychology of Winning,* you focus on building self-esteem, motivation, and self-discipline. Why are these so crucial to winning and success?

WAITLEY

They're so crucial they're misunderstood. I think especially the term "self-esteem" is misunderstood. We've spent a fortune and we had a California committee on it—we formed the National Council on Self-Esteem. What has happened, in my opinion, is that self-esteem has been misused and misjudged as being self-indulgence, self-gratification—a celebrity kind of mentality. We've put too much emphasis on the wrong idea about self-esteem.

Self-esteem is actually the deep down, inside the skin feeling of your own worth regardless of your age, ethnicity, gender, or level of current performance. It's really a belief that you're good enough to invest in education and effort and you believe some kind of dream when that's all you have to hang onto.

What's happened, unfortunately, is that we've paid so much attention to self-esteem it's become a celebrity and an arena mentality kind of concept. Most people are "struttin' their stuff" and they're celebrating after every good play on the athletic field, whereas, if you're a *real* professional, that's what you do anyway. A real professional is humble, gracious, and understands fans. I think that what we've done is put too much emphasis on asserting one's self and believing that you're the greatest and then talking about it too much or showing off too much in order to make that self-esteem public.

The real self-esteem has two aspects: 1) Believing that you deserve as much as anyone else and that you're worthy. Someone may look at you and tell you they see real potential in you. If you can feel that you have potential and you're worth the effort, that's the first step. 2) The second step is to start doing things to give you confidence so that when you do something and learn something it works out and you'll get the self-confidence that comes from reinforcing small successes. That combination of expectation and reinforcement is fundamental to anyone who wants to be a high achiever. That's what self-esteem is really all about—deserving on the one hand and reinforcing success in small ways to get your motor running and feel the confidence that you can do better than you have been.

Fears crop up and get in the way of our motivation. In my case I was afraid of success. Nobody had ever succeeded in our family and because they hadn't, I felt inadequate to be able to succeed. Whenever it would show up around the corner I would think, "Well, this is too good to be true for me—I don't deserve that." So I would feel a little bit doubtful of my abilities. When I would succeed, there would be an attendant, "Yelp!" I would feel because I would not believe I deserved what I had achieved.

I think fear is the thing that gets in the way of our motivation because we're all motivated by inhibitions and compulsions. You should be motivated more by the result you want rather than the penalty. That's why I've always said that winners are motivated by reward of success rather than inhibited or compelled by the penalty of failure. If you get this conviction that you're as good as the best but no better than the rest—I'm worth the effort, I'm not Mr. Wonderful, I'm not the center of the universe but I can do some things that I haven't done yet—and then apply this motivation to desire rather than fear, that is when self-discipline comes into play.

I'd have to say, David, I could spend the entire interview on self-discipline because I missed it as one of the most important ingredients in success. I've always been a belief guy, an optimism guy, a faith guy, and all the self-esteem things but I think, as time went on, I forgot the amount of discipline it takes for anyone who is a champion in any endeavor. I think I'm back on that track now.

WRIGHT

I can really appreciate the Flame Award you won from the National Council on Youth Leadership for helping high school leaders. I've got a daughter in college and I know how difficult and important it is. But in some circles, self-esteem has gotten a bad reputation. For example, in many schools, teachers won't reward high achievers for fear of hurting the self-esteem of others in the classroom. Many people feel this is not helpful to these children.

In your opinion, where is the balance between building healthy self-esteem and preparing kids and adults to cope and succeed in a competitive world?

WAITLEY

I think that there has to first of all be some kind of performance standard. A good example is the Olympic Games. The idea of the Olympic Games is to set a standard that you've tried to live up to in your own way as a world-class person, realizing that there can only be so many Olympians and so many gold medalists and so on. I think, on the one hand, it's really important to have standards because if you have a standard, then you have something tangible to shoot for or to measure against.

I think there's a problem, however, in that only so many people can be medalists and win medals at the Olympics. One of the reasons that the high jump bar, for example, is set so that everyone can jump over it the first time, is to experience the feeling of success that first jump produces. The feeling of success is working in the competitor before the bar is raised to world record height and to much higher standards than even the normal Olympian.

I'm one who believes in testing. It's difficult when you have a "No Child Left Behind" concept because many times today we're going pass/fail. We're moving people up through the grades regardless of their performance simply because we don't want them left behind and therefore feeling that they're not able to function simply because they can't compete with some students who've been given many more opportunities to succeed than others.

Having said that, I'd say that healthy self-esteem is gained by giving specific stair-step, incremental, bite-sized pieces; perhaps there needs to be several different standards set. Usually the grading system does that and the point system does that where you have someone who has a four point three grade average because of all the extra credits they're taking. Then you have those with a three point eight and then those who are just barely passing. Unfortunately then, what that does is enable only a few people to get into universities and the others have to go to community colleges.

What I will have to say, however, is that we in the United States have to be very careful that we don't dumb down or lower our standards for excellence in our schools. Traveling as much as I do, I have discovered information about this. For example, there are 300 universities in Beijing alone—just in one city in China. The way it goes internationally is that the public schools in Japan, for example, are much more competitive than the private schools. If you're in Japan going to a public school, you have to really perform up to the highest standards in order to ever think of qualifying for any kind of university. You'd have to go into a vocational school if you didn't compete in higher standards in public schools in Japan. The same thing is true in Singapore, China, and in the developing nations.

We have a situation brewing here where we've got global developing countries with really high standards in English, mathematics, engineering, and science. And we have educators in the United States who are more concerned about making sure that the self-esteem of an individual doesn't get damaged by this competitive standard. I think we have to maintain standards of excellence.

I wish we had kept dress codes in schools. I have found schools that have marching bands. A certain amount of uniformity not only encourages greater athletic performance but higher academic standards as well. The same is true globally. There's an argument that if you put kids in uniforms, you're going to limit their creative thinking. The truth is, if you can standardize the way people appear in their style, then you can focus more on substance—their experience, imagination, contribution, and their study. The core of an individual rather than the surface of an individual can be developed much better. It would be great if we could combine the more disciplined aspects of the developing countries with the more entrepreneurial, creative, free-thinking aspects of our society, which means we're critical thinkers (i.e., you throw us a problem and we'll try everything we can possibly think of to solve it). In the developing countries they'll use a textbook or an older person's experience rather than using critical thinking.

We're very entrepreneurial here in America, but I'm very much concerned that our standards are being lowered too much. If we're not careful, we're going to take our place in the future as a second-rate educational country and therefore forfeit the idea of being a technological and market leader.

WRIGHT

I also hear grumbling about motivation. I'm sure you've seen business people roll their eyes a bit at the mention of listening to "motivational" tapes or CDs. Some tire of getting all hyped up about change or sales goals, for example, only to lose their excitement and fail to reach their goals. Are they missing something critical about the nature or application of motivation?

WAITLEY

I really believe they are, David. I think they're missing the idea that what you *want* in life turns you on much more than what you *need* in life. Too often business managers even today focus on the hard skills because they say that the other skills are "soft skills." Well, there's no such thing as a hard or soft skill because you can't separate your personal from your professional life anymore. You get fired more for personal reasons—for being late, for your habits, for you hygiene, your behavior, your anger. This idea that technical training as opposed to motivation is the way to go is misguided.

I have found that employees are excited and are full of desire and energy because management listens to them, reinforces them, is interested in their personal goals, and is interested in keeping them inspired. That inspiration is what we remember. So, when we go to a meeting we remember how we felt about the meeting, not the specifics of the meeting.

I think this emotional component—keeping people's energy and desires foremost and doing a desire analysis of employees rather than just a needs analysis—is very, very important. I often think this is lost in the idea that we're giving a pep talk, or a quick fix, or a Band-Aid when, as Zig Ziglar has mentioned so many times, "Motivation is like taking a bath. You take a bath every day and you might say why take a bath—you're going to get dirty anyway." But the very nature of doing it, and doing it on a habitual basis, makes this positive energy continue to flow and motivation becomes habit-forming. I think you need a lot of it to keep these habits of excellence or else you'll just be running scared—you'll be afraid not to do well because you'll lose your job.

Believe it or not, we have a lot of employees in America who are working harder than they ever have before so they won't be fired. That's not really the way to go after a goal—constantly looking through the rear view mirror trying to cover your behind.

WRIGHT

If you don't mind, I'd like to change the focus a little to the topic of self-discipline. People seem to know what they should do and how they should change, but they just can't discipline themselves to take the necessary steps to do so. What is the secret to becoming a disciplined person?

WAITLEY

I think the secret is to get a team, a support group, a mastermind group because not only is there safety in numbers but there's accountability in numbers. When we are accountable to one another to maintain a certain standard of discipline, it's much easier to work out if someone else is getting up at six-thirty in the morning with you. It's much easier to have a support group if you're interested in maintaining a healthier diet, for example, because the temptations are irresistible to procrastinate and to fall off the wagon. That's why I believe you need a team effort.

It also has to be understood in an immediate gratification society that there is no "success pill" that you can swallow. There is no quick way to get rich and get to the top. There is this steady ratcheting to the top and that's why I think leaders need to say it's going to take us about a year to get any permanent change going. So, I think we should all understand there may be a little dip in productivity as we start this new program of ours—a little dip at first and a little uncertainty—but over time, over about a year, we're going to become like an astronaut or an Olympian. We need to engrain these ideas so they become reflexive. It takes about a year for an idea or a habit to become a reflex. This idea of being able to do it in twenty-one days is misguided. I don't think it takes twenty-one days to learn a skill. It may take twenty-one days to learn to type, it may take twenty-one days to begin to learn a skill, but it takes a year for it to get into the subconscious and take hold.

I think we have to learn that discipline is practicing on a daily basis for about a year so that it will become a habit—a pattern—that will override the old inner software program.

WRIGHT

I'm a big believer in the greater potential of the individual. I remember a fellow—Paul Myer—who helped me a lot when I was a young guy. He was in Waco, Texas, with a company called Success Motivation Institute. You may know him.

WAITLEY

I know him very well. Actually, he's one of the icons and pioneers in this entire field. He and Earl Nightingale were the first ones to ever have a recorded speaking message other than music. Earl and Paul were pioneers in audio recording and I have still a great respect for Paul. I spoke for his organization some time ago.

WRIGHT

He personally helped me a lot when I was younger and I just really appreciated him. In your book and program, *Seeds of Greatness*, you outline a system for nurturing greatness. Will you give us a brief overview of this program?

WAITLEY

It's taken me thirty years to get this thing to where I want it. I wrote the book twenty years ago titled, *Seeds of Greatness*, and sure, it became a bestseller but so did *One Minute Manager*, *In Search of Excellence*, *Iacocca*, and every other book at that time. I have trouble keeping that thing pumped up.

Over the years I've found that *Seeds of Greatness*, for me, has been a system. What I've had to do is go back through all the mistakes I've made as a family leader. I knew I was a father and not a mother *and* father so I had to find a mother who was also a good clinical psychologist and who had worked with every form of behavioral problem. We put our efforts together so that we had a man and a woman as family leaders with clinical and other experience who could give parents or leaders of the day a certain track to run on where they could coach their small children and adolescents on a daily basis.

I provided a perpetual calendar that gives coaching tips of the day—what I call "sign on the day" and "sign off the day"—for parents to use to communicate with their kids. Then I had to put nineteen CDs together—audio tracks—that covered these "roots and wings," which I would call the "core values" and the more motivational or, if you will, ways to set your kids free.

The idea of parenthood should be to lay the groundwork, make it safe to fail an experiment, and then send them off on their own as independent, not codependent, young adults so they can reach their own destiny. I divided it into "roots of core values" and "wings of self-motivation and self-direction" and tried to balance the two so that whether you're from a blended family, or a single parent family, and whether you're structurally religious or whether you're spiritually religious, it would work, regardless of your personal core belief system.

I'm very happy that we've finally put together a self-study program that can be taught by the authors or by people who are licensed facilitators. It's something that a family leadership group could take and work on their own at their own speed by watching, listening, interacting with their kids, and using a combination of a written book, the audios, the DVDs, and this coaching calendar to maybe put it all together so that over a period of six months to a year they might be able to effect some changes in the way they interact with their kids.

WRIGHT

Sounds great! Before our time runs out, would you share a story or two about your real life coaching and consulting experiences? I know you've coached astronauts and Super Bowl champions as well, haven't you?

WAITLEY

Well, I have. I've been lucky to work within the Apollo program in the simulation area. I found that simulation prevents failure of the first attempt. In other words, if you're going to go to the moon and they're going to shoot you up a quarter of a million miles up and back in a government vehicle, you had better have your rehearsal down and really pat. The astronauts teach you that the dress rehearsal is life or death. The Olympians teach you that at the moment you go to perform, you need to clear your mind so you can remember everything you learned without trying—you develop muscle memory and reflex.

Twenty-one years ago when Mary Lou Retton was doing the vault, she needed a nine point nine five to tie the Romanian for the gold medal in women's all around gymnastics. I asked her what she was thinking about when she went to vault and she said, "Oh gosh, I guess what everyone thinks about—speed, power, explode, extend, rotate, plant your feet at the end. When the pressure is on I get better just like drill. 'Come on, Mary Lou, this is your moment in history!'"

I thought, "Wow! That's not what everyone thinks. What everyone thinks is, 'Thank God it's Friday,' 'Why me?' 'Don't work too hard,' 'Countin' down to Friday,' 'Looking to five P.M.,' 'Romanians are better trained, probably on steroids,' " So I get these stories of Olympians who have internalized this wonderful running the race in advance and simulating as well.

I guess the one story that I'll share is about a ten-year-old boy. In about 1980 this boy came to a goal-setting seminar. He told me that none of the people who had paid their money were really working on their goals. They were really thinking about what they were going to eat and golf. I gave him a work book and told him to go back and do what they were supposed to do and write down his abilities and liabilities, what he was going to do this year and next year and five years from now and twenty years from now. He got all excited because he thought it was this wonderful game that you can play called, Write the Future, or Describe the Future.

So he ran back and worked on the project and forty-five minutes later he astounded the adults in the audience by saying he was earning money mowing lawns and shoveling snow so he could go to Hawaii on the fourteenth of July to snorkel on the big island of Hawaii's Kona Coast. Then he said next year he'd be eleven going into the fifth grade and he was going to build models of what was going to be a space shuttle and he was going to begin to learn more about numbers and math. In five years he'd be fifteen and as a tenth-grader. He said he would study math and science because he wanted to go to the Air Force academy—he was all excited about that. I asked him what he was going to be doing in twenty years and he said he'd be an astronaut delivering UPS packages in space.

I forgot all about him and twenty years later, sure enough, I saw him on the *Today Show* as they showed a picture of an astronaut on a tether line pulling the satellite into the bay of the space shuttle. I thought, "My gosh! This kid did what I only talk about in the seminars." He was a living, breathing example of someone who was focused on this. I said to my family, "Look at what he did!" And they said, "What have *you* been doing for the last twenty years?" I said I was a goal tender. They told me I should be a goal achiever too.

WRIGHT

What a great conversation. I always enjoy talking with you. It's not just uplifting—I always learn a lot when I talk with you.

WAITLEY

Well, David, I do with you as well. You've got a great program and you do a lot of good for people who read and watch and listen. I think you give them insights that otherwise they would never get. I'm just grateful to be one of the contributors and one of the members of your global team.

WRIGHT

It has been my sincere pleasure today to visit with a truly great American, Dr. Denis Waitley.

Denis, thank you for taking so much of your time to share your insights and inspirations for us here on *Stepping Stones to Success*.

WAITLEY

Thank you very much, David.

ABOUT THE AUTHOR

DENIS WAITLEY is one of America's most respected authors, keynote lecturers and productivity consultants on high performance human achievement. He has inspired, informed, challenged, and entertained audiences for over twenty-five years from the board rooms of multi-national corporations to the control rooms of NASA's space program and from the locker rooms of world-class athletes to the meeting rooms of thousands of conventioneers throughout the world. He was voted business speaker of the year by the Sales and Marketing Executives Association and by Toastmasters International and inducted into the International Speakers Hall of Fame. With over ten million audio programs sold in fourteen languages, Denis Waitley is the most listened-to voice on personal and career success. He is the author of twelve non-fiction books, including several international bestsellers, *Seeds of Greatness, Being the Best, The Winner's Edge, The Joy of Working*, and *Empires of the Mind*. His audio album, "The Psychology of Winning," is the all-time best-selling program on self-mastery.

DR. DENIS WAITLEY
The Waitley Institute

P.O. Box 197
Rancho Santa Fe, CA 92067
www.deniswaitley.com

CHAPTER SEVENTEEN

The Mind-Body Connection:
Steps to Take to Becoming Empowered Over Health Issues
An Interview with . . . **Evy Coppola**

DAVID WRIGHT (WRIGHT)

Today we are talking with Evy Coppola, a Certified Natural Health Counselor, nutritionist, herb specialist, registered yoga teacher and trainer, iridologist, kinesiologist, and craniosacral therapist. Evy brings more than twenty-five years of experience in the alternative health field.

Evy, welcome to *Stepping Stones to Success*.

What were the steps that led up to your becoming involved in the alternative health field?

EVY COPPOLA (COPPOLA)

First it was seeing my daughter suffer that had me really concerned about feeling so disempowered when it came to health. She started having severe headaches at fifteen years of age, which seemed to come on her suddenly. Traditional care recommended Valium and then consider a brain scan. Prior to her headaches, she also had skin problems that no amount of skin regimes, remedies, or prescribed antibiotics helped, much less cured. When my daughter turned twenty-one and had her annual Pap test, the results came back abnormal and our first gynecologist suggested she might have to have a hysterectomy.

Second was my own health issues, which I came to believe were common for everybody. These problems spanned a period of over twenty years and included having sinus infections and what appeared to be seasonal allergies, migraine headaches, sore throats, acidic stomach, pea-sized lumps in my breast, and sciatica. I was admitted to the hospital at nineteen years of age and put in traction for a slipped disc. I never received any permanent relief or cures for what I was experiencing. Continuing to treat the symptoms never really brought any permanent relief or answers. Overnight I developed pain in all my joints and was rushed to the emergency room. I was told they suspected Lupus Disease based on my symptoms. It turned out I was infected with Hepatitis B. I never took a drug in my life and couldn't imagine how I contracted this debilitating setback with my health until I found out my fiancé was a carrier. Traditional medical care gave me some of the following answers: antibiotics for the sore throats, sinus tablets for sinus, and some pain killer (I think it was Darvon) for migraines. Needles were injected into the breasts to remove the fluid buildup causing the painful fibroids and it was recommended that I have mammograms quarterly. I was instructed to take pain pills and muscle relaxants when needed for my back. I was given the impression it was "taboo" to have chiropractic care and no suggestion was ever made to have therapeutic massage therapy. I was further told to take some Maalox or baking soda for my stomach.

There was no cure for Hepatitis B. I had to have blood drawn weekly to see if my liver was failing. I asked what was the point of testing the blood and was told that if my liver totally failed, I would be put in the hospital and wait for a liver transplant.

The woman doctor I was seeing knew I had an interest in natural health and she ultimately told me that the liver stores vitamins from the food we eat to send out to where needed in the body and maybe this would be a good time to take some vitamins. I went home that day and took double doses of sport packets I had bought from a friend who was selling them. I took double the packets recommended for one week and when I went back to the doctor for another blood drawing, my liver count had come down by over 50 percent and continued to return to normal.

WRIGHT

Were you able to get the help you needed for your daughter's headaches?

COPPOLA

Yes. Do you know the expression, "When the student's ready, the teacher will appear"? Realizing that even at the young age of fifteen, school and life can be stressful, I took Michele to a health club for a massage with the intent of first ridding her of the headaches.

Traditional medical had suggested drugs for pain that neither she nor I wanted, as we both wanted to know why she was in pain and how to alleviate it permanently. She felt so much relief and less pain after the massage treatment, and while it wasn't the total answer it helped her tremendously. (As a side note, I think this opened the door for her to pursue her career first as a massage therapist and then in owning her own beautiful holistic day spa in St. Louis, Missouri.) The therapist also suggested Vitamin C might help her skin.

I took the advice of a co-worker who suggested Dr. Pine, an osteopathic physician she knew of, who helped people in a natural way to overcome pain and imbalance in the body. After the initial consultation discussing her diet and lifestyle, Dr. Pine then felt the base of her skull and asked if she had hit her head. She was on a swim team at school and his question reminded her that while swimming the backstroke a month before, she missed her count and hit the wall with her head, flipped under water, and continued the race. He called in his associate and gave her an adjustment much like what is used by a good chiropractor. He adjusted her neck and the base of her skull while he adjusted in one direction and his associate pulled in the opposite. He then went on to explain she had basically suffered a concussion with the pressure of the water locking the base of her skull out of alignment when she hit the side of the pool. She was immediately relieved of any further pain and without the use of drugs or weekly follow-up treatments or any other invasive or extensive treatments.

WRIGHT

What were the next steps you took to improve her skin?

COPPOLA

Her skin problems also became less of a problem when we consulted another alternative practitioner and nutritionist who specialized also in herbal therapies. He immediately recommended Vitamin C with Rose Hips and not the C with ascorbic acid that she had been taking. It appeared that the ascorbic acid was coming out through the pores in her skin creating cysts and much worse problems than the blemishes that she was fighting early on. Her skin started to improve in twenty-four hours.

We will never know for sure, but we believe eliminating Tab soda from her diet (I hadn't realized how much of it she was drinking) surely had a positive effect. It was much later when we learned about the importance of quality acidophilus. A common cause of infection is long-term use of antibiotics that destroy beneficial, as well as harmful, microorganisms in the body, permitting candida to multiply in their place. The resulting condition is known as *candidiasis moniliasis*, or a "yeast" infection. Quality acidophilus is important to avoid this condition when on antibiotics. Michele would have periodic yeast infections when being treated with rounds of antibiotics for her skin prescribed by a very qualified and highly regarded dermatologist. We were told that a good quality acidophilus could have balanced the friendly flora in her intestinal tract that caused the yeast infections from the overuse of the prescribed antibiotics. Once the acidophilus was introduced, we stopped the antibiotics, and she found the right natural skin care line that she uses in her own spa, resulting in healthy, vibrant skin.

WRIGHT

You said her Pap test came back abnormal? How did you find the right answer for such a serious health issue?

COPPOLA

Once again, when it came to the problem with the abnormal Pap test, the right door opened for her to have the best gynecological physician who basically developed a process to freeze the bad cells found in the uterus, which produced a melting affect, ultimately replacing good cells for the bad. She never had further abnormal Pap tests, she kept a healthy diet, and married five years later. She gave birth to two beautiful children sixteen months apart. She had already started into a vegetarian diet, which included fresh juices with the investment we made in a good juicer. She had no further female problems.

WRIGHT

What motivated you to continue your search for health answers?

COPPOLA

I was sick and tired of being sick and tired. I had gotten a glimpse of what I could accomplish with education and support to become empowered over my own health through getting answers for my daughter. The healthier I got, friends and even business associates asked me to help them improve the quality of their lives. My interest in less invasive and more natural approaches to finding answers to health on many levels continued to grow.

WRIGHT

Was it easy to find the right answers once you realized there was another way to go in order to get the answers you were seeking?

COPPOLA

No, it wasn't. So much of what we have to go through individually can take us to the next rung up the ladder to success if we just pay attention. I had no idea how much emotional trauma can play a part in getting or staying well until each of my sisters lost their sons six weeks apart in unrelated instances. They were twenty-six and twenty-seven. I was the one called upon and happy to help each through a very sad and emotional time in their lives.

When the funerals were over and I came back to my home in Florida, I found myself lacking energy, motivation, and my usual cockeyed optimism. I found it increasingly more difficult to take care of my business or life in general on a daily basis. I would manage to go to our neighborhood health store and get a fresh carrot juice drink or mixed vegetable or fruit juice and try and figure out why I lost my lease on life. It was on one of my short neighborhood jaunts to get my health drink, and after feeling so bad for about a month, when I saw an ad for a week's stay at a holistic health resort 250 miles away.

It was challenging but I thought I could make the drive. Besides, it was no coincidence that this information came to me at just the right time. When I called to inquire and register, much to my amazement, I had registered for the last space they had available for the week in Palm Beach. The ad showed that they offered education and fasting programs, various cleansing programs, and all types of natural approaches to getting well, including vegetarian diets.

While I barely had the energy to walk up three steps for check-in upon arrival, what transpired over the course of the next few days was nothing short of miraculous. I met a woman at the property's swimming pool who began to relate her experience at this miracle holistic treatment center. She had decided to check in as a private patient a month before, following a tremendous battle with cancer and before that, severe arthritis. She related that her aches and pains were gone, including symptoms of arthritis, which she had been told would never be alleviated. She was also told she would have to go on stronger medications since the others weren't relieving her pain prior to coming to Fineway House. She eliminated over thirty pounds and said she never felt better. She had also made lifestyle and dietary changes that would last a lifetime.

WRIGHT

Was it a big change for you to make to follow their dietary plan and other requirements?

COPPOLA

My introduction to vegetarian meals, fresh juiced fruit, and/or vegetable juices had started kicking in by my second full day at the "miracle center." I had more energy and felt as though I was becoming born again. It didn't take too long to realize I had been suffering with "depression" from what I had been through the previous month because of the death of my nephews.

I began the education process through the facilitator and learned about correct food combining, colon cleansing, eating meals in harmony, and the importance of working with the emotional aspects of any condition that can cause depression. Thus I was truly learning the meaning of the word "holistic" when it came to becoming empowered and healthy.

After a few days of a healthy diet, moderate exercise, and rest, I had more energy and felt better than I could ever remember. My head was clear. No more aches or pains. I started to perspire on our early morning walks, which was amazing. My lymphatic system had been blocked most of my life as it turned out, which was why I would turn beet red in the heat, but not sweat out the impurities in my body.

When I returned home, I continued on my path by finding a local therapeutic center to continue to work with cleansing programs, diet, and education. I then started having friends ask me what I had been doing because I looked like I had found the fountain of youth. I didn't sound like I had a cold anymore. My skin tone and whole appearance had changed and I now exuded health.

I knew I had to take advantage of the educational opportunities offered by the company whose products had given me a new lease on life. Luckily, twenty-five years ago, I was able to attend workshops and conferences in Utah and other parts of the country and gain the foundation and knowledge with which to help others. I met and worked with those who were pioneers in the field of non-invasive treatments. Every door opened and the very best in the fields wherein I needed certification, licensing, and education were the teachers I'd had on my pathway to wellness. It has been and continues to be an amazing journey with weekly miracles happening for clients.

WRIGHT

What types of complaints do you hear from the clients who come to you for help?

COPPOLA

There really isn't a common denominator, but there are many similarities and yet different answers for each. Among them are lack of energy, sleepless nights, weight gain, digestive problems that range from irritable bowel syndrome to acid reflux, constipation, bloat, and candida albicans.

Many have gone through surgeries and cancer treatments and want to change their habits and diet to learn how to better care for themselves and get healthy. Others have never gotten help with their complaints and just felt depressed and out of balance most of the time. Eventually many were being prescribed some antidepressant as a last resort. Other conditions include lowered immune systems, back problems, recurring respiratory problems, sinus problems, allergies, and feeling either hyperactive or lethargic. Many don't know how to even begin to break the cycle of poor dietary habits to start making better choices and others think there might be an herbal formula, homeopathic or energy treatment, or magic pill that will take all their complaints away. I am including a testimonial from a friend who became a client when she faced some very challenging times. Here's Martha's story:

"I never really thought about alternative health, because quite frankly, I never got sick and rarely visited a doctor. When a health issue, hyperthyroidism, crept into my life when I was in my forties, I did seek traditional medical help. The only alternative they offered was to radiate my thyroid. I started working with Evy Coppola, a friend and natural health consultant. Through a diet and herbal regimen the hyperthyroid condition went into remission, I kept my thyroid and never looked back. More recently, I was diagnosed with a fast-growing breast cancer and conceded to traditional approaches including chemotherapy, radiation, and surgery. During the treatment, Evy again helped me with a nutrition plan, herbal therapy, and homeopathic treatments. I started taking yoga (again) to keep my body as healthy as possible. My recovery was quick and I did not have the terrible side effects most people have from the treatments. When the cancer reoccurred a year later, I reluctantly started another round of chemotherapy, but after a few months, I decided to get my body strong and fight the cancer using herbs, homeopathic treatments, exercise, and diet. Although I am not cancer-free, the cancer is not active and I am feeling better than ever. My doctor is very pleased with my progress and is now asking me what I am doing to keep my health in check."

What do you offer your clients that traditional care doesn't?

The very first thing is taking the time to listen to the client. There is no one-size-fits-all approach that should ever be taken to help a patient or client. Four people can all have a lack of energy. One may be due to stress and do well with a Balanced B vitamin. Another is lethargic because he or she doesn't eat healthy and needs vitamins, while others are toxic and full of excessive waste and yet others could need blood support and exercise to oxygenate their blood stream.

I ask my clients how long they have been feeling bad or what discomfort and complaints they would like to improve. I know from my training that the two most important parts of the body to have in good working order are the digestion and elimination process. I learn about my clients' eating habits, including whether they are more drawn to salty foods, sweet, sour, hot, or full of spice. I also recognize that my clients usually fit the pattern of one of the four basic body types based on the endocrine systems.

An individual generally can be easily recognized as a Thyroid, Adrenal, Pituitary or Reproductive body type. While we start out at least with all those body parts in our systems, we don't all have the same dietary habits, sleep, or exercise patterns, and a few of us are very strongly influenced by more than one of our body's types, which does make it a bit trickier. But it's all about getting the person back into balance and having a new lease on life.

I will give you some generalized examples. Thyroid types tend to be breakfast skippers, especially when out of balance. They get a second wind of energy later in the evening, usually from a late night snack when they are out of balance. They especially like more carbohydrates such as fruits, vegetables, pastas, and then the refined carbohydrates like sweets. They are usually quite talkative and prefer exercises such as walking, yoga, and maybe swimming. They are generally lactose intolerant and need good quality calcium with magnesium and vitamin D in addition to digestive support.

Adrenal types like three good-sized meals a day. They like more aggressive sports, sugary foods, and tend to have more of an addictive personality, fitting the bi-polar pattern of highs and lows. They also tend to have more throat problems and are allergy prone. Bee pollen has been a great help for the Adrenal types along with pantothenic acid (B_5).

Pituitary types seem ageless, looking the same at fifty as they did at ten. They are usually the grazers when it comes to food and eat smaller meals throughout the day. Partners are important to this petite person and like regimen in their lives. Keeping their blood sugar level is an important step to keeping them healthy. Digestive enzymes especially targeting the pancreas are important support for the Pituitary types.

Reproductive or Gonadal types are the bigger boned men and women and those who have a lifetime of weight issues. Their nature is usually quite even especially if they get their comfort foods of pizza, ice cream, and lots of creamy and fatty foods. They are motivated to get off the couch by a good debate that gives them mental stimulation and challenge. They can maintain their health and weight well with workouts involving weight training and/or bodybuilding. Their system usually does well with higher protein diets to burn off the fat. Some of the supplements like amino acids are helpful for fat-burning as well as Spirulina.

They may have an easy time reproducing or a difficult time, but ultimately all these body types need support for their individual endocrine system, even though they may have a need to support other aspects of their body for imbalance such as back problems, lowered immune systems, etc.

WRIGHT

I have heard there are other types of non-invasive approaches to help individuals get to the core of their problems. Are you familiar with any others than what you described?

COPPOLA

I am so glad you asked, since I incorporate many systems into my evaluations and workshops. I think the work of Dr. D'Adamo has been extremely beneficial and insightful regarding blood typing. There are four blood types and each has distinct characteristics as to individuals' needs regarding food, exercise, personality, and health direction. I have directed many of my clients to include some of these principles and they did very well in accomplishing their health goals along with the right supplement, herbs or homeopathic remedies, and exercise.

For simplicity sake, in this type of non-invasive lifestyle change, those with type A blood tend to be drawn to more of a vegetarian diet. O's are the meat-eaters, thus they usually have an easier time with weight loss if they ditch the potatoes, breads, and pastas.

Of course there is that rare occasion when a person wants to gain weight and has tried everything. The right enzyme to support the digestive system is usually a big part of the solution. There are several enzymes and it is important to have competent professional guidance and not rely on your next-door neighbor, an article on the Internet, or a late night infomercial for the answer.

An example is someone who eats a good amount of meat may need a protein digestive enzyme, whereas a person with blood sugar imbalances would do better with an enzyme to support his or her pancreas. Yet another does even better with a carb-burning enzyme or fat-burning digestive enzyme.

We have Chinese formulas that are based on what is called Chinese Constitutional Body Typing, which is an amazing insightful look at the mind, body, and emotional nature of a person through understanding the theory of elements, described as having a nature of either stressed or weakened systems through influences and conditions such as Water, Metal, Earth, Air, or Fire. There is a questionnaire that when completed gives the client and facilitator basic information with which to proceed with specific Chinese formulas to bring about balance.

Then of course, there is Ayurveda. I have had the good fortune to stay and receive treatments at Ayervedic centers. The system of uncovering the individual's nature in Ayerveda starts with what is called a pulse point diagnosis. The right wrist is checked for males and left for females. This system recognizes that there are three distinct Doshas known as Vata, Pita and Kapha (I personally think there should be a fourth, which would be a person like me who is split right down the middle between two, but who am I to mess with the sages of thousands of years of knowledge and tradition?)

It is very interesting in this method to find that the Vatas generally have weaker digestion and Pitas have strong digestion. The Kapha is drawn to certain spices like Cardamom as well as the higher fat foods. Each has their own oils that work best on his or her skin and amazing results come about in a very short period of time when changes are made by understanding the person's own nature and leanings.

You can check people's tongues and see if they are toxic, lacking energy, over acidic, which is absolutely non-invasive. Tongue cleaners will only do so much to clean the tongue if the person has a diet that is wrong for them or their colon isn't functioning well.

There are also the marvelous books by Mioshi Kushi that describe the face shape, lines in the ear lobes, etc. All these relate to potential imbalances in the body. He also was the founder of the Macrobiotic diet. Some people swear that following his plan rid them of cancer and a myriad of other diseases.

We should not forget personality types. Before the Myers Briggs concept came along in business, which I think enhanced four basic personality types into sixteen, there were four personality types or "temperaments." For the sake of simplicity, I'll list them and give short descriptions. Melancholy types exhibit mood changes, Sanguine types are the life of the party, Phlegmatic types tend to be easy-going, and Choleric types are the go-getters. People become easy to recognize based on personality, size, shape, expressions, complaints, and habits, which quickly unfold in the consultation.

WRIGHT

What are some of the other ways people can get well in a less invasive way?

COPPOLA

There are different areas of the country that have four seasons. Many people find they feel better in a particular climate. When circumstances force them to make a change to a less friendly climate for their individual needs, many times health problems arise. Without breaking off a marriage or a relationship, they can create an environment that will help them adjust, mentally, physically, and emotionally.

I had a friend once who perspired profusely when eating. He developed a heart condition at a very young age. He would have been so much better off in a colder climate.

Another individual could be absolutely miserable in the heat and is highly allergic to mold. More than likely this person would do better in dryer climate.

This brings to mind the art of visualization and understanding the importance of creating a friendly and harmonious surrounding for oneself. If you are forced through circumstances beyond your control to live in a climate that is not your ideal, then have photos and drawings and other memorabilia that represents a climate that is the ideal for you.

My upcoming book on health for all seasons will give a great deal of insight into staying empowered on your quest and taking the right steps to success.

How many times do people get so caught up in making money, taking on more debt and responsibility that they forget to do the things that bring them joy? Draw, paint, sew, crafts, find a spiritual center if you don't have one and if you do, attend services and volunteer. Hike, dance, share time with family and friends, and just laugh out loud.

It brings joy to others when receiving as well as giving gifts or performing random acts of kindness. No one ever knew I left little tokens of appreciation for several volunteers at our yoga center several years ago. Those unrecognized gifts on my part were the best thing I inadvertently could have done. What I was going to get back certainly was the farthest thing from my mind and the recipients didn't feel pressured to reciprocate or be insincere in expressing appreciation. Another added benefit was realizing I only needed praise in the past and accolades from others because I wasn't taking care of me. It's all about balance.

WRIGHT

How important is a person's diet? What actually constitutes a good diet?

297

COPPOLA

The right diet for each individual is so important. There are so many choices and options today it can make your head spin. The old system of five food groups at a meal is probably one of the biggest causes of indigestion and allergies, in my opinion. There are so many people with lactose intolerance and perhaps it stemmed from feeding solid foods to them as infants prematurely before their little digestive tracts have fully formed. The mothers who are nursing need a really good diet to have a healthy, happy baby and that means plenty of fresh fruit in the morning, a higher starch meal at lunch when they need more energy, raw vegetable juice during the afternoon or protein snacks, depending on their body and blood types, and then a higher protein meal at night such as baked chicken or fish with two steamed vegetables or a green leafy salad, if they haven't had one yet for the day.

Nursing mothers should be able to produce enough milk to nurse their baby at least the full first year of life. Even working mothers can express their milk, which is still the best, and store it for use. But if the child is not satisfied and is cranky, chances are that Mom is not eating enough of the right foods to produce the nutritional components in her milk to satisfy the hungry baby. It is all so individualized. Of course mothers should also stay on a good prenatal vitamin for months after the birth of their little one.

A good way to tell if you no longer need a vitamin or perhaps it wasn't right for you in the first place, is that it doesn't digest well and you get an aftertaste from it. It is apparent that your body is rejecting it.

In my natural nutritional courses I learned the importance of not drinking liquids at meals, eating in harmony, and correct food combining. When you study this concept it makes a lot of sense. But most importantly, when people are willing to make some changes, they see immediate results.

Water and other liquids should be taken in between meals. For adults, protein should be the last meal of the day. Adults should eat a higher starch meal at lunch to maintain energy during the day when needed.

Think about the logic. You never give athletes a big steak before a race, they eat pasta or potatoes. The natural sugar in pasta or potatoes will burn off pretty quickly but will give them energy when needed.

There are people suffering with lack of energy and even depression who can be helped tremendously by diet. The first thing that has to change when a person is diagnosed with diabetes, heart problems, high blood pressure, and many other ailments is to reduce intake of sugar, salt, alcohol, etc. So logically, if you changed your diet and ditched the desserts and bacon and egg breakfast, you could avoid the disease.

I think it is important to notice if there are severe cravings for things like chocolate, it can mean that you are actually lacking in magnesium. If you crave excessive salt, you might be lacking natural sodium, which is found in a little herb called dandelion. Dandelion is also a good source of support for the liver. When the smell of dirt makes you salivate, you can be lacking minerals. When you add the right mineral formula into your diet it greatly helps with osteoporosis and other types of arthritis.

We must not forget exercise. Not everyone is drawn to the same kind of exercise. Walking for up to two miles at least three times a week is a good start and the only investment is the right shoes. Others do well with swimming, dancing, or yoga. The adrenal type personalities who may have a sedentary job look forward to their kickboxing or aerobic classes.

Many people think it's such a horrendous job to make changes and find every excuse in the book to not do it such as their significant other wouldn't like any changes made to the meal plans, they work too late to exercise, they would have no time for church, and on and on it goes. Instead they rely on their health care professionals to come up with a magic pill to take away their lack of involvement in their own health.

I took the advice of a wise health nut one time when I was told to just start reading labels on the foods I was going to purchase. If I couldn't say the word, don't buy the product. It was amazing. Something as simple as applesauce was my first experience. Some were loaded with corn syrup and other ingredients and when I found one that said organic and only contained apples and water, I was elated. It was and still is the best applesauce I've ever had. You could actually taste the apples.

Making necessary changes becomes easier and step-by-step it brings the success strategies to living a healthy quality empowered life.

ABOUT THE AUTHOR

EVY COPPOLA, Certified Natural Health Counselor, nutritionist, herb specialist, registered yoga teacher and trainer, iridologist, kinesiologist, and craniosacral therapist brings more than twenty-five years of experience in the alternative health field. She also offers business consulting and training for individuals and companies through presentations, consulting, and workshops to enhance their lives and become empowered over their health. Evy brings firsthand experience and a wealth of knowledge to her clients and students to gain the tools to lead a balanced personal and professional life. She is a business owner, an author, professional speaker, award-winning sales and marketing specialist, and former member of the National Speakers Association in Missouri.

EVY COPPOLA, CNHC, E-RYT500

Pathways To Wellness and Steps for Success Workshops
617 Everhart Road
Corpus Christi, TX 78411
(361) 985 9642 or (361) 549-0095
www.path2wellness.com

CHAPTER EIGHTEEN

Stepping into Wellness

An Interview with . . . **Mindy Schrager**

DAVID WRIGHT (WRIGHT)

Today we're talking with Mindy Schrager who has over twenty years' experience managing cross-disciplinary programs, processes, and communities. She has a bachelor's degree in French, a master's degree in Business Administration, and a coaching certificate from the Ford Institute at JFK University. Her career interests in diversity, transformation, and collaboration grew out of her desire to make life better and have people understand the synergy in diversity. Her interest in wellness grew during eighteen years of studying modalities to improve her own emotional, physical, and relationship wellness. Both paths helped Mindy see the gift and impact in a childhood of being bullied. Bullying is happening not only in our schools, but in families, the workplace, primary relationships, and within ourselves. Her new passion is to support others in their journey to love, accept, and appreciate themselves and create a life they love. She facilitates this through coaching, NLP, a network of incredible practitioners, and some healthy products.

Mindy, welcome to *Stepping Stones to Success*.

MINDY SCHRAGER (SCHRAGER)

Thank you, David.

WRIGHT

So what do you consider to be the key areas of wellness?

SCHRAGER

There are some people who look at wellness—personal wellness—as physical health. I've also heard it referred to as mind, body, spirit. So key areas of wellness include mind, body, and spirit.

However, through my journey to wellness over many years, I've come to believe that wellness manifests in the area of physical health, emotional health, and the health of our relationships.

WRIGHT

So why do you think it's important to take a holistic view?

SCHRAGER

I think it's important to take a holistic view because as humans we are whole beings.

I remember being treated for a thumb injury. As the therapist was doing ultrasound on my thumb I could feel the pain in my elbow. When I mentioned this, the therapist said that the doctor's orders allowed her to only treat my thumb. She wasn't treating me as a whole being, even though I could feel the wholeness of my being. I've seen situations where a massage therapist worked on the right foot, but I felt the referred pain in my left shoulder. That's another example of us as whole beings.

Our emotions are part of our whole being. You may hear someone say over and over, "I can't stand being around that person," and then suddenly develops back

302

pain. Or someone may say, "I cannot stomach that situation," and then develops ulcers. These are examples of how people's emotions can affect their physical health.

In my case, I've been on a call where I'm being coached and I'll go into a feeling of fear and then have an allergy attack. In NLP, I've heard it said that allergies are phobias of the immune system, so that would be a fear playing itself out. I really see that there is a connection with all parts of our being.

WRIGHT

So how do people know if they're unwell if there are no physical symptoms?

SCHRAGER

Well, people may be in an unhappy relationship or feel depressed because they are in a job they don't enjoy. They may not have any physical symptoms, but they have those feelings of unhappiness or depression. They may feel stuck or unfulfilled. From my point of view, those are a part of being unwell, just as much as having a physical illness.

This could be the perfect time for them to get assistance because the next step might be for that unhappiness or depression to manifest as an illness in the physical body. I've seen instances where people were unhappy in a relationship or they thought they were in a dead-end job and then developed a physical illness. It was at that point when they decided that life was too short to not pursue the life of their dreams and they left the dead-end job or unhappy relationship. Illness and sometimes facing death forced them to look at what they really wanted to do.

WRIGHT

What are some of the ways that people sabotage their well-being?

SCHRAGER

I think sabotage of yourself can actually be very overt—out in the open—or it can be sneaky and covert. Examples of overt self-sabotage would be addictive behaviors such as drinking too much, chain-smoking, or doing drugs. There are other ways of self-sabotaging like intentionally making your significant other angry at you because you know he or she is going to do something when angry. Or maybe someone puts off studying for an exam—an exam necessary in order to move into a field the person wants to enter, so he or she procrastinates, sabotaging success. Other instances might be less obvious where people run negative internal dialogue, constantly telling themselves that they're not good enough, or telling themselves how stupid and worthless they are. I'm not sure most people would necessarily think of that as self-sabotage until they really step back and see how self-destructive it is.

WRIGHT

So low self-image would be a way to sabotage one's well-being?

SCHRAGER

Absolutely. Choosing unhealthy eating habits and not exercising are two other ways people sabotage themselves. There are many ways to sabotage yourself.

WRIGHT

Why is it that some people seem to find a "miracle cure" while others continue to search?

SCHRAGER

I really believe everyone has a path he or she is on—a path he or she is meant to follow. From my experience, there are some people who find an approach that works; sharing that approach becomes their life's work. Maybe their "miracle cure" is what they're meant to do. But for others the journey is part of their healing. So it isn't just a one-stop journey, it's all the different stops along the way.

I also believe that some people choose an easy path in life and others need to do a lot of work on their issues, making their journey longer. It can also be something as simple as what they believe. For instance, if someone believes that what he or she needs is not out there, that person is going to have a very long journey, and will potentially continue searching and searching for something he or she doesn't believe exists.

WRIGHT

So if I'm looking for someone to love me just as I am, and I've never been able to find that person, the probability is I'm not going to.

SCHRAGER

Right, and if you don't love yourself, the likelihood is even less. If you don't believe it exists and you don't believe it within yourself, you may be on a very long journey to find it.

WRIGHT

To extend that, I suppose you could say if I never do find it, that's just more proof that there is no one out there.

SCHRAGER

Exactly, so you get to continue to reinforce the belief that you have about yourself, and then you can create circumstances that allow you to continue to sabotage it as well.

WRIGHT

I remember someone telling me years ago that I was one of the best problem-solvers they had ever seen. I took it as a great compliment and thanked him. He said, "Wait a minute! I didn't mean that as a compliment. I meant that you're such a great problem-solver that when things go well in our life, you screw it up so you will have a problem to solve.

SCHRAGER

That's one aspect to being a problem-solver for sure—creating problems that you get to solve.

WRIGHT

So how does community and family play into someone's wellness?

SCHRAGER

Earlier I mentioned relationships as a key part of wellness. So let's take a few examples. Say you're in a primary relationship where your significant other tells you how fat and ugly you are. You may begin to take on those negative thoughts. Then you may start to overeat, and you may stop exercising and do other things that result in your creating the image that your significant other has of you.

Another example could be in a job situation, where you don't quite fit in because you are a creative type working with mostly analytical types. This may lead you to doubt your ability to be effective or belong, which could affect your emotional health and that may actually contribute to physical unwellness.

Or take the opposite side. If you're a child who is being bullied but you come home to a very supportive environment where you have nurturing and loving parents who are good problem-solvers and help you work through those issues, then you may not be as affected because that community is very supportive of you and can help you work through what the impact is. So I've seen very strong instances both where your community and relationships can make you better, and others where they can make you less well.

WRIGHT

You mentioned in your biography that you were bullied. What have been some of the long-term effects of that in your life?

SCHRAGER

I think that having been bullied I kept myself in the victim role for many years, and I didn't actually know it. It kept me in a place of questioning what was wrong with me, which had a negative impact on my self esteem. There were some specific events that happened that resulted in my keeping myself invisible and not standing out, so I hid. That was one of my self-sabotaging behaviors.

It was only recently through the incredible teachings of Debbie Ford when I was actually able to stand back from the experience and see what a gift it was. Someone may wonder how can there be a gift in being bullied? Well, who better to facilitate groups of people than someone who was an outcast and felt different? Because of my experience, I can really help people to work together, see the value in each other, and support them in working together.

One of the things it helped me to see is that there is synergy in diversity—strength in our wholeness. When you take all those different qualities and put them together, you have so much power—as long as you accept that it's all worthwhile.

WRIGHT

For our readers to be clearer about the term bullying, what are some of the ways that bullying is manifested?

SCHRAGER

I think there are different kinds of bullying, but if you look at the experience of childhood bullying I think it's primarily done through words. A lot of it is done by mocking others and putting them down. There can be physical aspects to it—some kids get kicked and hit and can't defend themselves. I'm not as close to it these days, but there seems to be a lot of bullying that happens through cyber media.

WRIGHT

I've always thought bullying was physical.

SCHRAGER

My experience with it was mostly verbal. There was some physical, but it's really being in a place where you are just uncomfortable all the time. I think that is why you see in the media instances of kids who were bullied where they saw no way out.

WRIGHT

I remember being bullied as a child. It's a terrifying experience and one that takes a long time to get over, or at least it did in my case.

So do you believe that bullying transcends the classroom and our childhood years?

SCHRAGER

Yes absolutely.

I was at an equine learning workshop several years ago. The first thing we did was describe our current circumstances. I was describing a job situation and the workshop leader said to me, "That sounds like adult bullying." I had never thought of it that way because my experience of bullying had been as a child. How could it happen outside the classroom? Then, when I started looking at the whole concept of adult bullying, I started finding other instances that you really can consider to be bullying. Sibling rivalry can be both physical and emotional, one sibling bullying another. Or spousal abuse—isn't that really someone bullying another person? Then in the workplace—if one person is too intense or nerdy or uncommunicative, what do his or her colleagues do? They bully the person for not being "normal."

Then there is something I've started calling "bully marketing." Those are the offers you get where you must sign up *today* because if you don't, it will never be offered at this price ever again. I think we've all experienced that one.

Then what I realized most recently is that we actually bully ourselves—we eat unhealthy food, we beat ourselves up for how we handle situations, and we put ourselves in situations where we can be a victim. I really think that all of these are examples of bullying. I'm sure there are others I haven't thought of.

WRIGHT

What have you found gets in the way of teams or groups being successful?

SCHRAGER

Well, there are general things that get in the way like lack of a clear goal, no ground rules, a weak leader, or poor team facilitation, but I think a lot of it is how people treat each other. I mentioned the example where one person on the team is creative and the other person is analytical. Then, as opposed to working together, they may clash and say, "Well, I don't know why you think that; it's too artsy." And then the other person says, "Well, that's too rigid and following the rules." If they were to come together and say, "How do we create synergy?" then they might work together better.

Another example can be found in what NLP calls "representational systems" (visual, auditory, and kinesthetic). If you have a visual person and he or she uses visual terms such as "I see" or "I get the picture," that may be challenging for a kinesthetic person who uses a term such as "I get the feeling." Another behavioral aspect of representational systems is the visual person tends to talk really fast, where a kinesthetic person may be a little more thoughtful and take pauses. Have you ever seen people who just sit there and say, "Can you hurry up?" That is a way of teams not working together because they don't understand the differences. So a lot of it can be people getting annoyed with people in the room because they're different. Differences could be in a Myers Briggs type or a right brain/left brain preference or a visual versus kinesthetic representational system orientation. People can sometimes clash, which affects the team's dynamic and ability to work together.

WRIGHT

Do you find that there are some common approaches in the techniques you have studied?

SCHRAGER

I found that there are several commonalities in what I've studied and experienced. For instance, many of the modalities, including NLP, Debbie Ford's Shadow work, and Voice Dialogue, among others, highlight the fact that we have parts of ourselves that fragment during traumatic events or other negatively received events in our lives. Those fragments can keep us stuck and living in past events.

There are many modalities today, including the Law of Attraction, that highlight the importance of beliefs. What you believe is what you manifest unless you change your beliefs. Beliefs are typically formed when we are quite young by a compelling or repetitive experience. Then once a belief is in place, we create experiences that reinforce the truth of that belief until we change our thinking.

Emotion is another common factor I've seen. There is awareness of our emotions—how we manage them and how we can use emotions to educate ourselves as to what we need to change. In NLP there is the concept of "state

309

management" where you learn to observe the emotional state you are in and then take action to shift or manage your emotional state.

The fourth commonality is that many of these modalities are about energy. The pervasive belief is that we are energy beings—our emotions are energy, our physical bodies are energy, and illness has an energetic blueprint.

I would say that beliefs, parts, energy, and emotional state are the modalities that are common.

WRIGHT

What are some of the approaches you recommend to others?

SCHRAGER

I've tried about eighty different healing modalities. Some have worked and some have been interesting and have worked for others but not for me necessarily. The ones I love the most include NLP, Family Constellations, the work of Debbie Ford, and Shamanic healing. I found that energy modalities, along with The BodyTalk System and Equine Inspired Coaching at Birchwood Farm, were breakthroughs for me as well.

For physical health, Phytobiodermie, kinesiology, and Regulation Thermography have been very effective for me. I've also found some great products related to physical wellness, which, along with practitioner referrals, can be found on my Web site. But again everyone has his or her own journey and those are just some of the approaches that have worked for me.

WRIGHT

"Family Constellation" is a term I'm not familiar with.

SCHRAGER

Family Constellation Work was developed by Bert Hellinger and looks at the energetic imprint of the family. One approach is to attend a workshop with a trained practitioner who can facilitate different constellations. I've experienced constellations in a workshop with twenty people and remotely with just myself and the facilitator on the phone. The facilitator helps you identify the family imprint and then supports you in shifting it. If you have a physical illness or you're stuck at work, there may be something in your family imprint that is keeping you there. It's very interesting.

WRIGHT

Almost like heredity?

SCHRAGER

Yes, I have seen a constellation go back only one generation and others that go back four or five generations. In attending the workshop, you may be called upon to be a representative in another person's constellation and see and feel what the person you are representing experienced.

WRIGHT

And BodyTalk?

SCHRAGER

The BodyTalk System is based on quantum physics, I believe. You tap into your body's innate wisdom to discover the underlying source of issues and identify potential solutions across many facets of your life. It's similar to other modalities except some of the things you uncover may be even deeper than your subconscious. The facilitator helps bring out these issues based on talking to your body through kinesiology.

WRIGHT

I have participated in kinesiology experiments where you test the deltoid muscle and given certain words or certain products to make the entire body weak without touching it. Is that what you're talking about, or are you talking about biofeedback?

SCHRAGER

It does use kinesiology, although there's a variation in terms of how they do the testing. There are a lot of modalities that use kinesiology such as food testing, allergy testing, CRA, and many others.

311

WRIGHT

I have found that to be very effective.

SCHRAGER

I have, too.

WRIGHT

And it's almost never wrong. It's rather scary. When I show it to people, they think it's a parlor trick. Most people get nothing from it.

SCHRAGER

I think it depends on the practitioner, too.

WRIGHT

Could be.

If you were able to give one piece of advice as to where someone should start, what would that be?

SCHRAGER

I really think the most important place to start is within yourself.

WRIGHT

To be well?

SCHRAGER

Yes. You may need others to facilitate your process. For example, you mentioned kinesiology. You're most likely not doing kinesiology on yourself, although you could. You may need another person to facilitate it, to hold the space, to ask questions, or to problem-solve. But you alone have lived your life and you alone know your experience, so you're the only one who can provide the answer.

I once wrote something that went like this: The way to wholeness starts from within because when you love yourself, believe in yourself, and trust yourself, anything is possible. Your body knows what you need as long as you are willing to listen. Your soul knows what you are destined to do, as long as you're willing to listen. Your heart knows the right people for you, as long as you're willing to listen. So it *really* is about listening to yourself.

WRIGHT

Well, what a great conversation. I could talk about this all day; I've been taking notes copiously here. I really do appreciate the time you've taken to answer these questions. I think our readers are going to learn a lot from this chapter. It may even present more questions than answers, which might encourage them to learn more.

SCHRAGER

There's never a shortage of questions or answers.

WRIGHT

I appreciate your time here.

SCHRAGER

And I appreciate your help.

WRIGHT

Today we've been talking with Mindy Schrager. Her passion is to support others in their journey to love, accept, and appreciate themselves and create a life they love. She does this through coaching, Neuro-Linguistic Programming, a network of incredible practitioners, and some healthy products.

Mindy, thank you so much for being with us today on *Stepping to Success*.

SCHRAGER

Thank you, David.

ABOUT THE AUTHOR

MINDY SCHRAGER has over twenty years' experience managing cross-disciplinary programs, processes, and communities. She has a bachelor's degree in French, a master's degree in Business Administration, and a coaching certificate from the Ford Institute at JFK University. Her career interests in diversity, transformation, and collaboration grew out of her desire to make life better and have people understand the synergy in diversity. Her interest in wellness grew during eighteen years of studying modalities to improve her own emotional, physical, and relationship wellness. Both paths helped Mindy see the gift and impact in a childhood of being bullied. Bullying is happening not only in our schools, but in families, the workplace, primary relationships, and within ourselves. Her new passion is to support others in their journey to love, accept, and appreciate themselves and create a life they love. She facilitates this through coaching, NLP, a network of incredible practitioners, and some healthy products.

MINDY SCHRAGER

Cary, NC
919-303-2945
waytowholeness@yahoo.com
www.itisallaboutwellness.com

CHAPTER NINTEEN

Pebbles of Thought

An Interview with . . . **Patrick Ratchford**

DAVID WRIGHT (WRIGHT)

Today we're talking with Patrick Ratchford. Patrick has been motivating people, groups, and organizations for several decades both as a motivator, keynote speaker, and sales trainer. A captivating speaker—whether in the classroom, auditorium, or the boardroom—he will leave you with a lasting impression and, more importantly, a game plan for success in your endeavors. Patrick has authored several books and audio programs on goals, sales, motivation, and achievement. He achieved financial independence and enlightenment early in his life from entrepreneurial activities and has since dedicated the next decade to inspiring others to do the same. Mr. Ratchford won't just help you reach your goals—he'll show you how to catch them.

Patrick, welcome to *Stepping Stones to Success.*

PATRICK RATCHFORD (RATCHFORD)

Thank you, David.

WRIGHT

How do you define success?

RATCHFORD

My definition of success is people's ability to reach their own specific goals that they have set for themselves, not goals set by their parents or their friends or neighbors or coworkers or employers; but rather, goals that they have specifically set for themselves.

If your goal is to be a housewife with a home and raise two children and have a puppy dog and you achieve that goal, you are a success. On the other hand, if your goal is to have a log cabin up in the mountains and live off the land and you achieve that goal you are a success, just as much as the individual who set the goal to become a millionaire, billionaire, professional football player, or rock star. Each of them is successful because each set his or her own goal and achieved it.

WRIGHT

So why are you so motivated?

RATCHFORD

We see the bumper sticker stating life is short, and it certainly has become a part of Americana, but I have literally taken it to heart. In comparison to how long the Earth has been here, our time on this Earth literally is short. Statistically our lifespan is perhaps seventy or eighty years. If we take good care of ourselves, we may be able to extend that by one or two decades, but nonetheless, even with that extension, life is still short. So in essence I'm in a race against time, not against an individual, but against time. Since I have taken to heart that my experience here in life is very limited, I continually strive on a daily basis to set my goals, to attain those goals, and to set new goals.

I will share an experience with you that has influenced my life since childhood. It is about a young man who was seeking the secret to success. As he was taking his

316

normal stroll by the ocean, there stood a man gazing across the ocean, with a presence about him of great success. As he got closer to the gentleman, he did indeed recognize him as one being truly successful. He said, "Sir, you're a success, would you share with me the secret to your success?"

Without hesitation, the man said, "Yes," and, putting his arm around the shoulder of the younger man, he began to walk into the ocean. The water was up to their knees and they continued walking. Then the water was waist high and soon it was chest high. Just as the water reached the tip of his chin, the man's grip tightened around his shoulder and the younger man was pulled beneath the water. In shock he didn't even take a breath. He began to kick and wave his hands about frantically. Just as his body was about to go limp, he was pulled from the water. He was breathing hard, coughing up water, and his eyes were red.

He managed to call out to the man, "I asked you the secret to success and you pulled me out here in this water and tried to drown me!"

The man stared him straight in the eye, paused, and said, "Young man, what did you want more than anything when I held you under that water?"

"You old fool, I wanted to breathe!"

The gentleman said, "When you want to succeed as much as you wanted to breathe when I held you underwater, that is when you will succeed!"

So that is where my motivation to succeed came from. It is defined by that kind of passion and has that essence.

WRIGHT

How do you stay positive on a daily basis?

RATCHFORD

That part is somewhat easy for me, I guess, because of my background. It's easy to stay positive because I set goals for myself, not just short-term goals or long-term goals, but also tangible and intangible goals. I reevaluate on a daily basis: Do my goals still apply? How can I tweak them? How do I dot the I's or cross the T's?

On the flip side of that coin, it's very important not just to live in the future, as far as goals are concerned, but to take time to reflect upon the past, to take from that experience, confidence and at the same time to not just look at the future or to live in the past or reflect on the past, but to sincerely live in the present. It's important to enjoy the relationships you have, to enjoy the job that you're involved in, to enjoy the business that you're operating, to reward yourself, take in a movie, go for a walk in the park, or along the beach or take the dog for a walk or go visit a family member and have a stimulating conversation with a loved one. That's living in the moment and that's how I stay motivated.

WRIGHT

So would you share with our readers what is your secret to success?

RATCHFORD

I know there has been a lot of excitement and a lot of advertising using the term "secret." My colleagues and I always chuckle when we hear that because we don't think it's a secret at all. It's great for marketing, but setting goals should not be a secret at this point in most people's lives, going after goals should not be a secret, so my direct answer is it's truly not a secret.

I set goals—short-term and long-term, tangible and intangible. I reevaluate, I tweak, and I adjust until the goal is achieved. So sincerely, whoever is reading this, if you simply set goals and write them down, you will succeed.

After you set a goal, the key is to take it a step further by writing your goal down. When you write it down it adds magic to it—it gives it life. Once that ink or that lead hits that paper, your goal gets a life of its own. It will then motivate you and it will get you out of bed in the morning. It will enable you to stay later; it will enable you to share with others what your goals and dreams are. That will carry you to achieving your goal.

One of my favorite quotes that provides clarity for the process goes like this: "Whatever you vividly imagine, ardently desire, sincerely believe, and enthusiastically act upon must inevitably come to pass." That was shared with me over twenty years ago by Paul J. Meyer. I committed that to memory back then and have used it to realign myself from time to time. In many ways it is an extension to Napoleon Hill's, "What the mind can conceive and believe it will achieve." I've applied those two philosophies to relationships, businesses, cars, houses—you name it—with great success. The more rapidly you hone those points is a reflection of the pace in which you achieve your own goals. This goes hand in hand with the breathing analogy shared earlier.

WRIGHT

So how do you maintain a healthy, growing relationship?

RATCHFORD

There is an acronym, CANI, that stands for Constant And Never-ending Improvement. This was originally coined by Tony Robbins who was influenced by Dr. W. Edwards Deming. Dr. Deming was an American in charge of rebuilding Japan after the war. I believe the original Japanese term was Kaizen. Kaizen means change and good. "Kai" means "change" and "Zen" means "good," hence "Kaizen."

I would suggest that you ask yourself, "How can I change in a way that is good? How can I be a better boyfriend, a better husband, a better uncle, a better cousin, a better friend, a better neighbor, a better employee, a better employer? By asking yourself these questions, sometimes on a monthly basis, a weekly basis, or if need be on a daily basis, you will see improvement in your relationships. It's important to ask yourself these questions, not just on your birthday, not just on New Year's Eve, but to ask yourself these questions on a consistent basis.

Then take this a step further, in a cordial way, and share these questions with someone you have a close relationship with. Ask these questions while you're walking in the park or walking the dog or sitting on the couch, or waiting for the movie to start while you're sitting in the theater. Both of you ask each other: What would make me a better person for this relationship? What would make me add happiness to our relationship? Then listen to those answers. Make sure you are not asking the questions in a confrontational tone and not in a confrontational manner. You'll be surprised at the answers you'll get. You can combine them with the answers you provided when you asked yourself those questions. Therein lies the core of improving and maintaining a successful relationship.

WRIGHT

Things are tough in our country right now; all we hear is bad news from the media. How do you stay successful in a down economy?

RATCHFORD

If you're referring to the recession we are currently in, we've had about a dozen or so of since 1857. So I say with growth comes corrections or retracements, so this too shall pass. I literally take to heart that this is the opportunity to test myself, this is the moment we've been training for our entire life, this is the reason why we've read the books we've read, this is the reason why we've attended the schools or seminars we've attended. We've engaged in conversations about this and we set goals for ourselves that address this problem. This is the time we prove our metal.

If you are a pugilist, whether you're a professional boxer or a mixed martial artist, you can be in the gym punching the bag and shadow boxing and jogging around the block and sticking to a specific diet, but the day your car breaks down and it's late at night and you're walking to the nearest gas station and you are accosted by someone who threatens you, that moment is when you really have the opportunity to apply all the skills you've been practicing in the gym.

Likewise, in a down economy this is the time when you have the opportunity to truly put yourself to the test, to set and pursue goals, to show your ability to maintain a winning attitude and your ability to overcome procrastination. This is the time to apply those skills.

That gives me the satisfaction and the fulfillment to welcome each day because now it's more challenging and "the game is afoot."

WRIGHT

Would you share with our readers the most remarkable moment in your professional life?

RATCHFORD

Most remarkable moment? I think that would be twofold: One was in a materialistic arena. Was it remarkable to earn in a single day what the average

American earns in a typical year? Sure, but esoterically speaking to have people come up and say, "Hey, I heard your CD a couple years ago" or "I heard you speak a few months ago" or "I read your book and it had an impact on my life," that's what's remarkable. Being a businessperson I know that when you treat people well, you rarely hear about it. Most often it's when you mess up or when there is a complaint do people take the time to give you feedback. So to receive positive feedback from time to time from people is just incredible. Complimenting someone takes a lot of courage in my opinion. Telling someone that he or she had a positive effect on your life is incredibly remarkable. Receiving comments like that is better than monetary success.

WRIGHT

When did you feel you had reached success?

RATCHFORD

I was going through some papers in my office and I found a goal sheet I had written in my late teens. It was incredible that the majority of the goals I had written then have been, in fact, achieved. So when I look back on that I thought, "Wow these are the goals I set out to achieve in the next decade or two and 95 percent of them were achieved. The ones that weren't achieved, in many respects, were adjusted.

So when you look back at a goal list (I think the proper term now is "bucket list"), if you find that there are fewer things to check off, you feel successful.

WRIGHT

So who were some of the most inspirational people in your life?

RATCHFORD

I know a lot of individuals would think their parents would head this list, and I too would begin with that. I had a mother who was very supportive regardless of what my goals may have been, from operating a lemonade stand as a child or going door to door selling candles or selling magazine subscriptions for different organizations while in school or supporting different businesses while I was still a child. Regardless of what I did and what I came to her with, she was always supportive. She never said, "Don't be silly" or "We can't afford it" or "You should spend time doing something else." She was always a constant support.

Then I was fortunate enough in junior high to run across a book by Napoleon Hill. I know many readers are familiar with the classic *Think and Grow Rich,* but I took it to heart. Sure, everyone has aspirations for financial independence but it was so well rounded that it enabled me to not just think and grow rich in the monetary sense, but it encouraged me to think and grow rich in my personal life and relationships as well as in business. That concept resonated with me.

Then secondly, I would probably mention James Tolleson. I don't know if many people are familiar with him. He was one of the early speakers on success education. Later in high school I was fortunate enough to run across an introductory tape where he actually had the audacity to state that you should have a goal to become financially independent in eighteen months. That definition of independence in his mind was a million dollars. For others it might be hundred thousand, for others it might be ten million, for others it might be a hundred million.

I took that to heart, just like with Napoleon Hill's work. I took it to heart that I should have the goal that within eighteen months, I should have the business I want to have, and within in eighteen months I should have the relationship I want to have, and within eighteen months I should take my dream vacation.

So those who have influenced me are a combination of my parents, and the work of Napoleon Hill and James Tolleson.

WRIGHT

Why did you choose speaking as a profession?

RATCHFORD

Growing up I used to watch late night television with my parents. It consisted of infomercials, different evangelists, and different talk show hosts. I was always captivated by their ability to persuade an audience. Then I ran across a poll of what the greatest fears people had and learned that the number one fear was death and the number two fear was the fear of public speaking. I thought to myself that if I could master public speaking, then I wouldn't have a fear of doing anything else.

I had butterflies when I first started, of course, but one of my early mentors said, "Patrick, everyone will have butterflies but the key is to have the butterflies fly in formation." So that is what I strive to do. Yes I do have butterflies from time to time, but they're at a minimum because I am prepared when I speak. I am also open-minded enough to know that when you're dealing with new material or you want to raise the level of your game, you will have some excitement, you will have some discomfort, but you exploit that and use it to your advantage.

So to answer your question directly, it was exposure to different speakers on late night television and, most importantly, accepting the challenge that if public speaking was one of the top two fears that if I mastered that, everything else would be a piece of cake.

WRIGHT

So do you think anyone can be motivated?

RATCHFORD

Can anyone be motivated? I do have people tell me, "Patrick, you're a motivator right?"

"Well," I'll reply, "I'm primarily a businessman. I can share with you techniques that I have used in my life to succeed. I can share with you stories that have been effective in my life—stories that can enable you to learn from my experiences and philosophy." But we must also be cognizant that many like to proclaim that they have twenty, thirty, or forty years of experience when, more often than not, they simply have one year of experience repeated nineteen times. Rarely is it decades of constant improvement.

As a businessperson (or Renaissance man more aptly), that serves as a constant reminder to me in my evolution through life to constantly improve. This being said, I know that whatever your goals may be, whether on a personal level or on a business level, I can spark the fire, but you must be able to maintain it.

I had a colleague a couple of years ago. We were debating whether anyone, could be motivated. He said, "Patrick, if you take an imbecile and you motivate him, you have a motivated imbecile."

I don't think my philosophy is as strong as his in that respect. I believe that people can initially be motivated by observing what I do or by reading books or listening to CDs or watching DVDs or listening to a lecture, but that next day, they're the ones—not me, not some other motivator—who are going to have to get themselves out of debt. They're the ones who are going to drive themselves to their job. They're the ones who are going to have to pick up that book, approach that future mate, take that class, and ask those questions on how to improve their relationship, their business, or their life. So can I provide the spark? If you want to refer to that as motivation, yes, but the maintenance of that spark is totally reliant on the individual.

WRIGHT

So what's in store for Patrick Ratchford? What does the future hold for you?

RATCHFORD

Will I continue to develop books, and CDs and DVDs and seminars and give lectures? Sure, but not for the monetary aspect. I do it for the fulfillment that comes from contributing to the world and the satisfaction of contributing to the human race. Each day I ask myself these questions: How can you communicate more effectively? How can you help yourself and others reach their goals more effectively. How can you improve your relationships? I carry that philosophy into my career. Will my next talk be better than my last? Yes. Will my next CD be more effective than my last? Yes. Will the DVD and the next book be better? Yes. So it ties into constant and never-ending improvement in my life and recognizing that I am in a race against time. So for my limited time here on this Earth, I want to have the most dynamic impact possible.

WRIGHT

Well, what a great conversation, I really appreciate the time you've spent here with me today. You've given me a lot to think about and I'm sure you've given our readers good information. I appreciate your taking all this time to answer these questions.

RATCHFORD

I thank you for your time as well, David.

WRIGHT

Today we've been talking with Patrick Ratchford. Patrick is a motivator of people, groups, and organizations. He's a captivating speaker whether he's in the classroom, auditorium, or in the corporate boardroom. He has authored several books and audio programs on goals, sales, motivation, and achievement. I think he knows what he's talking about because what he has said makes a lot of sense to me.

Patrick, thank you so much for being with us today on *Stepping Stones to Success*.

RATCHFORD

Thank you David, cheers.

ABOUT THE AUTHOR

PATRICK RATCHFORD has been motivating people, groups, and organizations for several decades both as a motivator, keynote speaker, and sales trainer. A captivating speaker—whether in the classroom, auditorium, or the boardroom—he will leave you with a lasting impression and, more importantly, a game plan for success in your endeavors. Patrick has authored several books and audio programs on goals, sales, motivation, and achievement. He achieved financial independence and enlightenment early in his life from entrepreneurial activities and has since dedicated the next decade to inspiring others to do the same. Mr. Ratchford won't just help you reach your goals—he'll show you how to catch them.

PATRICK RATCHFORD

P.O. Box 620496
Las Vegas, NV 89162
702.947.1211
sales@canspeakwilltravel.com
www.canspeakwilltravel.com

CHAPTER TWENTY

I Want to be the Best Boss You Ever Had!

An Interview with . . . **Robert Alderman**

DAVID WRIGHT (WRIGHT)

Today we are talking with Robert Alderman, Certified Professional Behavioral Analyst and CEO/President of Performance 2000 Inc. Robert has over forty-five years of business experience. A University of California trained teacher, he has utilized his former California teaching credential as a springboard to teaching throughout his business career.

Robert is a Certified Professional Behavioral Analyst. His assessment company, Performance 2000 Inc., is one of the most successful in the United States. His coaching practice is always full with a wait list. To date he has made over eighteen thousand one-on-one coaching calls. He has been named one of America's twenty-five most influential coaches as well as being selected Coach of the Year out of eight thousand affiliates at Target Training International.

In his business career, he has been a top level sales executive in several organizations before starting his own company. He has been a successful solo entrepreneur for forty years. He has worked extensively around the world as well as in the United States.

Robert is a member of the international faculty of TTI specializing in the arena of corporate leadership. Additionally, he is a well-recognized speaker on candidate selection, sales, and sales leadership.

Robert, welcome to *Stepping Stones to Success.*

The title of your chapter is "I Want to be the Best Boss You Have Ever Had!" Why do you believe this is an important statement for a manager-leader to make?

ROBERT ALDERMAN (ALDERMAN)

This simple statement, genuinely stated, has the power to radically transform the working relationship between a manager and his or her direct report. It can take the relationship to a whole other level that fosters inspiration, motivation, and performance far beyond standard operating procedures. It has the ability to create a truly synergistic relationship that shows up in increased output and profits and decreased turnover. Yet there is zero cost of business associated with implementing it.

Amazingly, in over twenty-two years of coaching, I am still waiting for one person to tell me, *yes,* my boss has said that to me: "I want to be the best boss you have ever had." Not one person I have talked to has ever heard these kinds of words or messages from his or her manager.

In the course of working over thirty years in corporate America as well as clocking more than eighteen thousand hours of corporate coaching, it has struck me that the relationship between the supervisor/boss and the subordinate tends to be structured in a very impersonal, even sterile way.

This glaring irony lends itself to a lack of trust and synergy and is an invitation for misunderstandings, conflict, and missed opportunities—opportunities that ultimately and inevitably affect the bottom line.

By having the authentic boldness to say to an employee, "I want to be the best boss you have ever had," you are stepping out of this outdated top-down mold that has traditionally put the onus only on the *employee* to prove that they have the goods. You're stating I am stepping up to walk my talk, give in kind what I am asking and expecting to get, and I have the confidence and courage to want to be the best boss you have ever had.

WRIGHT

Why is that important to you?

ALDERMAN

Because if I am, in the eyes of my employee, the best boss she or he has ever had, there is a very high probability that the person will be fully engaged. While the term so commonly used today is "engaged," I would like to see an expanded definition: to be *fully passionate* about his or her job. My ultimate goal is to have an employee who when his or her alarm goes off in the morning, he or she will be excited about showing up. Imagine a company, division, or a team full of committed and passionate individuals! You can bet the output is going to be a lot more exciting and fruitful than when merely "engaged."

WRIGHT

Where did this idea come from?

ALDERMAN

Many years ago I was a sales manager heading up a group of one hundred salespeople. I had established in my own mind that I wanted to be the best boss they'd ever had. It was an internal goal and while I never stated it outwardly to them, I let my actions dictate it so I was living that statement.

WRIGHT

What resulted from that goal?

ALDERMAN

Word got out throughout the company that I had a great deal of success with my sales force. When someone was faltering and on the verge of being fired, other divisions of the company would send these troubled employees to me as a last resort. These are employees they had given up on. If, upon interviewing them, I came to the decision I could save them, then I took them in.

They knew they were close to being terminated. I would sit them down and open the conversation saying, "I believe that in a different environment you have the potential to be a superstar and I'd like you to join my team."

That statement alone creates motivation. Nobody shows up to fail. They were failing in one environment but I was in charge of a different division. One of these people who was almost terminated went on to be a very highly successful executive in the financial industry and is now a VP for Morgan Stanley. He has been managing my money for the past twenty years. This is a guy who was on the way out the door. Think of the losses my sales organization would have incurred if they had just taken the easy route and fired him. They would not only have had the expense of replacing him and training someone else, but they would have experienced the loss in superstar revenues that he ended up generating for the company, not to mention the motivation and inspiration his story generated for other salespeople.

WRIGHT

What did you experience as a result?

ALDERMAN

Twenty years after I left the company, a core group of my salespeople had a party in my honor. People flew in from all over the country. That is something you don't usually hear of. In fact, it was the Morgan Stanley guy who organized the party.

I empowered, trusted, and believed in them. I acknowledged them in front of their peers, but criticized them in private. These are the basics of a *respectful* relationship.

By introducing a more synergistic relationship, the end result is creating an environment where the employee is extraordinarily empowered and fully passionate to do his or her work. Not only do employees do their work, but they to do it beyond the boundaries that were previously established. We are talking about a shift in the corporate culture, one relationship at a time.

WRIGHT

What do you mean when you say "the culture shift"?

ALDERMAN

This means to shift the company culture from the standard "I am the boss, you're the subordinate and therefore you do what I say" to "we're in this together." It means creating a synergy where people feel they're on an equal playing field—they're partners. In fact, I find the word "subordinate" to be a negative term because it conveys that someone is on one level and the other is below them, which can undermine trust and *security,* which are the basis for a healthy, harmonious relationship as well as constructive motivation. We're just talking basic relationship development.

WRIGHT

So you're really talking about a paradigm shift?

ALDERMAN

Absolutely. We're talking about changing the way in which the senior employee relates to the junior employee and vice versa—creating *freedom* on the part of the employee to participate in my success as a manager-leader by helping me to be the best boss I possibly can.

But let me say this: just because it is a shift—a departure from the current mode of operating—it doesn't mean it is rocket science or that it has to be hard or challenging. It is a shift to greater authenticity and freedom.

WRIGHT

What kind of freedom?

ALDERMAN

This kind of freedom is one where there is free exchange of dialogue about how are *we* doing? You're also opening the door for your reports to have the freedom to be real about what is going on for them, where they might be experiencing frustrations or needing your expertise, guidance, *coaching,* and/or advice. When you've leveled the playing field, your employee is more likely to share and seek out performance improvements on his or her own, proactively. Now that is a bonus.

We're talking about taking proven winning strategies in personal relationships to the work relationship. Create a space that is safe and authentic for open dialogue and healthy communication.

WRIGHT

So it's a freedom coming from open dialogue?

ALDERMAN

Yes. It is important to have a boss with whom you can share your feelings. Living in a one-sided, closed communication work relationship with no one to share your feelings can create negative physical reactions. One study conducted over a twenty-year period with thirty-seven thousand people found that a person is twice as likely to suffer sickness or death when isolated from open dialog. I believe a large part of this can be work related.

If you are the best boss a person has ever had, you will have opened the door for the employee to share and release angst, fears, and dissatisfaction. You can contribute to the overall well-being of every employee by utilizing an open relationship leadership style.

The boss and the direct report should be communicating in a way in which the sound is like the most successful speakers—the static has been pushed out. When you reduce static, you reduce stress. Stress is a physiological and psychological time bomb. If you continue to manage or work in an environment of stress, you will eventually implode either physically, psychologically, or both. People working with a low level of stress have reserves of positive energy to accomplish extraordinary things in the workplace and in their own lives.

WRIGHT

How can the "Best Boss" approach affect the work relationship?

ALDERMAN

Well, the first thing that happens is that it transforms a concept that people have lived with throughout their entire work career about the boss-employee relationship, which is typically a top down, undefined but distinct wall between the two parties. Hearing from their manager, "I want to be the best boss you've ever had," they realize that they have just stepped into something brand new. This is not just another boss. This is an exceptional person. This is a different kind of company. This is going to be a different kind of work experience.

If you heard this from your boss, all of a sudden there will be a psychological shift in your head. You're sitting across from someone who actually cares what your work experience is like and what kind of support you're going to experience on the job. You're going to produce higher than in the past. All of a sudden you're in a new universe.

WRIGHT

What happens when this is said on the first day?

ALDERMAN

Whether it is a new hire or someone newly promoted, saying, "I want to be the best boss you've ever had" on the first day of work establishes that this person now has a job in a very different company or division and has a different work environment. You're conveying to your new report: "We're different because we care about you." You have just conveyed an authenticity and transparency that makes this picture crystal clear.

You are empowering your new employees from day one, setting them on a path of productivity and profitability that will empower them to reach beyond themselves and travel to places never before imagined. Your approach will change them forever, along with yourself.

WRIGHT

Talk about some simple Best Boss practices.

ALDERMAN

We can sum up Best Boss practices with these four concepts: Believe, Recognize, Trust, and Share.

BELIEVE

First, really believe in your employees' ability to super perform, and support your employees to believe in themselves. Terry Cole said: "Believe in your ability to do great works." We're extending that saying to your workforce—believe in their ability to do great work. Expectancy theory has shown that people rise or fall according to the expectations set by others. Not only believe in their ability, but believe that *they,* in fact, want to do great work.

RECOGNIZE

Empower them and regularly catch them doing things right. *The One Minute Manager* had it right: "Catch your people doing something right." Now that will mean you always only see the wins, but you're setting up something like a scale of justice. With my sales force, I was always building up their self-esteem because sooner or later I was going to have to reprimand them for something. But I had earned the right to do that because I had empowered them along the way.

TRUST

If the only thing you get is "the last report you did was sloppy," or "your sales in the last two weeks stinks," you have no motivational chits. If you had told them the three weeks preceding that "I really appreciated your staying late to finish the report" or "Thanks for training that new hire," you would then have *earned* the right to reprimand and criticize them.

Just because you're the boss, you don't have the right to criticize. As a manager, there are going to be times you need to call someone to task for under performance but if that is all you ever do, it becomes a very negative event. If you view it as a scale of justice, on one side, you're building up their self-esteem so you earn the right to critique them when they fail to meet specific certain standards. If all you do is critique, what are you creating? You are creating negativity. That isn't why people come to work.

Stephen Covey talks about this in terms of the emotional bank account. You have to make deposits if you want to make withdrawals and ultimately stay in the black. Once you're in the red, you have lost your credibility and ability to constructively motivate. Once you've established trust, you've set the stage so that they can comfortably receive constructive feedback. So now you're sharing from a place of trust.

SHARE

In my coaching practice, I utilize behavioral assessments as a way to shortcut identifying and understanding strengths, weak spots, and opportunities. Here is a radically powerful Best Boss practice to share: "I have a copy of your behavioral assessment and have had a chance to look at it. Now, I'd like to take mine out so you can see my strengths and soft spots." What a way to create a higher level of understanding and rapport. What is the takeaway that employee will have after experiencing this with his or her boss? Here is someone who is confident, transparent, and a straight-shooter.

One of the hot buzzwords is "retention." If you're creating or contributing to the kind of environment where your employees are feeling nurtured, why are they going to leave? You know other environments don't do that. I've been using assessments with a Fortune 500 company for eighteen years and have had the opportunity to implement these strategies. I've seen how they work long-term to retain and grow talent. It is all about creating a synergistic relationship and an empowered employee who will be passionate and not just "engaged" in their work.

WRIGHT

Why use a behavioral assessment?

ALDERMAN

The right behavioral assessment can be a Best Boss's best friend. Simply, it is an instruction manual on how to create and raise the quality of your company through people. You will build great relationships that drive your company's success. When you use the right behavioral assessment, you leap-frog this process. On the first day, you're exchanging assessments and establishing a shared language by which you're able to glean things from each other's profiles.

(Note: you don't have to use behavioral assessments. In my professional view, it is a handicap not having this information. Utilizing and sharing assessments makes for a stronger, more viable strategy.)

An assessment can provide instructions and tools for how to speak to your employees, how to motivate and how to lead them. It is a type of shortcut for really becoming self-actualized yourself and for deeper understanding of your new-hire or newly promoted employee.

WRIGHT

Why share profiles with an employee?

ALDERMAN

New-hires will see that you have soft spots and areas for improvement, just like they do. The boss just stepped off his or her pedestal and came down to earth to join the new employee at ground zero. This leveling sets the stage for an important buy-in from your employee.

WRIGHT

Why is this kind of buy-in important?

ALDERMAN

Getting buy-in from an employee, whether a new-hire or not, establishes a two-way dialogue and a sharing of ideas, behaviors, and goals, which establish a foundation for a successful working relationship. You can say these words: "I cannot be the best boss you have ever had without your help. Together we can grow and prosper." Not only are you saying this, you are encouraging your new employees to help you be the best boss you are capable of being.

WRIGHT

So how does this look?

ALDERMAN

When you hire someone on the first day, call the person into your office and say, "The reason I would like to spend some time with you is that my goal is to be the best boss you've ever had. One of the ways I think we can develop that kind of relationship is to share our assessments. I'd like to go over yours to see if there is anything you don't agree with; but I'd also like to give you mine. I have my soft spots, just like you do; but if we respect each other and honor each other's strengths and weak spots, that will be the next step to creating synergy and for us to get on track with each other. Then I can be the best boss you've ever had and you will be the best employee I have ever had."

WRIGHT

Are there some risks with this particular strategy?

ALDERMAN

Well, there are risks getting up in the morning and walking to your car. The risk can be in lack of trust or someone who abuses this inappropriately, but that usually backfires.

I've seen perceived risk show up as resistance. Sometimes there is a pretty strong push-back when I ask managers to catch their people doing something right. They will say, "Oh yeah, I do that," but when they're questioned, they really aren't doing that. The outcome I know that will show up is when they start to empower their employees through their words of catching them doing something right, the feeling that they receive from doing that will transform them. Even if the boss is receiving this from *his* boss, there is no reason why he wouldn't pass this on down the line.

WRIGHT

Where does push-back come from?

ALDERMAN

I see this when there is a certain degree of pessimism or with someone who is not warm and friendly. This is where people have to adapt their behavior because the end result is going to have a powerful effect on them. When you give that recognition (ideally in front of peers), you have given them a gift much more important than extra money or days off. Making someone feel good and thus engaged is many times more effective than other superficial motivators. It hits a core psychological need, which is to be loved and liked. This is where many people have a hole.

WRIGHT

What does a "Best Boss" look like?

ALDERMAN

A Best Boss oriented manager-leader is someone who is very focused on the company goals, company agenda, and on treating his or her people respectfully, fairly, and openly. He or she treats everyone equally and is genuinely supportive. The bottom line here is that you can't be the best boss your employees have ever had if you don't respect them and if you're a boss who is just a people-pleaser and is letting people run over them because of a high need to be liked. The best boss has above average EQ.

WRIGHT

What does emotional quotient (EQ) have to do with this equation?

ALDERMAN

Best Bosses are comfortable enough within themselves and will have a highly developed sense of confidence. There's a distinct inner development where the person can't be afraid to say this and mean it. It is about being able to be authentic, reach out, and connect with another human being in a genuine, present way.

WRIGHT

What are important qualities for a "Best Boss"?

ALDERMAN

This is someone who is willing to show vulnerability, openness, and to be respectful and fair. What words would we use for a good husband? Ethical, honest, trusting, and willing to compromise. Why don't we take all these relationship skills and qualities and transfer them into the work environment? I think that taking words from a good marriage is applicable here because we're creating a marriage between us—the manager-leader and the employee. Another key quality for a Best Boss is self-efficacy.

WRIGHT

Why is self-efficacy a key Best Boss trait?

ALDERMAN

Self-efficacy is believing that we can control events and deal with the challenges of life as they appear in front of us. Remember when I told you I took the throw away employees and turned them into superstars? Somewhere inside, I had a high sense of self-efficacy—an internal belief that I could turn these people into stars.

If managers-leaders can adapt the strategy of opening themselves to creating a more dynamic, effective relationship, then they'll create a higher degree of self-efficacy. The outcome of this is a manager who will stretch, take chances, and constantly be raising the bar.

Albert Bandura from Stanford University says: "People's beliefs about their abilities have a profound effect on those abilities. Ability is not a fixed property; there is a huge variability in how you perform. People who have a sense of self-efficacy bounce back from failures; they approach things in terms of how to handle them rather than worrying about what can go wrong." Helping employees is the greatest gift they can ever receive.

An epitome of self-efficacy is Warren Buffet. He manages billions of dollars but in a way that demonstrates how to bounce back and manage his mindset of not dwelling on the negatives—always looking at the glass half full. He has an internal strength that makes him America's most successful investor. If you ever hear or read Warren Buffet, it becomes crystal clear how much he has control of his own psychology. Warren Buffet is a genius when we apply the constructs of Emotional Intelligence to his behavior.

WRIGHT

How difficult or easy is this?

ALDERMAN

In my experience, coaching hundreds of executives, this is one of the easiest, quickest, most effective tools available. One thing is certain. You can't force someone to practice this approach. It must be voluntary. If a manager has a developed sense of self-efficacy and is open to change, to learning, experimenting, and getting outside of how he or she has been operating within the corporate box, then it will be simple. Remember, emotional intelligence can be coached, developed, and parlayed into new strategies and new techniques for becoming a very powerful leader. But the manager has to be comfortable within himself or herself. That is one of the keys.

WRIGHT

Why would someone resist this?

ALDERMAN

The funny thing with the Best Boss tool is that it is infectious. If you start this at level four, then all of a sudden the person above you starts to see what is happening. Maybe he or she is going to incorporate your management style. The idea is to have this start with the CEO or President. Starting at the bottom is not ideal, but start where you can start. It will affect any manager who tries this.

WRIGHT

Why don't people say this to their subordinates?

ALDERMAN

Very good question. I've asked it at least five thousand times and am still waiting for someone to tell me he or she does. It seems like such a natural thing.

WRIGHT

What is the down side to the Best Boss approach?

ALDERMAN

Can you tell me what is wrong with saying this? One hypothetical answer could be: "Because I don't want to open the door to be criticized." I say that's too bad, then you have work to do on yourself." This is not for everybody—it's for those who can see the benefits and for those not afraid to take risks and who are forward thinking.

If we took a hypothetical company and had everyone doing this, I find it hard to believe they wouldn't be flourishing and successful. Is there something deleterious to the bottom line if everyone is happy and excited to be there? I don't think so.

What's in it for the boss? By showing up genuinely wanting and willing to be the best boss your employee has ever had, that employee will attempt to be the best employee you have ever had. If a manager has six direct reports all trying to be the best employee, what has happened to the boss's performance and self-esteem? How empowered is he or she as a leader? See how this can take someone from being a manager to a true leader?

WRIGHT

So being a Best Boss can cultivate leadership?

ALDERMAN

Absolutely. You step out of just managing and start leading. A manager just sees that you get to work on time and get your work done, and that you're "engaged." A leader takes you to new places you never knew existed. As a Best Boss, you then earn the right to be a leader. Make no mistake, being a leader is an earned position that comes from respect and trust. This is the groundwork you've been laying in setting your intention to be a Best Boss.

Go beyond where your employee has ever gone before. Of course, this only happens when you provide the right environment so the employee will become extraordinarily passionate—beyond engaged. Create a work team that will not keep looking at their watches to see who can get out the door first. I am a big believer in a balanced life but I'm also a big believer in passion on the job.

Real leaders—truly effective leaders—have the gift of connection. They have what is called "irresistible attraction" or "interpersonal polish." People want to be around them. They admire them, trust them, and many times want to model themselves after real leaders. And keep this in mind: an inspired employee *wants* their boss to be successful and wants to support him or her in being successful. This is the payoff you receive from being a Best Boss leader.

WRIGHT

Give an example from your experience.

ALDERMAN

Here is a scenario. I'm using the Best Boss strategy and you're my peer but have chosen not to implement the Best Boss approach. Two of us have equal divisions of twenty employees. We give them a survey and ask this question: "If Manager B (that's you) were to leave the company and start his own business would you follow him?" The answers they give will tell you which one of us is leading and which one of us isn't. Remember, if you're out for a walk and no one is following, then you're not leading.

I have a client who has seven direct reports and when they were asked this question, none would follow her—zero. What did that feedback do for her? It was like getting hit on the forehead with a baseball bat. It was a gigantic wake-up call to start implementing Best Boss practices. Now I am getting calls from her CEO telling me there's been a huge transformation and that people are starting to admire and respect her after just two months of implementing the Best Boss approach.

Changing one key person to a Best Boss can play itself out to the whole organization.

This is simple, quick, and easy to implement. This is not top grading that takes ten hours to do. You just put it out there and you get a lifetime of return on your investment. One of the questions is: "What does it cost you to say these words?" If you measure this, it will be the best investment you can make because your cost of being a Best Boss is zero.

WRIGHT

Are there any other Best Boss tools you can share?

ALDERMAN

One of my favorites is the Mary Kay *"Necklace Technique."* You have a box of invisible necklaces based on the number of direct reports you have. These necklaces are labeled "make me feel important." You take them and hypothetically place them around the necks of each direct report so each of them is walking around with an invisible jeweled sign, "make me feel important." For one month or a year you are aware of making them feel important. You see the invisible sign and it reminds you to catch them doing something right. In other words, you are making them feel good about being at work. I have experienced miraculous shifts in people with this simple technique. It will be a seed that changes the culture of the company.

WRIGHT

What are some simple "Best Boss" goals?

ALDERMAN

To create a work environment so full of positives that when employees awaken in the morning they are totally excited about coming to work. If I am successful in being the best boss they have ever had, then there is a high probability that the employee may just become the best direct report I have ever had.

Best Boss goals include being trustworthy, ethical, fair, and being an "endorser." That means making them feel good about who they are and their role at work. When people have a higher belief in their own potential, the barriers to their success are removed.

Everyone has the potential to be a Best Boss. You need an inner drive to stretch yourself. You can't be the best boss someone's ever had without stretching yourself. You're asking for a high level and quality of production from employees, but in turn you're willing to raise your level of contribution as well. This is a two-way street. Remember, the boss has more responsibility than the employee.

WRIGHT

What are key take-aways from the Best Boss strategy?

ALDERMAN

This is a strategy that truly reflects the old adage of win-win, but in this modern version it is bigger. The new-hire wins, the leader wins, the customer wins, the other leaders win, the employees win, and all the executives win along with the company. It permeates throughout the culture. This can work in any size company. One person can change the entire culture.

Watching this special relationship dynamic based on mutual trust and respect take hold and flourish creates the miracle we call leadership success.

The person feels enriched when they walk through the door at work. Create an environment whereby when your employees get on the road to work they are looking forward to arriving, creating, participating, and accomplishing, not just going through the motions. Nurture their self-esteem and catch them doing things right. Empower your people. Empower, empower, empower.

WRIGHT

Can you summarize Best Boss strategies?

ALDERMAN

- Believe in Success
- Recognize Accomplishments
- Establish Trust

- Share through Open Dialogue

So in conclusion, the Best Boss strategy is a simple, easy, quick way to:

- Demonstrate that you have the confidence and courage to want to be the Best Boss.
- Create motivation for your employees to participate in *your* success as a manager-leader.
- Transform you from standard manager to standout leader.
- Inspire a "best employee."
- Transform the workplace and work relationships.
- Generate bottom line payoffs and talent retention.

About the Author

Robert Alderman has over forty-five years of business experience. A University of California trained teacher, he has utilized his former California teaching credential as a springboard to teaching throughout his business career.

Robert is a Certified Professional Behavioral Analyst. His assessment company, Performance 2000 Inc., is one of the most successful in the United States. His coaching practice is always full with a wait list. To date he has made more than eighteen thousand one-on-one coaching calls. He has been named one of America's twenty-five most influential coaches as well as being selected Coach of the Year out of eight thousand affiliates at Target Training International.

In his business career, he has been a top level sales executive in several organizations before starting his own company. He has been a successful solo entrepreneur for forty years. He has worked extensively around the world as well as in the United States.

Robert is a member of the international faculty of TTI specializing in the arena of corporate leadership. Additionally, he is a well-recognized speaker on candidate selection, sales, and sales leadership.

Robert Alderman
Performance 2000 Inc.
2945 Stonefield Drive
Jamul, CA 91935
619.920.8299 (cell)
619.579.0200 (office)
www.managingyoursuccess.com
www.performanceprofiles.net
drdisc_2006@yahoo.com